father smith instructs jackson

father smith instructs jackson

by Archbishop John Francis Noll, D.D., LL.D.

*Revised in the Light of Vatican Council II
and the Credo of the People of God
by Albert J. Nevins, M.M.*

OUR SUNDAY VISITOR, INC.
Publisher
HUNTINGTON

Nihil obstat: Rev. Lawrence Gollner, Censor librorum
Imprimatur: ✠Leo A. Pursley, D.D., Bishop of Fort Wayne-South Bend
January 15, 1975
The Nihil Obstat and Imprimatur are official declarations that a book or pamphlet is free of doctrinal or moral error. No implication is contained therein that those who have granted the Nihil Obstat or Imprimatur agree with the contents, opinions, or statements expressed.

ISBN 0-87973-864-2
Library of Congress Catalog Card No. 75-628
FIRST PUBLISHED IN 1913
THIRD REVISED EDITION

PRINTED IN U.S.A.
Our Sunday Visitor, Inc., 200 Noll Plaza, Huntington, Indiana 46750

Table of Contents

PART III
The Means of Grace

PART IV
Approved Devotions
and Religious Associations

Introduction

The course of instructions contained in this book—in dialogue form—is intended both for Catholics who were deprived, during their youth, of a sound and orthodox training in the science of God, or who are confused about what they are supposed to believe, and for non-Catholics who are interested in learning what the Catholic Church teaches officially concerning religious doctrine and practices.

But it must ever be remembered that one may have a vast store of religious knowledge gathered from study and still lack faith—because faith belongs to the supernatural order and is a gift of God. Catholics who are convinced that they possess the true Faith, should frequently thank Almighty God that He has so blessed them and should show their gratitude by striving to interest others in their religion. The convert to the true Faith, also especially blessed by God, should show his or her appreciation by making an effort to share it with non-Catholic friends.

Both the Catholic and non-Catholic, while exercising an apostolate for the cause of Christ and of souls, should pray daily that God may draw to Himself those who are near and dear to them. If they are prayed for in this way, indifferent Catholics will be best impelled by God's grace to take a greater interest in their religion, and non-Catholics will become better disposed to hearken to the voice of God's Church.

An inquiry into the claims of the Catholic Church, such

as you are about to make, has resulted in the conversion of hundreds of thousands of citizens of the United States — men and women who sought truth and found it.

Despite the prejudices in which so many have been reared, despite the stricter religious discipline under which Catholics are expected to live, the Catholic Church grows faster than all the major Christian churches combined.

As you continue your inquiry you will learn that the Catholic religion claims to be *essentially* different from others —because it is divine in origin, divine in character, divine in its means of sanctification.

Perhaps to some the above may sound triumphal, in this, as it is called, age of ecumenism. However, true ecumenism recognizes the sincerity of the beliefs of non-Catholics and respects that sincerity. It is a reality that Christian sects partake in God's truth, but the fullness of that truth resides only in the Catholic Church, as this book will demonstrate. The fullness of truth can never be diluted or silenced in order to bring about better relations with others. We respect our fellow Christians, and out of love for them we pray that God will give them that fullness of His truth which resides solely in the continuing apostolic Church that Christ founded, namely, the Catholic Church and the Catholic Faith.

Your instructor may question you from a more formal catechism, but if you master this book, which, I believe, you will find at least interesting, you will be able, in your own words, to answer practically all questions contained in a typical Catholic catechism.

One final note. There are many controverted opinions among today's theologians. Speculative argument among experts is to be encouraged. Unfortunately, some of this argument reaches the ordinary faithful and leaves them confused. This book is not concerned with such argumentation or with possible theories. What we are presenting here is authentic doctrine of the Catholic Church. Sometimes we express it in the words of the Second Vatican Council which was an official teaching council and sometimes in the words of the Credo of the People of God of Pope Paul VI. But always it represents the authentic teaching of the magisterium (or teaching body) of the Catholic Church.

PART I

God's Church and Her Teachings

"I will build my church . . ." Matt. 16:18.

"The Church of the living God, the pillar and bulwark of truth." 1 Tim. 3:15.

"If he ignores even the Church, then treat him as you would a Gentile or a tax collector." Matt. 18:17.

"He who hears you, hears me." Luke 10:16.

"Go, therefore, and make disciples of all nations . . . and behold, I am with you all days, even unto the consummation of the world." Matt. 28: 19-20.

"It is he who is head of the body, the Church." Col. 1:18.

"So too we, though many, are one body in Christ." Rom. 12:5.

"No more than a branch can bear fruit of itself apart from the vine, can you bear fruit apart from Me." John 15:4.

"I went to extremes in persecuting the Church of God." Gal. 1:13.

"Why do you persecute Me?" Acts 9: 4-5.

Getting Acquainted

We believe in one only God, Father, Son and the Holy Spirit, Creator of things visible such as this world in which our transient life passes, of things invisible such as the pure spirits which are also called angels, and Creator in each man of his spiritual and immortal soul. —*Credo of the People of God.*

Mr. Jackson. Good evening, Reverend.

Father Smith. Good evening; come in. What can I do for you?

Mr. J. My name is Jackson. I came to see you about taking instructions in the Catholic religion, if you have the time.

Father S. Certainly I have the time; and if I didn't, I would make the time; instruction is an important part of my work. If I am frank with my explanations and you are equally frank with your observations and questions, our conversations should be interesting. Just a few preliminaries. Have you ever been baptized?

Mr. J. No, Sir.

Father S. Have you been reared in any religion?

Mr. J. No, Sir.

Father S. Are you going with a Catholic girl?

Mr. J. No, Sir; at least not yet. But I am impressed by the age, the bigness of the Catholic Church, and by the religious unity among its people.

Father S. Well, that means that you are not prejudiced as some are.

Mr. J. I try, Sir, to have an open mind. Pardon me for forgetting to address you with your proper title. You know, I am not accustomed to addressing a priest.

Father S. That's all right. Do you happen to know why Catholics call their priests "Father"?

Mr. J. No, I do not, although I heard a Catholic friend give a good answer to a non-Catholic, who contended that the priest had no right to that name.

Father S. What was the answer?

Mr. J. Well, the non-Catholic quoted Christ as saying: "Call no man 'Father'," and the Catholic answered: "What do you call your 'Dad'?"

Father S. That was more than a clever come-back. St. Paul furnishes the principal reason why the priest is called "Father": "You have only one father. It was I who begot you through my preaching of the Gospel." (1 Cor. 4:15). The priest's office is like that of St. Paul—he is an instrument in God's hands for the imparting of a new kind of life, a *supernatural* life, to the soul, just as the parent whom you call "Father," was God's instrument for giving natural life to you. God is the *principal agent* in both instances, and that is what Christ meant when He said: "Only one is your father, the One in heaven" (Matt. 23:9). The priest's very purpose in life is to serve the spiritual needs of his parish, just as a father does the temporal needs of his family, and hence merits the title "Father."

Mr. J. Father, since we have touched on this subject, would you mind giving the Church's reasons for requiring her priests to remain single? Understand me: if I asked you why *you* are not married, you might tell me that it is "none of my business," but I suppose it's legitimate for me to ask why the great body of Catholic priests does not marry. Non-Catholics do not understand this requirement of your Church.

Father S. I'll gladly explain it. A priest is particularly called or chosen by Christ. "It was not you who chose me," Jesus told his Apostles; "it was I who chose you." The priest is more than merely a preacher of the gospel; he is "another Christ," dedicated to God by a special consecration, and may never be anything else thereafter; and he sees himself as *called* by God from tanglements with the world and human ties. In the words of St. Paul: *"Every high priest is taken from among men and made their representative before God, to offer gifts and sacrifices for sins"* (Heb. 5:1). He is ordained *for men,* and hence his time, his talents, his life should be at their disposal. To be free from all earthly ties is quite essential for wholehearted work in the cause of God. St. Paul was not married. He obviously recommended that all ministers of the Gospel remain unmarried in order to devote themselves wholly to the work of God. In fact, he positively states this: "I should like you to be free of all worries. The unmarried man is busy with the Lord's affairs, concerned with pleasing the Lord; but the married man is busy with this world's demands and occupied with pleasing his wife" (1 Cor. 7:32-33). There is no doubt that an unmarried clergyman who has no family ties, can imitate the unmarried Christ more closely, has no family demands on his time, can minister to people afflicted with contagious diseases better than a married one. He should be able to get along with less financial support.

Mr. J. Those are strong arguments in favor of an unmarried clergy, and I don't think that they are weighed by most non-Catholics.

Father S. Some believe that it is impossible to live a chaste unmarried life. Catholics, who know the character and duties of the priesthood, heartily believe in a single life for the priest. The priest's daily Mass and meditation, his other prayers which take proportionate time each day, should alone keep the priest close to God. The frequent "tippler" might find it difficult to let drink alone, but not the one who never tasted it. So it is with those who have always been single, but solemnly pledged to remain chaste.

Mr. J. But so much literature represents the priest and nun as being anything but virtuous.

Father S. That's true, but it emanates either from professed enemies of the Catholic Church, from disgruntled former priests and Sisters who attempt to justify their own disobedience and weaknesses, or from men and women who find it financially profitable to attack the Catholic Church. I admit that many of those who have left the priesthood because of the rigorous demands made upon them are a problem to many. Invariably, those who desert the priesthood follow a definite pattern — a loss of prayer life, an involvement in the world, and then an abandonment of their vow of celibacy. Because they are oddities, they get press attention for a period and then are soon forgotten. No one talks about the many thousands of priests who are faithful to their calling. Everyone knows who Judas was but I wonder how many could name the other eleven Apostles? Some present-day religions were started by ex-priests who rejected their vows. You would not have any respect for the Catholic religion if it had such an origin.

Take this book and read the first few lessons very carefully, then some night this week come back for your first instruction. On page 288 you will find certain prayers, some of which we should like to have you learn by heart. You need not commit them to memory at once, but read them every night as a night-prayer, and in a short time you will know them without much study.

It's important that you do some praying while taking instructions, because true faith is a gift of God, which you must seek from Him by prayer. *The Lord's Prayer,* the *Hail Mary,* and the *Apostles' Creed* practically came from Heaven. That is why we want Catholics to know them by heart. *The Lord's Prayer* was composed and taught to His followers by Christ Himself; the first part of the *Hail Mary* contains the words which the angel, as a messenger of God, addressed to Mary; also the words spoken to her by her cousin Elizabeth, speaking under the influence of the Holy Spirit; and the *Apostles' Creed* is the most ancient Christian profession of faith which contains a summary of the chief truths taught by Our Lord through His Church. Hence we cannot improve on these three prayers. In addition, we wish our people to know *some form* of the Acts of *Faith, Hope, Charity* and *Contrition.*

Mr. J. I note that to nearly all public prayers said by clergymen, the congregation answers "Amen." What does that mean?

Father S. It's a Hebrew word that means "So be it," and expresses approval of and firm belief in the prayer said. But even the one who prays privately usually closes with that word.

In our discussions I am going to make frequent quotations from the Bible because God's revelation to us is fundamental to faith. I am also going to refer frequently to the documents issued by Vatican Council II. This Council which was composed of all the bishops of the Catholic Church gives the most up-to-date and authentic statements of what Catholics must believe. We will not use the decisions of the Council Fathers as proofs but solely as statements of Catholic beliefs. Our proofs will be drawn mainly from Scripture because non-Catholics are familiar with the Bible and place great confidence in it. We shall also refer to Apostolic tradition.

Be sure to ask me any questions that occur to you during your instructions. We have nothing to hide and would not receive you into the Church unless you could assure us that you are thoroughly convinced.

Mr. J. Well, Father, I'm certainly much obliged to you for the information you have given me tonight, and I'm looking forward to my first instruction.

Father S. Can you come on Tuesday night?

Mr. J. Yes, that will be fine.

Father S. But *pray* while you study. I want God to become especially interested in you, just as you, prompted by His grace, are beginning to become interested in Him.

Mr. J. I promise to do that.

Fundamentals of Christian Faith

We believe that this only God is absolutely one in His infinitely holy essence as also in all His perfections, in His omnipotence, His infinite knowledge, His providence, His will and His love.

He is *He Who Is,* as He revealed to Moses; and He is Love, as the Apostle John teaches us: so that these two names, Being and Love, express ineffably the same divine Reality of Him Who has wished to make Himself known to us, and Who "dwelling in light inaccessible" is in Himself above every name, above everything and above every created intellect.

God alone can give us right and full knowledge of this Reality by revealing Himself as Father, Son and Holy Spirit, in Whose Eternal Life we are by grace called to share, here below in the obscurity of faith and after death in eternal light.

The mutual bonds which eternally constitute the Three Persons, Who are each one and the same Divine Being, are the blessed inmost life of God Thrice Holy, infinitely beyond all that we can conceive in human measure. We give thanks, however, to the Divine Goodness that very many believers can testify with us before men to the Unity of God, even though they know not the Mystery of the Most Holy Trinity. — *Credo of the People of God.*

Mr. J. Good evening, Father Smith. I'm ready for our first session.

Father S. Good evening. Take a chair. Have you done any praying for Divine assistance, as I suggested?

Mr. J. Yes, I have prayed in my own way for God's direction, and have committed to memory the *Lord's Prayer,* the *Hail Mary* and the *Apostles' Creed.* I do not yet know those other forms called the "Acts."

Father S. That's good progress. Learn the "Acts" by reading them once a day. Of course, you *could* say them in your own words.

Mr. J. Will there be any special order to the instructions I shall receive?

Father S. Yes, there will be; otherwise you would never know when you were through. We shall relate our discussion (1) to matters of *Faith;* (2) to God's *laws* or Commandments; and (3) to the *helps* Christ provided for man's salvation. Members of the Church must believe all Christ taught, observe God's laws, and use the means of grace Christ instituted.

Mr. J. Well, as far as my instruction is concerned, you had better start at the very beginning.

Father S. Yes. I'll try to give you as much information as possible during these instructions. Religion, like everything else, must have a foundation and the foundation of all religion is the recognition of a Supreme Being, belief in the existence of an almighty, all-holy, all-wise, all-merciful and just God. You believe in God, do you not?

Mr. J. Yes, Father; but I must admit that I take it for granted and I would have difficulty proving He exists.

Father S. I'll give brief proofs. Of course, practically every page of the Bible speaks of God, but there are reasons apart from the Bible. Here they are:

(1) The universe is governed by perfect laws. These laws are responsible for the ever admirable *order* in the universe. There are billions of immensely large heavenly bodies, most of which move in space with almost lightning speed and also revolve round one another, yet there are no disorderly collisions such as we have with automobiles, for instance, despite

traffic signals and State laws to control driving. By knowing and using these laws we were able to put men on the moon and bring them home. Everything in the universe, except human beings, observes faithfully the laws imposed by the Creator. It would go badly with us if it were not so. But such laws did not make themselves. They imply a Law-Maker with a supreme intelligence that planned those laws and a supreme power that put them into effect.

(2) Belief in God is so natural that it has always been the universal conviction of mankind. All men are endowed with reason and the world about them is so manifestly dependent upon its Author that their minds almost instinctively rise to God. No rational man is a born atheist. To become an atheist, he must set himself apart from other men of all times and try to persuade himself that they are wrong; yet no such person has brought forth one *valid* proof that there is no God.

I mentioned earlier that I was going to quote frequently from Vatican Council II. Well, in its Decree on Revelation it tells us that God can be known by reason alone. Recalling Paul's Letter to the Romans (1:20) where he writes that God can be known for certainty from created reality by the light of human reason, the Council adds that those truths which are not accessible by human reason can easily, certainly and truthfully be known through revelation.

(3) It is much easier to believe in God than to try to account for the universe without God.

(4) Another most convincing proof of the existence of God is that voice within us which tells us that certain things are wrong, and which disturbs our peace when we do certain evil things. If there were no God, to Whom we are accountable, there would be no reason to be thus disturbed.

Mr. J. May I ask you how you would answer the believers in evolution?

Father S. Have you ever stopped to realize that while most men consider evolution a *fact,* it is still only a *theory,* unproven and leaving many unanswered questions. But if scientists ever actually *proved* the theory that everything material in the universe, including plants and animals, evolved by slow processes from original atoms or gases, the Church would not oppose them. Because even that original element must have been created. Every effect must have a cause; the first thing must have been produced from nothing, which only a God could accomplish.

Mr. J. You imply that the human soul could not be accounted for by evolution.

Father S. It certainly could not. Since every effect must also have an *adequate* cause, the soul of man, whose nature is altogether spiritual, could not evolve from an animal or anything material. A spirit could be produced only by the Supreme Spirit, God.

Mr. J. A friend of mine calls himself an Agnostic. What is meant by that?

Father S. One who does not deny God's existence, but contends that he does not know whether there is a God or not. Usually he is not anxious to know, because he is not in the mood to keep the commandments of God.

A German writer (Dennert) published a book in Berlin some years ago, in which he shows that of 300 of the greatest scientists of the last three centuries, 243 were firm believers in God, and saw harmony between science and their faith. Herbert Spencer says: "The existence of this inscrutable power (God) is the most certain of all truths." Alexis Carrel, the inventor of the artificial heart, was a skeptic as a young man but the greater a scientist he became, the greater grew his belief in God. Werner Von Braun, "father" of the space program, was a firm Christian. Astronauts read the Bible while traveling to the moon. A priest, Gregor Mendel, is the founder of modern genetics. Doctor Albert Zahm was a prime developer of our aerodynamic industry and a believer in God. Thomas Killion, a Catholic physicist, was responsible for the development of our Polaris submarine program. None of these men found any conflict between religion and science.

Actually, the question of God's existence is not a question for physical sciences to answer at all. The scientist's work is to study things as he finds them and the laws which govern their operation. He is *not* concerned about their *ultimate origin*.

Mr. J. My question is answered as far as I am concerned, but my difficulty is that I don't know much about God.

Father S. We can best know God by knowing some of His perfections. First of all, He is an infinitely perfect spirit. This means that He has perfect understanding and free will, but there is nothing material about Him. He hasn't a body, and He will never die, for He is immortal. He possesses every perfection without limit and to the utmost degree. He does not owe His existence to another, but is in every way self-sufficient. This is true of no other being, for all other beings owe their existence to Him, hence they are dependent and limited in the perfections that they possess. Moreover, God never changes and He is eternal—which means that He always was and always will be. He is all-good; He is infinitely lovable and showers His blessings upon us. There is nothing that He cannot do, because He is almighty. He knows all things perfectly: the present and the future; even our most secret thoughts, words and actions. Although He cannot be seen by our bodily eyes, He is everywhere, for it is His power that keeps everything in existence. Thus, as a loving Father He cares especially for His human children and provides for them. This loving care is called Divine Providence. Do not these facts about God give you some idea of how far above His creatures He is, yet how close He is to every one of us?

Mr. J. I'll say they do.

Father S. Now, although our reason demands the existence of a Supreme Being, to Whom we owe our life, on Whom we are dependent for all things, and Whom we must serve, as things stand it cannot know enough about the nature of God, nor about the precise service He wants from us. These latter things depend wholly on His will, which it was necessary for Him to make known to us. We call this divine *Revelation*. God has revealed much about Himself and what we must believe and do in order to reach our eternal destiny.

Religion is a form of elementary justice which obligates us to give God the recognition and honor which is His right and which we owe Him as private individuals and as members of human society. All people are obliged to recognize their Creator by religious practice. It should be clear also, I think, that the Almighty should want to be known alike and served alike by the whole human family.

Mr. J. Yes, Father, it seems that He should.

Father S. Then He would have to tell enough about Himself for the purpose, and define in pretty clear terms what He wants of us. He revealed Himself to the first human creatures, and frequently thereafter to their descendants, and 2000 years ago, when the world was in sore need of a dependable teacher, He appeared on earth in human form, and founded a Kingdom, or Church in which His revelation would be authoritatively and universally taught until the end of the world. Now, in the course of our instructions, you will become acquainted with the nature of this Church, with her teachings, with God's laws, and the God-given helps which she possesses for the purpose of leading men to eternal happiness. But before proceeding to this, we shall see what Revelation (much of which is contained in the Bible) says about God's creation of, and His dealings with, the first intelligent creatures He made. While fashioning this visible world, the temporary home of man, He made a multitude of angels to share His happiness in Heaven. Some liberal theologians today question the existence of angels. However the Bible frequently mentions them, they are companions of Jesus (Matt. 25:31), and Vatican Council II in its Constitution on the Church (49, 69) accepts angels as essentials of Catholic teaching. The Sacramentary even has Masses in their honor. You have often heard of angels, have you not, Mr. Jackson?

Mr. J. Yes, Father; and I have often seen them pictured as beautiful figures with wings.

Father S. Actually, they have no wings; they do not even have a body which could support wings. They are pure spirits (Pope Paul's Credo) resembling God much more closely than a human soul, which is also a spirit.

Mr. J. But why are angels pictured with a body and with wings?

Father S. Well, they could not be represented at all without a body; there is no way to draw an invisible spirit. Then, angels have frequently been sent as messengers of God to men, at which times they appeared in a human form. Artists represent them with wings to convey better the idea of how they pass from heaven to earth and of the swiftness with which they carry out God's wishes.

Mr. J. If the devils are fallen angels, they have no bodies either?

Father S. No; though they are often represented as hideous figures, with horns, cloven feet, etc. Of course, the devils have become as hideous and deformed by their fall as the angels have become beautiful and god-like by their loyalty to God. Hence devils cannot be pictured too ugly. Vatican II in The Church Today (13) refers to the devil as Personified Evil.

Mr. J. When you say angels are pure spirits, that doesn't give me a very definite idea of them.

Father S. Well, I'll try to be more definite. Angels are persons, made in such a way by their Creator that they do not need and do not have bodies. They are persons because they are individuals highly endowed with intellectual powers and free will; and since there is nothing material in their make-up, they are purely spiritual persons.

Persons of this kind reflect the perfection of their Author more clearly than do any other creatures and are capable of sharing His happiness through knowledge and love.

The fact is that some of the angels attained that happiness and some failed. God does not force such happiness on His free creatures. There can be no love without free will. He sought their choice by testing their loyalty. At the beginning of their lives, all the angels were tried and the outcome determined whether their everlasting careers were to be spent happily associated with God or separated from and opposed to Him. Some, disregarding His will in this matter, and with proud thoughts of independence, chose to part company with God, but the majority cast their lot with their Maker. The result was the Devils of Hell and the Angles of Heaven. All are angels, but some are faithful, some fallen.

Mr. J. Did they all have an equal chance?

Father S. Yes, all the angels had an equal chance. They were created sinless with the opportunity of attaining life in Heaven, the liberty of the Sons of God and the happiness that was their divinely appointed goal. Their fall came when they deliberately chose a state that has come to be Hell. For it was then that the punishments of Hell were first prepared. Fixed in their determination to be separated from God, they are fixed in their opposition to Him and all His plans, even for men. Hence they strive to separate men from God with all the efforts that God permits them to exert. That is why St. Paul tells us: "Put on the armor of God so that you may be able to stand firm against the tactics of the devil" (Eph. 6:11).

By their loyal obedience, the Angels of Heaven deserved to be familiarly associated with their Maker and to secure forever their share of His life and happiness. In Heaven they have a willing part in His plans to lead each and every one of us to that same happy state by their prayers, by acting as His messengers to men, and serving as our guardians. (Ps. 91:11; Heb. 1:14).

Mr. J. I never gave much thought to any possible interest they might have in me.

Father S. As a matter of fact, the invisible world of angels is lined up for and against us. Our guardians cannot compel us to do good, but they help us, especially when it is humanly impossible for us to help ourselves. Our tempters solicit us to sin in ways that the evil world about us and the evil inclinations within us can never use, but they never compel us to do wrong.

This is why St. Peter tells us: "Stay sober and alert. Your opponent the devil is prowling like a roaring lion looking for someone to devour" (1 Pet. 5:8). This explains the temptation of our first parents by the devil, to which we shall refer in our next instruction.

Fall of Adam, and Original Sin

We believe that in Adam all have sinned, which means that the original offense committed by him caused human nature, common to all men, to fall to a state in which it bears the consequences of that offense, and which is not the state in which it was at first in our first parents, established as they were in holiness and justice, and in which man knew neither evil nor death.

It is human nature so fallen, stripped of the grace that clothed it, injured in its own natural powers and subjected to the dominion of death, that is transmitted to all men, and it is in this sense that every man is born in sin.

We therefore hold, with the Council of Trent, that original sin is transmitted with human nature, "not by imitation, but by propagation" and that it is thus "proper to everyone." —*Credo of the People of God.*

Father S. Well, Mr. Jackson, have you had any difficulty in accepting what you were taught in the last instruction?

Mr. J. No, Father; only I was impressed by what you said about the fallen angels—the poor devils, who have lost Heaven for good.

Father S. It does seem sad, but it was all their own fault. They knew what would be the consequences of their rebellion, and possessing free will, could have chosen to obey the Almighty. They surely could not have expected to be rewarded, and rewarded eternally, for rebellion against their Creator, their only Lover, the One Who drew them out of nothingness, clothed them with beauty and offered them happiness indescribable in His own Heavenly home. Eternal reward had no alternative but eternal separation from God; if they could not have Heaven, they must be excluded from Heaven, which is the worst torment of Hell.

The Almighty dealt quite similarly with the first human creatures He made. God gave us free will, and it can be our salvation or our undoing. He tested the loyalty of our first parents with a promise of Heaven for fidelity and a threat of Hell for disobedience. We shall take this up presently. According to the Bible (Genesis 1-5), God made the universe and all it contained in six days, beginning with purely material things, followed by the lower kind of living things, then by animals, and finally by man, who was to have only a temporary home here below. Our final destiny, like that of the angels, would be Heaven; but like the angels, we would receive it only as a reward for service. God could deal honorably with us in no other manner and still leave us what we are, free beings.

Mr. J. Was the whole structure of the universe really formed in six days?

Father S. Not likely. Most experts in the interpretation of Sacred Scripture are inclined to support geologists who contend that the word "day" used by Moses, could not have been the brief period spanned by 24 hours. Not that God could not have produced all in six days or even six seconds, but they say facts are against the literal "day." We measure our days from sunrise to sunrise, but, according to the Bible, the sun was not made until the fourth day. The word "day," as used by the biblical writer, in the absence of a better word, may have covered a very long period of time. The Church does not oppose this view. What we wish to note is that Adam, who appeared on the scene, differs from all other living creatures of the visible world in this, that he was made to serve God here and win for himself eternal happiness with God hereafter. Speaking of the creation of human beings: after material things were formed, according to Genesis 1:27, God created humans after his own image — which refers chiefly to the human soul, for God does not have a body. Our soul is like God in these respects: it is a spirit, immortal, and endowed with understanding and free will.

Mr. J. Do not scientists hold that the human body evolved from lower forms of life?

Father S. Some hold that as a theory, but they do not offer convincing proof for it. The most renowned scientists have considerably modified their ideas of evolution. There is a long list of scientists who reject total evolution. If science itself cannot agree it behooves theologians and catechists to beware of basing teachings on uncertain foundations. And even if the evolutionists were right, we are not contending that we differ so much from the animals as to body, but as to soul. The difference between us and animals makes us differ from them not only in *degree* but also in *kind*. Our very conversation proves the spirit within our bodies. Every effect shows the nature of its cause. Our thoughts, whether expressed in words or not, are spiritual; they certainly are not material, for they cannot be seen or handled. Therefore their source, the soul, must be spiritual. And a spirit cannot die (Wisdom 3:1-4). It is not made of parts into which it can dissolve or corrupt. Hence, whether God made Adam's body out of the earth or not, matters little. The Bible says, and reason proves it, that God breathed into his body a *living* soul, a spirit that would ever live, and hence excel in value the whole material creation. This fact itself explains why God should have so interested Himself in the creature Man.

Mr. J. Does your Church have any official teaching on Adam?

Father S. Yes. Some of it is defined doctrine and some traditionally accepted explanation. It can be summarized thus: a) Adam and Eve had the same kind of human nature we do; b) they enjoyed certain gifts we do not have; and c) Adam had certain supernatural gifts which he lost by original sin. Regarding the Fall of humanity, Pope Pius VI expresses the teaching of the Church in the words from his Credo, in the section I shared with you at the start of this session.

Mr. J. But I have heard some people say that the whole creation story is just an allegory.

Father S. You used two key words there, "story" and "allegory." The latter is a poor word to use to describe the literary form used under divine inspiration to convey certain truths God wishes to be revealed. It would be an error to assume that there is no human historic value in the first chapters of Genesis. The more science learns, the more we marvel at the knowledge of the authors of these chapters. In story form, Genesis tells us of the origin of man, his elevation to grace, his fall from grace. The Church teaches these facts without ambiguity or equivocation.

Mr. J. This seems important. Can you go into it in more detail?

Father S. Certainly. We must first understand what God's original intention was concerning all mankind, providing our first parents would not disobey Him. God not only gave to them all that belonged to a complete human nature, such as keen intelligence of mind, physical health, and sharp senses of body, but He elevated their nature by causing them to share in His own divine life, and hence were objects of His intense love. But that was not all God did for our first parents, and was ready to do conditionally for all their descendants. He intended that earth should be a veritable paradise for them. They lived in a state of complete earthly happiness because God gave them full knowledge befitting their position; they were in no way disturbed by evil inclinations of their bodily desires for the pleasures of food or sex; they were free from all bodily suffering and hardship, and would never die. These perfections were *gifts* which were not due to them, but by which God generously corrected the natural imperfections which their nature would have had. However, these gifts would be lost by them for themselves and their descendants—the entire human race to come—if they, like so many of the angels, would not prove themselves loyal to their creator.

Mr. J. Does the Bible really say that we should not have had to die, had Adam not sinned?

Father S. Yes. In the Book of Wisdom 2:23-24, we read: "For God formed man to be imperishable; the image of his own nature he made him. But by the envy of the devil, death entered the world." And St. Paul, Rom. 5:12, speaks most plainly: "Just as through one man sin entered the world and with sin death, death thus coming to all men inasmuch as all sinned." That death would follow only as a consequence of sin is evident from the very threat of God to Adam: "From that tree you shall not eat; the moment you eat from it you are surely doomed to die" (Gen. 2:17). Even the necessity of wearisome labor for the maintenance of life is a consequence of our first parents' sin: "Because you listened to your wife and ate from the tree of which I had forbidden you to eat. . . . By the sweat of your face shall you get bread to eat, until you return to the ground, from which you were taken; For you are dirt, and to dirt you shall return" (Gen. 3:17-19).

Vatican II writing on the Church (2) says: "By an utterly free and mysterious decree of His own wisdom and goodness, the eternal Father created the whole world. His plan was to dignify men with a participation in His own divine life. He did not abandon men after they had fallen in Adam, but ceaselessly offered them helps to salvation, in anticipation of Christ the Redeemer 'who is the image of the invisible God, the first born of every creature' " (Col. 1:15).

Mr. J. But, Father, to me this sin does not appear to have been so bad. If I understand the case rightly, our first parents plucked from a tree and ate fruit, which God forbade them. Or is the "eating of fruit" a figure of speech to express something more vile?

Father S. That's what the Genesis story says but what difference does it make? They disobeyed God. It must be remembered that their loyalty was on trial; it was a matter of principle; God was testing their obedience; His commandment was easy to observe, but it was grave because so much depended upon their observance of it. God, in effect, said to them: "I am the Lord, your God, Who made you for Myself; Heaven is offered to you in reward for a slight act of obedience; but as free beings you are at liberty to disobey. The consequences of disobedience will be the loss of My friendship and the withdrawal of the gifts of freedom from death, pain and evil passion from yourselves and all your descendants."

God permitted one of the fallen angels, who envied Adam and Eve their opportunity to gain heaven, to tempt Eve. And she heeded, in disregard of God's command, as we read in Genesis 3:6: "The woman saw that the tree was good for food, pleasing to the eyes, and desirable for gaining wisdom. So she took some of its fruit and ate it; and she also gave some to her husband, who was with her, and he ate it."

Mr. J. And what happened?

Father S. As far as Adam and Eve were concerned, they lost the grace that made them friends of God and worthy of living the life of Heaven which had been promised to them. Besides this they became subject to death, to suffering and to a strong inclination to evil; also they were expelled from the earthly paradise in which they had dwelt.

Let me read this Council quotation to you. The Church Today (13): "Although he was made by God in a state of holiness, from the very dawn of history man abused his liberty, at the urging of personified Evil. Man set himself against God and sought to find fulfillment apart from God. . . . His senseless mind was darkened and he served the creature rather than the Creator."

As far as Adam's descendants are concerned, we have come into the world deprived of grace and inheriting his fallen state and punishment as we would have inherited his gift had he been obedient to God. This state in which we are born is called *original sin* because it is inherited by us through our origin or descent from Adam.

Vatican Council II speaking on The Laity (7) puts it this way: "Affected by original sin men have frequently fallen into multiple errors concerning the true God, the nature of man, and the principles of the moral law."

Mr. J. But does it seem just that the whole human race should be punished for the disobedience of Adam?

Father S. Yes, if you look at it in the right way. Original sin does not deprive us of anything to which we have a *strict right* as human beings, but only the free gifts which God in His generous goodness would have bestowed on us if Adam had not sinned. All God owes to the soul are its natural endowments, namely: immortality, free will and understanding. The supernatural beatification of the soul by grace, the preservation of the body from death, sickness, evil inclinations of the body passions, etc., were *gifts,* which God was free to give or withhold; and He chose to withhold them from the posterity of our first parents, if Adam, the fountainhead of the human race, disobeyed. In that one act, mankind was on trial. We have inherited our human nature from Adam in its *fallen* state.

An example may help to clear this up. What if I, as your personal friend, of my own free will presented you with a large farm which would remain yours and go to your children on a certain condition? You do not fulfill this condition, and hence lose the farm. Your children are also deprived of the same. They cannot blame me, although they might well blame you. I did not owe the farm even to you. Its retention by you, and its transmission to your children, depended wholly on your compliance with my demand. By your refusal to comply with my terms, you forfeited the same for yourself and descendants.

Mr. J. But only our temporal and not our eternal welfare was affected by our parent's sin.

Father S. That's not true. Our souls, being deprived of the supernatural beauty of grace, are not in a condition to enter a state of supernatural glory — not even the soul of a little child who has no personal sin, but has inherited "original sin."

Mr. J. I never knew that Catholics taught "infant damnation."

Father S. We don't. We do not believe that the soul of a child who dies without the grace of God because unbaptized, will be consigned to positive punishment and suffering. In fact, we believe that it enjoys a happiness which far exceeds any natural happiness here—but it can be only a *natural* happiness, or a kind that fits the soul's capacity.

Mr. J. Will parents and unbaptized children be reunited after death?

Father S. We know nothing about human relationships beyond the grave. All we do know is that we will possess everything necessary to make each of us fully happy.

Mr. J. Well, how is it that grown-ups can fare better than children?

Father S. All grown-ups do not fare better than children, and many of them not as well. But God, in His goodness and mercy, has come to our rescue. Original sin can be removed, and the souls of both children and adults can receive the grace in which they would have been created had Adam not sinned.

In our next instruction we shall explain what God did to reinstate us in His friendship, and how we can be made capable and worthy of living the life of Heaven.

Mr. J. Were Adam and Eve jointly responsible for original sin?

Father S. Both violated God's command, but Adam alone, as head of the human race, is responsible for its transmission through the ages.

INSTRUCTION 3

God's Plan to Save Mankind

We believe that Our Lord Jesus Christ, by the Sacrifice of the Cross redeemed us from original sin and all the personal sins committed by each one of us, so that, in accordance with the word of the Apostle, "where sin abounded, grace did more abound" (Rom. 5:20). — *Credo of the People of God.*

Father S. Well, Mr. Jackson, where did we leave off with our instruction? You see, I have a number of persons coming for instructions and I easily lose track of what progress we have made.

Mr. J. Why, you told me that you would explain how it became possible for those who are born in a state of original sin to recover the friendship of God by receiving Sanctifying Grace.

Father S. Oh, yes; and this lesson will present God to you as an infinitely good, loving and merciful Father. But for a proper understanding of the matter it will be necessary for you to know something about the Trinity. Do you know what that word means?

Mr. J. No, Father.

Father S. It means that in the One God there are three Divine Persons, called respectively, God the Father, God the Son, and God the Holy Spirit.

Mr. J. You are telling me two things which I do not quite see through: (1) that God is a person; I thought only creatures were persons, and (2) that the One God is Three.

Father S. In answer to your first difficulty, let me remind you that not only human beings are persons, but all *spirits,* because possessed of intelligence and free will, are persons. The angels, therefore, are persons, and so is God. We human beings are *persons* only because we too have intelligence and free will. Our personality, therefore, arises primarily from our souls and their powers of reasoning and free choice. If merely our bodies made us *persons,* animals would be persons.

As to the second difficulty, you do not quite catch the teaching of the Church; God is ONE in *nature,* but three Divine persons possess that divine nature. Vatican II expresses it thusly: "Our union with the Church in heaven is put into effect in its noblest manner when with common rejoicing we celebrate together the praise of the divine Majesty. Then all those from every tribe and tongue and people and nation (Apoc. 5:9), who have been redeemed by the blood of Christ, who have been gathered together into one Church, with one song of praise do magnify God One and Three" (The Church 50).

Mr. J. I am afraid you will have to express yourself somewhat more clearly, Father; that is over my head.

Father S. That's not surprising. Not only you, but I, and the most learned theologians, fail to fully comprehend what Christ has revealed concerning the Trinity.

That God is Triune, one and three, is a truth we only know by revelation. "Indeed the Lord Jesus, when he prayed to the Father 'that all may be one . . . as we are one' (Jn. 17:21-22), opened up vistas closed to human reason. For he implied a certain likeness between the union of the Divine Persons and in the union of the children of God in truth and charity" (The Church Today 24). The Trinity is one of the few revealed truths which we cannot fully grasp. No created intelligence can fully comprehend God's nature. God would not be God, He would not be infinite, but finite, if creatures whose powers of intellect are limited could fully comprehend Him. I said that it is *one of the few* teachings of faith which we cannot grasp. The wonder is that such truths are not innumerable because if we consider the countless number of things in *nature* which we do not understand we should expect to find very much of the mysterious in the *supernatural* order. The Trinity is a mystery, or a truth which we believe on God's word, but which we cannot fully fathom with our reason.

Mr. J. Where does the Bible refer to the Trinity?

Father S. In Matt. 28:19 we read Christ's last command to His Apostles that they should preach to all nations and "Baptize them in the name of the Father, and of the Son, and of the Holy Spirit." Then we read in Mark 1:9-11: "During that time, Jesus came from Nazareth in Galilee and was baptized in the Jordan by John. Immediately on coming up out of the water he saw the sky rent in two and the Spirit descending on him like a dove. Then a voice came from the heavens: 'You are my beloved Son. On you my favor rests.' " There are many other passages in the New Testament which refer to the Father, Son and Holy Spirit, together and separately.

Mr. J. Then it seems that they are separate Persons.

Father S. Yes, they are three Divine Persons really distinct from one another. The Father is not the Son, neither is the Holy Spirit the Father or the Son. In our soul, though a spirit, and hence an indivisible thing, the understanding is not the will, neither is the memory, yet each of these distinct powers belongs to the very nature of the soul. But as I have said, you must not expect to grasp this, nor expect that I should be able to explain the "how" to you. However, we do know that the three Divine Persons are perfectly equal to one another because they are one and the same God, and they are one and the same God because they all have one and the same divine nature.

Now, we can start the promised instruction. After Adam, the head of the human race, sinned, and involved us all in his loss of God's friendship and grace, Heaven was closed against all mankind, because as we have already seen, the possession of Sanctifying Grace is a condition for the enjoyment of the vision of God. Had the Almighty shown no mercy, Adam and Eve would have met the same miserable everlasting fate as the rebellious angels, since they knowingly committed a similar sin. However, because our first parents were tempted from an external source, and there was question of future billions being involved who did not sin actually, God in His unbounded mercy, opened a way for the possible salvation of the human race.

As the Decree on Liturgy (5) states: "God, who 'wishes all men to be saved and to come to the knowledge of truth' (1 Tim. 2:4) 'in many and various ways . . . spoke of old to our fathers by the prophets' (Heb. 1:1). When the fullness of time had come He sent His Son, the Word made flesh, anointed by the Holy Spirit, to preach the gospel to the poor, to heal the contrite of heart (cf. Is. 61:1, Luke 4:18) to be a bodily and spiritual medicine, the mediator between God and man (cf. 1 Tim. 2:5). For His humanity, united with the person of the Word, was the instrument of our salvation. Thus 'in Christ there came forth the perfect satisfaction needed for our reconciliation, and we received the means of giving worthy worship to God' (Verona Sacramentary)."

Mr. J. This is certainly a consolation.

Father S. A consolation to us, but mind you what it cost God to accomplish it!

Mr. J. What it cost God! Could He not simply have pardoned Adam and let that end it?

Father S. He could have; but because God is all-just and cannot be indifferent to sin, He required that the demands of justice be met; He required that the sin be fully atoned for, and Adam could not do it.

Mr. J. Why could not Adam do it? It would seem that the one who sins could undo his sin by repentance.

Father S. No, Mr. Jackson, a creature endowed with

reason and free will can disobey God, but only a person of infinite dignity can repair that offense.

Mr. J. I don't grasp that.

Father S. Well, you see, offenses are greater as the dignity of the one offended is greater, so the offense involved in a sin against God is measured by the greatness and dignity of God, Who is offended — and God's dignity is limitless and infinite. Now, no good human work can be greater than a person's own powers, which are limited; and there will always be an immeasurable distance between our best works and what God is actually entitled to by strict justice.

Mr. J. It is plain to me, now. We human beings are born with a limitless debt to pay and only limited means to pay it.

Father S. That's right. The Son of God, the Second person of the Trinity, took unto Himself human nature and was born of the Blessed Virgin Mary. "The Son, therefore, came on a mission from His Father. It was in Him, before the foundation of the world, that the Father chose us and predestined us to become adopted sons, for in Him it has pleased the Father to re-establish all things (cf. Ephesians 1:4-5, 10). To carry out the will of the Father, Christ inaugurated the kingdom of heaven on earth and revealed to us the mystery of the Father. By His obedience He brought about redemption. The Church, or, in other words the kingdom of Christ, now present in mystery, grows visibly in the world through the power of God" (The Church 3).

The Son of God was not always man, but He became man at the time of the Incarnation. Now by that term "Incarnation" is meant that the Son of God, remaining God, took unto Himself a body and soul like ours in Mary's womb. Thus Jesus Christ was truly God because He had the same *divine nature* as His Father, and He was truly man because, as Mary's son, He had a *body and soul like ours.* He was one person — the Second Person of the Trinity, who became man and here on earth offered an adequate atonement for the sins of mankind to His Heavenly Father. That is why we speak of

Him as the Savior of all. With God atoning for sin, the reparation was as infinite and limitless as the sin which attacked His infinite majesty. St. John calls the Second Person of the Trinity "the Word," and refers to the "Incarnation" thus: "In the beginning was the Word; the Word was in God's presence, and the Word was God. . . . The Word became flesh and made his dwelling among us, and we have seen his glory; the glory of an only Son coming from the Father, filled with enduring love" (John 1:1, 14).

Mr. J. That was surely mercy and goodness on the part of God, of which we were wholly unworthy. Was He the Son of God in the flesh, Who, on earth, was known as "Christ"?

Father S. Precisely.

Mr. J. But did not thousands of years elapse between Adam and Christ's time?

Father S. Yes, according to the way the Bible reckons time, over 4,000 years. But we must remember that the biblical writers were not scientists. What they are really speaking of is ages. Through Carbon-14 tests and other modern methods we know the human race to be very old. Evidence of campsites found in Africa go back 2,600,000 years. The more scientists discover, the more their discoveries support the testimony of the Bible. Our ancestors became wanderers, spreading over the face of the earth.

Mr. J. That is another puzzle to me. Did all the descendants of our first parents, who lived during those centuries, get the benefit of God's atonement?

Father S. Yes, God promised a Savior to Adam and Eve, and often thereafter through others — the prophets — and in anticipation, He applied the merits of the atonement of Christ to their souls on the condition of faith in the Redeemer to come and the fulfillment of other conditions, such as observing the Law.

Mr. J. I now understand Christ in a new light! Who He was and what He did never dawned on me. That makes Mary important, too, doesn't it?

Father S. Yes, and I'm happy that you are beginning to grasp God's plan for us. Mary is the next logical step. When, in eternity, God willed to become man, He evidently thought of the one from whom He would take His flesh and blood. She must be as worthy of her dignity as a creature could be. Hence at the moment He would create her soul, He would apply to it the merits of His atonement and preserve it from original sin. It would not be fitting that she, from whom He would take His human nature, in which He would atone for sin, should herself ever have been infected with sin. You will hear us speak of Mary's *Immaculate Conception,* by which we express our belief in her preservation from original sin when she was conceived, at the first moment of her existence.

Mr. J. Is the Immaculate Conception the same as the "virgin birth"?

Father S. No. Mary was *born* in a natural way of human parents as all other human beings are. It was Christ Who had a "virgin birth," since His body was formed in the womb of a virgin by the power of the Holy Spirit (Luke 1:35).

Mr. J. I now understand better that little prayer I read the other night called *"Hail Mary";* there Mary is spoken of as being "full of grace."

Father S. Yes, those are the words of the Angel Gabriel, who was sent by Almighty God to announce to Mary her exalted vocation, and receive her consent to the will of God. I wish you would read this incident in the first chapter of St. Luke's Gospel. There it is recorded that Mary was a *virgin,* and blessed among all women — both because she did not inherit original sin and because she was chosen from among all women to be the Mother of the Son of God. There it is told how Mary hesitated at the angel's message, because she could not understand how she could become a mother and still remain forever a virgin consecrated to God. Then the angel made known that by a miracle, by the power of the Holy Spirit, she would conceive and bring forth a Son Who would be called "Son of the Most High." The *Apostles' Creed* expresses this mystery in the words "Who was conceived by the Holy Spirit, born of the Virgin Mary."* Thus Christ had no human father, but St. Joseph, who was Mary's husband, was His guardian or foster father.

Mr. J. Father, you told me at the beginning of this instruction that you would present God as a good and living God; He must certainly be that. I would not leave off this study for anything, for while God seems greater and holier to me than ever before, yet I feel nearer to Him. I begin to picture Him as intensely interested in me.

---

*The Credo of Pope Paul VI expresses the Church's doctrine in this regard succinctly and scholarly:

"We believe that Mary is the Mother, who remained ever a Virgin, of the Incarnate Word, our God and Saviour Jesus Christ (13), and that by reason of this singular election, she was, in consideration of the merits of her Son, redeemed in a more eminent manner (14), preserved from all stain of original sin (15) and filled with the gift of grace more than all other creatures. (16).

"Joined by a close and indissoluble bond to the Mysteries of the Incarnation and Redemption (17), the Blessed Virgin, the Immaculate, was at the end of her earthly life raised body and soul to heavenly glory (18) and likened to her risen Son in anticipation of the future lot of all the just; and We believe that the Blessed Mother of God, the New Eve, Mother of the Church (19), continues in Heaven, her maternal role with regard to Christ's members, cooperating with the birth and growth of divine life in the souls of the redeemed(20)."

(13). Cf. Dz.-Sch. 251-252. (14) Cf. Lumen Gentium 53. (15) Cf. Dz.-Sch. 2803.
(16) Cf. Lumen Gentium 53. (17) Lumen Gentium 53, 58, 61. (18) Cf. Dz.-Sch. 3903.
(19) Cf. Lumen Gentium 53, 56, 61, 63; Cf. Paul VI, Alloc. for the Closing of the Third Session of the Second Vatican Council, AAS LVI (1964) 1016; Cf. Exhort. Apost. Signum Magnum, Introd. (20) Cf. Lumen Gentium 62; Cf. Paul VI, Exhort. Apost. Signum Magnum, P.1, n.1.

Principal Events in Christ's Life

We believe in Our Lord Jesus Christ, Who is the Son of God. He is the Eternal Word, born of the Father before time began, and one in substance with the Father, homoousios to the Father, and through Him all things were made.

He was incarnate of the Virgin Mary by the power of the Holy Spirit, and was made man: equal therefore to the Father according to His divinity, and inferior to the Father according to His humanity, and Himself one, not by some impossible confusion of His natures, but by the unity of His person.

He dwelt among us, full of grace and truth. He proclaimed and established the Kingdom of God and made us know in Himself the Father. He gave us His new commandment to love one another as He loved us. He taught us the way of the Beatitudes of the Gospel: poverty in spirit, meekness, suffering borne with patience, thirst after justice, mercy, purity of heart, will for peace, persecution suffered for justice' sake. Under Pontius Pilate He suffered, the Lamb of God bearing on Himself the sins of the world, and He died for us on the Cross, saving us by His redeeming Blood.

He was buried, and, of His own power, rose the third day, raising us by His Resurrection to that sharing in the divine life which is the life of grace. He ascended to heaven, and He will come again, this time in glory, to judge the living and the dead: each according to his merits — those who have responded to the Love and Piety of God going to eternal life, those who have refused them to the end going to the fire that is not extinguished.

And His Kingdom will have no end. — *Credo of the People of God.*

Father S. This evening we are going to discuss the life of Christ, at least the important events. Most of our instruction will deal with Him, His teachings, and what He means to us. Soon we shall prove that He was truly God. But now I should like to ask how much you know about His life while He was on earth.

Mr. J. I know something, because after your suggestion, I read St. Luke's Gospel.

Father S. We derive our historical knowledge of Christ chiefly from the books of the Bible which, besides being the inspired word of God, can be proved to be reliable historical records. The Bible makes mention of only a few incidents up to the time He began His public teaching, when He was 30 years old. But nearly the whole New Testament is concerned with Him, His teachings, His miracles, and so on, from His thirtieth to His thirty-third year. You know where He was born, Mr. Jackson?

Mr. J. Near a little town called Bethlehem, in Palestine. But, Father, didn't Mary live at Nazareth?

Father S. Yes. I suppose you are not acquainted with the sad circumstances associated with the birth of the Savior. It must be remembered that He came from Heaven not only to teach us, and to give the human race divine help for the attainment of salvation, but He came to atone for *sin by suffering;* and He wanted that suffering to begin with His entrance into the world, and continue uninterruptedly until He would die in acute agony on the Cross. Hence, it was providentially arranged that He should be born away from home—be born in a stable or cave outside the town of Bethlehem, whose every house on that day was filled with people, who like Joseph and Mary, went to register their names for the census. The census then was not taken up as it is here in our country. Instead of agents going from house to house to get the information, people went to what we might call the "County Seat" and registered. Bethlehem was the town to which Joseph had to go; Mary went with him, and while away on this mission, the birth of Jesus took place. Do you know how Heaven showed its interest in the birth of the Savior? (Luke 2:1-20).

Mr. J. Do you refer to the appearance of an angel to the shepherds, and the coming from Heaven of a multitude of angels to honor Jesus in the crib?

Father S. Exactly. And the angel announced that this event gave great glory to God, and would give peace to people on earth. For the first time since the dawn of creation, God was fittingly honored on earth; it was an infinite honor. And it opened the way for peace between the human race and God.

Mr. J. How do you explain all the wars which have taken place since then?

Father S. By the evil will of people who still rebel against God. However, absence of war is not what the angel meant by "peace." He meant peace in the hearts of men, and among all men if they would love one another as brothers.

Mr. J. Did not the Son of God do enough by the mere act of assuming human nature, without subjecting Himself to 33 years more of humiliation and suffering following His birth?

Father S. It would have been sufficient to redeem us, but not to satisfy God's love. God would furnish further proof of His unlimited love for us, and impress on us forcibly the lesson of the awful malice of sin. Hardly was Christ born when there was scheming for His death. King Herod, who ruled over Judea at the time, fearing that Jesus wanted to become an earthly king, who might dethrone him, ordered a massacre of all infant boys as a sure way of killing the child Jesus. Mary and Joseph received a warning from Heaven to this effect, and escaped with the Child from Herod's frightful anger. They went over into Egypt, where they endured the terrible affliction of living for several years amid pagan wickedness, and where they likely suffered the severest poverty and privations.

It is true that Christ could have prevented all this, but it was part of His plan for a superabundant reparation for the sins of mankind. Now, Mr. Jackson, what is the next reference to Christ in the Gospel story?

Mr. J. I believe it bears on His coming up to Jerusalem with His parents at the age of 12 (Luke 2:42-52).

Father S. Yes, and His stay there for three days after Joseph and Mary had left for home. He intentionally allowed Himself to be lost from them.

Mr. J. What was His purpose in doing this?

Father S. The Savior wished to teach people for all time that his "Father's business" must have our attention before anything else, even if we must slight our nearest relatives or our dearest friends. It was the Father's will that Jesus should avail Himself of this opportunity to prove to the Doctors of the Jewish Law that it was time for the appearance of the Messias, by which name the Jews referred to Him Who was to come. It was also the Father's will that He should teach all of us how we should love to spend time in the house of God.

Mr. J. But I cannot understand how Joseph and Mary could have gone far without missing Jesus.

Father S. The city of Jerusalem was surrounded by a wall, as were almost all cities at that time, and there were roads which went out over the country from different gates; it was not unusual that for groups traveling together men would travel with men, women with women, or for husbands and wives to split up and travel with different groups of relatives. This is what happened to Joseph and Mary, and each thought that Jesus was with the other, until they met at some point after having walked a whole day. Then upon discovering that Jesus had not accompanied either, they returned together to Jerusalem, probably stopping at every house to inquire whether a boy answering His description had been seen. "Sorrowing" they sought Him in vain until they had returned to the temple, where Jesus was enlightening by His heavenly wisdom, men who were supposed to be well versed in the Old

Testament Scripture and law. The question is sometimes raised of how much the man Jesus knew of His calling, of how much the human nature knew of the divine nature. Luke shows clearly in his Gospel narrative that even as a child Jesus was definitely aware of His divine mission. His surprise was that others were not. Just as it was the Father's will that Jesus should have remained there for a purpose, so now it was the Father's will that He should teach the lesson of obedience and respect to parents by returning home with them; in fact, the Bible sums up the home life of Jesus by the words: "He was subject to them"—His parents. After this there is no allusion to Our Lord—until when?

Mr. J. Until, if I remember correctly, He was baptized by St. John in the River Jordan, after which He spent 40 days fasting in the desert. I do see, Father, that Christ was most severe with Himself, and of course, for our sake, because He personally stood in no need of such works of penance.

Father S. Yes. And after that, what did Christ do?

Mr. J. He began a public ministry lasting three years.

Father S. That's correct. During this time it was not so much His aim to be a true teacher, and assist the people with whom He came in contact, as to prove His divinity and prepare the way for the instruction and sanctification of the people of every nation until the end of the world. We shall treat of this later. Do you know some of the ways by which Jesus proved that He was God?

Mr. J. Yes, if they can be believed.

Father S. Why, you surprise me, Mr. Jackson. You have already expressed your firm belief that Christ was the Son of God in human form.

Mr. J. Yes, Father, and I am *not* beginning to doubt it now.

Father S. You are, in effect; for you do not know whether to believe that He changed water into wine, multiplied the loaves, cured the blind, the crippled, the deaf and dumb, raised the dead to life, etc.

Mr. J. It does seem that if He was God, He could do these things as well as He could have fashioned the universe. But I have often heard that there are no such things as miracles.

Father S. You wish, therefore, to be convinced that Christ actually wrought the miracles ascribed to Him. How about letting proof of Christ's divinity and of His miracles go until our next instruction? For the present, let us suppose that the New Testament relates true history, that Christ, the Son of the living God, came that He might save His people from their sins (cf. Matt. 1:21) and that all men might be made holy. (Decree on Bishops 1). What does it say about Christ's death?

Mr. J. It tells us that He went freely to His death; that He sweat blood caused especially by mental agony; that He was scourged, His head crowned with thorns; that He was mocked, and cursed, and bore a cross to Mt. Calvary, was nailed to it, and died on it, hanging between thieves, after three hours of intense suffering.

Father S. And after His death, what?

Mr. J. He arose again, remained on earth 40 days, then ascended to Heaven.

Father S. Where did His soul go when He died?

Mr. J. The *Apostles' Creed* says it went to Hell, but that seems unreasonable.

Father S. Well, that needs some explanation. "Hell" is a translation of Hebrew *sheol*, "abode of the dead." Recent Bible translations use instead the wording "Nether World" (Rev. 1:18). You have already learned that Heaven was closed against all people until Christ's death; that those who, before His coming, lived holy lives, believed in the Redeemer to come, and dedicated themselves to Him, would not be lost. Jesus did not go to where the souls of those who died outside God's grace are damned. He went to those who were waiting for Him. Because Jesus would die for men God had forgiven Adam and had given him and his descendants the grace to live as His sons. All those who chose to love and obey God were waiting in what we call limbo. They had died in God's grace; but they could not go to heaven until Christ Himself should take them there. After His death He came down to them; "It was in the spirit also that he went to preach to the spirits in prison," said St. Peter (1 Peter 3:19). Although they died in God's grace they were really in prison, in the kingdom of death. The devil had brought sin and death into the world; that was his great victory. These souls were in limbo instead of heaven through his power.

When Jesus broke into the kingdom of death, He told the souls there the good news that He had won the victory for them by offering His Sacrifice, and that soon they would be taken out of their prison to heaven. These souls who had been saved through the grace He had won them received Him as their Lord and Redeemer and their God. The *Apostles' Creed* means that place by the word "Hell."

Mr. J. One last question, Father. What does the Creed mean when it says that Christ sits at the right hand of God, the Father Almighty?

Father S. By those words we profess our belief that in Heaven, Christ as God is equal in power to the Father Almighty and that as man He shares the power and glory of His Father above all the Saints and exercises the supreme authority of King over all creatures forever. This will be especially manifest to all on the last day when He will judge every one who ever lived in this world. It expresses a special relationship between Father and Son. The Credo of the People of God puts it this way: "We believe then in the Father who eternally begets the Son, in the Son, the Word of God, who is eternally begotten, in the Holy Spirit, the uncreated Person who proceeds from the Father and the Son as Their eternal Love. Thus in the Three Divine Persons, co-equal and co-eternal, the life and beatitude of God perfectly One superabound and are consummated in the supreme excellence and glory proper to uncreated Being, and always 'there should be venerated Unity in the Trinity and Trinity in the Unity'."

Proof That Christ Is God

God, who "wishes all men to be saved and to come to the knowledge of truth" (1 Tim. 2:4) "in many and various ways . . . spoke of old to our fathers by the prophets" (Heb. 1:1). When the fullness of time had come He sent His Son, the Word made flesh, anointed by the Holy Spirit, to preach the gospel to the poor, to heal the contrite of heart (cf. Is. 61:1, Luke 4:18) to be a bodily and spiritual medicine, the mediator between God and man (cf. 1 Tim. 2:5). For His humanity, united with the person of the Word, was the instrument of our salvation. Thus "in Christ there came forth the perfect satisfaction needed for our reconciliation, and we received the means of giving worthy worship to God" (Verona Sacramentary).

The wonders wrought by God among the people of the Old Testament were but a prelude to the work of Christ our Lord in redeeming mankind and giving perfect glory to God. He achieved His task principally by the paschal mystery of His blessed passion, resurrection from the dead and glorious ascension whereby "dying he destroyed our death and rising He restored our life" (Easter Preface). — *Decree on Liturgy, 5.*

Father S. Tonight, Mr. Jackson, I am going to present to you proof, plain and convincing, that Jesus Christ was truly God.

Mr. J. Why, Father, I have no reason to doubt that.

Father S. That may be true, but I want you to be able to

defend your faith by arguments. Even if a person did not believe that the Bible was inspired, you could prove your point from it, because it is certainly reliable history. You would refer to Old Testament prophecies, fulfilled in Christ, to New Testament miracles, supporting His claim, and especially to Christ's resurrection from the dead. And if your objector were so unreasonable as to spurn any argument taken from the Bible, you could prove the divinity of Jesus from what he is prepared to admit concerning His character.

Mr. J. I need just such an argument for a man who works with me. He contends that ignorant and too credulous men wrote the Bible, and that their testimony is unreliable.

Father S. They were far from being too credulous. They were accused by Christ frequently of being too slow to believe, they wanted to see and feel, and even then doubted; they would have been "fools" to doubt longer. Regarding the charge of ignorance, this was in their favor. God purposely chose the unlearned to convince the learned, because it would better prove that the cause they advocated was divine. It is easy for sharp and learned men to "deceive" others, while there is no testimony so strong as the convincing kind which comes from unlearned and simple folk. Unlearned and simple witnesses at a court trial always testify best when they relate what they actually saw or heard. Beware of the sharp fellow, if he has no conscience.

Mr. J. What proof of Christ's divinity do the prophecies of the Old Testament furnish?

Father S. In harmony with the traditions of every nation of antiquity, they tell of a Redeemer Who would descend to earth from heaven, and they clearly describe His person, character, the principal circumstances of His life and death.

Mr. J. Just what is a prophecy?

Father S. It is the definite prediction of events, the occurrence of which depends upon either the free will of man or of God, and which could not, therefore, be foreknown by man or angel, but only by God.

Mr. J. Were there many prophecies that Christ fulfilled?

Father S. Yes. I'll give you some references in the Scripture and you can compare the prophecy concerning Christ in the Old Testament with its fulfillment in the New. For instance:

He would be a *King:* Isaias 9:7; Luke 1:32. He would be a *priest:* Psalm 110:4; Hebrews 7:24. He would give *a universal form of worship:* Malachias 1:10; to *all men:* Isaias 2:2; Luke 22:4; Mark 16:15. He would *descend from David:* Jeremias 23:5-6; Luke 3:32; Matthew 1:6. He would be *born of a virgin mother*: Isaias 7:14; Luke 1:35. He would be *born in Bethlehem*: Micheas 5:2; Matthew 2:1. He would *confirm His teaching by miracles*: Isaias 35:4-6; Matthew 9:4-5.

In a most striking manner of circumstances His suffering and death were foretold: that He would be betrayed for *30 pieces of silver:* Zacharias 11:12. That he would be *flogged and spit upon*: Isaias 50:6. That His *hands and feet would be transfixed*: Psalm 22:17. That He would *die between criminals:* Isaias 53:12. That he would be *mocked:* Psalm 22:8 and *given vinegar and gall to drink:* Psalm 69:22; that His *garments would be divided:* Psalm 22:19. That His legs *would not be broken:* Numbers 9:12.

It is evident that Christ was the promised Redeemer because the fulfillment of all these prophecies in Him could not have been due to chance or human trickery, but must have been the work of God.

The doctrine of the Church resulting from all this is summed up this way by Vatican II. "The Son, therefore, came on a mission from His Father. It was in Him, before the foundation of the world, that the Father chose us and predestined us to become adopted sons, for in Him it has pleased the Father to re-establish all things (cf. Ephesians 1:4-5, 10). To carry out the will of the Father Christ inaugurated the kingdom of heaven on earth and revealed to us the mystery of the Father. By His obedience He brought about redemption. The Church, or, in other words the kingdom of Christ, now present in mystery, grows visibly in the world through the power of God" (The Church 3).

Mr. J. How do the miracles related in the New Testament prove that Christ was God?

Father S. As already noted, a miracle can be worked only by the omnipotence of God. It is an effect that is traceable to God alone. Now the New Testament records dozens of miracles which were performed by Christ *with a view to prove His claim to divinity.* They were wrought in open day, and almost always in the presence of a large number of people; yes, most of them were wrought in the presence of His very enemies—the Scribes and Pharisees—who did not doubt the genuineness of His miracles, but were envious of His success when they saw the people come to Him from far and near with their blind and deaf, their paralytics and lepers.

For the past 1800 years, criticism, the most severe, has been trained on the miracles of Christ, but with only one result, namely of establishing their truth. Well could the Savior say to His enemies: "the works the Father has given me to accomplish. These very works which I perform testify on my behalf that the Father has sent me" (John 5:36). "If I do not perform my Father's works, put no faith in me. But if I do perform them, even though you put no faith in me, put faith in these works, so as to realize what it means that the Father is in me and I in him" (John 10:37-38).

Mr. J. You said that the "Resurrection" offers the best proof.

Father S. Yes, Christ's own Resurrection, in support of which there is greater evidence and more weighty testimony than there is for any other fact of ancient history, ought to establish His divinity for even the most skeptical. For how could Christ, in accordance with His prediction, return to life of *His own power,* unless He were God? His Resurrection is attested by nearly a dozen contemporary historians, who either witnessed or were positive of His death, and then saw Him alive later. And as I say, they were men who themselves were slow to believe; in fact, they believed only after they saw Him, spoke to Him, ate with Him, touched Him. After they were convinced they appealed to the Resurrection as the foundation of all faith in Christ; they would accept no successor to Judas except one who could bear witness to Christ's death and Resurrection; they braved every danger and cheerfully laid down their lives in defense of their Master's glorious triumph over death.

Mr. J. Are there clear statements in the Scripture in which it is claimed that Christ was truly God?

Father S. 1. Yes, Our Lord Himself claimed to be God. On Good Friday morning, standing before the High Priest of the Jews, He was asked: "Are you the Messiah, the Son of the Blessed One?" Then Jesus answered: "I am; and you will see the Son of Man seated at the right hand of the Power and coming with the clouds of heaven." At that the high priest tore his robes and said: "What further need do we have of witnesses? You have heard the blasphemy. What is your verdict?" They all concurred in the verdict "guilty," with its sentence of death (Mark 14:61-64). Before He suffered, He uttered this prayer: "Do you now, Father, give me glory at your side, a glory I had with you before the world began" (John 17:5).

2. Scripture gives Christ the name of God. "In the beginning was the Word; the Word was in God's presence, and the Word was God" (John 1:1). Furthermore, this Word became the man who is Christ. "The Word became flesh and made his dwelling among us, and we have seen his glory; the glory of an only Son coming from the Father, filled with enduring love" (John 1:14).

3. Christ claimed all the powers and perfections of God: "All that the Father has belongs to me" (John 16:15). In particular, Scripture attests to His knowledge. St. Paul, speaking of Christ, says: "In whom every treasure of wisdom and knowledge is hidden" (Col. 2:3).

4. According to Scripture, divine honor is due to Him. This is plain from Our Lord's own words: "The Father him-

self judges no one, but has assigned all judgment to the Son, so that all men may honor the Son just as they honor the Father. He who refuses to honor the Son refuses to honor the Father who sent him" (John 5:22-23).

Mr. J. This is surely abundant proof for anyone willing to believe, but what if my objector refused to believe that the Bible was written by the ones to whom we ascribe the various parts?

Father S. Tacitus and Pliny, pagan historians, who lived during Christ's time, wrote about these things, and reported to the Roman Emperor their effect on the people who lived far from Palestine. Then, from profane history you could prove that the historical character, called Christ, actually lived, and was regarded as the most perfect character ever known to the world. Infidels admit this much, and this admission alone contains proof that He was God.

Mr. J. How so, Father?

Father S. Well, they grant that He was everything short of God, a model of the highest perfection, the holiest person that ever lived, etc. Now if Christ was not what He claimed to be, i.e. God, how could He have been a "model of perfection"? Would He not rather have been the "most impious, the most irreverent, the most blasphemous man that every lived" if His very profession was a lie? If Christ was not God then He was not only a false teacher, but the very greatest of the world's imposters.

We cannot weigh the beautiful things the enemies of Christianity say about its Founder without discovering the clear, even if implicit, admission they contain of His divinity. And hence logic forces us to conclude that if His enemies do not, like Peter, recognize in Him the "Son of the living God," it is because they are not willing, like Peter, to fall down on their knees and worship Him as their Lord and Master.

To sum up: The Gospel relates how on one occasion Christ asked the Apostles what the people had begun to believe concerning Him. The people were aware of Christ's sanctity and of His miracles, and hence knew Him to be an extraordinary personage; but seeing that in His exterior He resembled other men they regarded Him as another great prophet, some believing Him to be John the Baptist, others Elias or Jeremias returned to earth. Then Jesus asked the Apostles what they, by this time, believed concerning Him; whereupon Peter, speaking for all, answered: "You are the Messiah, the Son of the living God" (Matt. 16:17). Both the Apostles and the people were right, for Christ was both God and man. Had He not been God He could not have redeemed the world from sin; and had He not been man He could not have lived on earth, among humans, nor have died for them.

When we weigh the evidence furnished by Holy Scripture, history and reason in favor of Christ's divinity, and the groundless arguments adduced by the infidel to disprove the same, we become at once convinced that it requires vastly stronger faith to be an infidel than to be a believer in Christ's divinity. The Christian sees Jesus foretold hundreds of years before He was born upon earth; sees the whole world anxiously awaiting His coming; hears even pagan philosophers tell that the world must have a teacher from Heaven; sees fulfilled in Jesus all that the prophets have foretold concerning the Messias; has before him the incomparable personality and the sinless life of Christ; hears of His many miracles and of His Resurrection, from a dozen simple-minded, holy men, who were His daily companions for several years; sees His religion planted, though all the powers of kings and emperors were employed to prevent it; sees millions of men and women of every condition of life not only honor His memory, but seek their happiness and find it in surrendering to Him their entire hearts.

And it was from Christ that came God's Church. In the Liturgy Decree (5) Vatican II puts it most beautifully: "For, it was from the side of Christ as He slept the sleep of death on the Cross that there came forth the wondrous sacrament which is the Church."

Correct Concept of God's Church

We believe in one, holy, catholic, and apostolic Church,
built by Jesus Christ on that rock which is Peter. She is the
Mystical Body of Christ; at the same time a visible society
instituted with hierarchical organs, and a spiritual community; the Church on earth, the pilgrim People of God here
below, and the Church filled with heavenly blessings; the
germ and the first fruits of the Kingdom of God, through
which the work and the sufferings of Redemption are continued throughout human history, and which looks for its
perfect accomplishment beyond time in glory. —*Credo of
the People of God.*

Father S. Now, Mr. Jackson, we have seen that Christ
was truly God, that "He so loved the world" as to die for it.
This is known as the Redemption. Christ offered His sufferings and death to God as a sacrifice in satisfaction for the sins
of men and regained for them the right to become children of
God and heirs of Heaven. But the mere fact of Christ's death
will not save all people.

Mr. J. I should not think so, although some of my friends
tell me that they *are* saved now. It seems to me that if all people should be saved no matter how they live, merely because
Christ died for all, the Redemption would give encouragement
to sin, which I understand God must hate.

Father S. Exactly, Mr. Jackson. But there are many who

believe that by merely recognizing Christ as their Savior they will be saved. This would do away with both the Church and God's Commandments.

Mr. J. As I understand it, the Redeemer's death merely gave man a new *chance* for Heaven, made the attainment of eternal happiness with God *possible*.

Father S. And you understand it rightly. For example, every town has a central water supply that contains far more water than any one family needs. Yet each individual family must lay pipes to connect into that water supply. It is even conceivable that a family might choose not to take part in the community water system. In like manner, Christ's merits are more than ample to save all mankind, but the individual must still become a member of Christ's Church, keep God's Commandments, and receive divine help through the channels of grace Christ provided.

Mr. J. I see the point, Father. Even such people as are good in their own way might not benefit by Christ's merits, because they have not complied with all terms which He Himself has laid down.

Father S. Exactly; and doctrine which contradicts this forms one of the greatest errors of our day.

Mr. J. I myself have been like a house wired for electric light, but never connected with the line which brings the current from the powerhouse. The house might just as well never have been wired as far as benefit goes.

Father S. You grasp the idea well. The world is filled with people who contend that they can work out their own salvation in their own way. They fail to recognize that Heaven is a *supernatural* reward — one which can be attained only by works having *supernatural* value from grace. The best works of man have only a natural value unless the person performing them is in union with God by grace.

Now, Mr. Jackson, I should like to know whether you understand in what manner the Savior provided for the instruction of us who live in America in this century.

Mr. J. Well, the impression I have received is this: Christ came not only as *Redeemer,* but also as a *Teacher.* He had a message which He wanted to teach all people until the end of the world, even though He Himself only taught in the little country of Palestine. And if I understand it rightly, He spent most of His time instructing twelve men, whom He intended to send to other nations with His message. Am I correct, Father?

Father S. As far as you have committed yourself; you have told how the people of the first century might come into possession of the teaching of Christ. But how would it come down through the centuries to our day with the stamp of absolute genuineness on it? How can we be sure it is authentic?

Mr. J. Well, the twelve Apostles instructed by Christ wrote down what they were taught and left it for future generations in the Bible, didn't they, Father?

Father S. No, Mr. Jackson. I feared that you *might* have a wrong idea here, as most non-Catholics have. Because Protestants constantly appeal to the Bible only in support of their personal beliefs, those who have given no extensive study to religion get the impression that the Founder of Christianity wrote this book Himself, or ordered His Apostles to write it for the instruction of all future generations everywhere.

Mr. J. That was my impression, Father.

Father S. It is wrong. Christ did not write a word of the Bible, nor did He order His Apostles to write. But Matthew, Mark, Luke, John, Peter, Paul, James and Jude — not all Apostles — were inspired by God Himself to write what He wanted written, so that He is, in reality, the author of the Bible. However, it was never intended that the nations should be taught and saved by it alone.

Mr. J. What do you mean by saying the Scripture writers were "inspired by God"?

Father S. I mean that the Holy Spirit moved and directly assisted them to write what He wanted written. The Credo of the People of God states it this way: "We believe all that is contained in the Word of God written or handed down, and that the Church proposes for belief as divinely revealed, whether by a solemn judgment or by the ordinary and universal magisterium."

I do not want you to get the impression many people have, namely, that the Catholic Church makes little of the Bible. I suppose you have heard this, have you not?

Mr. J. Yes, Father, I have heard that Catholics are not encouraged to read the Bible.

Father S. You can probably hear worse than that. The fact is that Catholics are urged to study the Bible. How do you think the Bible endured over the centuries for Protestants to use it? Only because the Church protected it and preserved it for the generations. Any student of reliable history should know that the Catholic Church gave the Bible to the world; that only on her authority the world knows that this book contains inspired writing; that her most learned sons for many centuries spent their lives copying by hand the whole Bible and translating it into different languages.

But we shall come back to the subject of the Bible later. For the present I want you to have the right idea of God's plan for the salvation of all people. You were right, Mr. Jackson, when you said that for three years Christ trained the Apostles whom He chose from the rank and file of His disciples, in order that they might be able to present His true teaching to the people of other lands in their day. But these twelve men were the first teachers for the real and visible organism, society, or Kingdom, which was to have continued existence until the end of the world: "and his reign shall be without end" (Luke 1:33). Christ called this Kingdom His Church: "I will build *my church*" (Matt. 16:18), and promised to be ever with it: "And know that I am with you always, until the end of the world!" (Matt. 28:20). You see, Mr. Jackson, the Church was to represent Christ not only as Teacher; it was to perpetuate all His works — which the Bible would be incapable of doing. *The Church produced the Bible, and not the Bible the Church.* The New Testament was written only after the

Church was fully organized and hard at work preaching Christ.

Christ organized the "body" of the Church during His three years' ministry, then ten days after His return to Heaven, the Holy Spirit in accordance with Christ's promise was sent to animate it, to be the source of its divine life, to protect it from error, etc. Well then is this Kingdom of God upon earth spoken of by Saint Paul as: "The Church of the living God" (1 Tim. 3:15). How plain that it must be "the pillar and bulwark of truth" (ibid)? How plain that "the jaws of death shall not prevail against it" (Matt. 16:18)? How reasonable: "If he ignores even the church, then treat him as you would a Gentile or a tax collector" (Matt. 18:17)? How reasonable, too: "He who hears you, hears me" (Luke 10:16)?

How could this "Church of the living God" with Christ's identical mission, have less authority to teach than Christ Himself? Or less power to remove sin? How could it lack divine helps to sanctify man? "As the Father has sent me so I send you" (John 20:21).

Mr. J. You leave no room for argument. Now let's see if I grasp it all. Christ was to continue His work of teaching, forgiving sins, and sanctifying man through an institution which would be divine, not only because He stated it, but because the Holy Spirit would dwell in it. He Himself would ever abide with His Church as its invisible Head, operating through successors of His original Apostles.

Father S. Yes, you have a good hold on the fundamental outline, Mr. Jackson. The Church would be international, and hence its teaching, guidance and divine helps would be extended to all people; on all would rest an obligation to become members, and in return they would enjoy its divine helps and be led to eternal salvation.

Mr. J. Of course, all that does not tally with the present-day state of religion. Most people talk as if all the religious denominations are the Church. Could that possibly be?

Father S. No, Mr. Jackson; the Church of Christ today must be in nature, in power, in teaching, what it was when it served men through the twelve Apostles. It is to this Church that all are obliged to belong in order to be saved. Those people who, though doubtful, deliberately refuse to seek out the true Church, or knowing it, refuse to join it, cannot be saved. Vatican Council (The Church 14) said the Catholic Church is the ordinary means of salvation: "This sacred Synod turns its attention first to the Catholic Faithful. . . . It teaches that the Church now sojourning on earth as an exile is necessary for salvation. For Christ, made present to us in His Body which is the Church, is the one mediator and the only way of salvation. . . . Whosoever, therefore, knowing that the Catholic Church was made necessary by God through Jesus Christ would refuse to join it or to remain in it would not be saved."

Mr. J. What about those who, through no fault of their own, remain outside the Church?

Father S. The same document (15) states: "The Church recognizes that in many ways it is linked with those who, being baptized, are honored with the name of Christian, though they do not profess the faith in its entirety or do not preserve unity of communion with the successor of Peter." They can belong to the soul of the Church, because they can be in the state of grace and can save their souls by making use of the graces which God gives them.

Mr. J. Cannot the charter of Christ's Church be stated clearly enough to remove all doubts about its nature, its commission, its authority and its powers?

Father S. It is stated most clearly by Christ Himself: "Full authority has been given to me both in heaven and on earth; go, therefore, and make disciples of all the nations. Baptize them in the name of the Father, and of the Son, and of the Holy Spirit. Teach them to carry out everything I have commanded you. And know that I am with you always, until the end of the world!" (Matt. 28:18-20).

The above words were addressed to eleven men corporately known as the Apostles, whom Christ had personally instructed. Their names are:

Peter,	Philip,	James the Lesser,
James the Greater,	Bartholomew,	Jude Thaddeus,
John,	Matthew,	Simon the Zealot.
Andrew,	Thomas,	

Since one of the Apostles, namely Judas Iscariot, had betrayed his Master and taken his own life, there were only eleven commissioned by Christ to go out into the world and propagate the religion of the New Law intended for all nations.

Mr. J. Wasn't someone chosen to fill the place of Judas?

Father S. Yes, not long after Christ so addressed the eleven, these gathered together and elected one of His disciples to succeed Judas; one who had also been a close follower of His teaching from the beginning of His public life and thus was able to testify to His Resurrection and Ascension. His name was Matthias.

Mr. J. What other commission did Christ give to the Apostles and to the Apostles only?

Father S. Some very important ones. On the night before He died, after offering the *first Sacrifice of the New Law,* and after giving Himself in Holy Communion to the Apostles, He commissioned them to do what He had just done, namely, to *continue* that sacrifice. He empowered them to convert bread and wine into His body and blood, and then to distribute it to others — "Do this as a remembrance of Me" (Luke 22:19).

Three days later, on the day of His Resurrection, He gave the eleven (Judas was dead) *power to forgive sin.* Since only God can forgive sin, that power must have been delegated by God to the Apostles. Hence we read: "Then he breathed on them and said: 'Receive the Holy Spirit. If you forgive men's sins, they are forgiven them; if you hold them bound, they are held bound' " (John 20:22-23).

The very name by which Christ was foretold, namely, the "Messias" means "one to be sent." He, as the "Son of Man," was "sent" into this world first to reconcile all mankind with Heaven, and secondly to found a spiritual Kingdom, to which would be committed His teaching, a remedy for sin, and divine ordinances for imparting and nourishing the supernatural life, known as the Sacraments.

The words of Christ: "And I am with you always until the end of the world" would have no meaning *unless the original corporate body* of the Apostles *was to be perpetuated* through their successors.

St. Paul states definitely what should be clear to everyone, namely, that no one may constitute himself an Apostle or a divinely commissioned teacher (Rom. 10:15). After the Apostles, only those are commissioned and empowered to do the things delegated to the original body, who are *legitimate successors* of those Apostles.

Relation of Bible to Church

This sacred Synod earnestly and specifically urges all the Christian Faithful, especially Religious, to learn by frequent reading of the divine Scriptures 'the knowledge of Christ which surpasses all knowledge' (Phil. 3:3). 'Ignorance of the Scriptures is ignorance of Christ' (St. Jerome). Therefore they should readily put themselves in touch with the sacred text itself, whether it be through the liturgy, rich in the divine word, or through devotional reading, or through instructions suitable for the purpose and other aids which in our day are commendably available everywhere, thanks to the approval and active support of the Shepherds of the Church. — *Vatican II, Revelation, 25.*

Father S. We have seen, Mr. Jackson, that just as Christ was God and Man, so the institution, which He established to continue His work, consists of human members, but has a divine origin. Just as Christ "was sent" by the Father, to perform divine works through His human nature, so He in turn would "send" others, through them continuing His mission of "saving His people from their sins" (Matt. 1:21). By this arrangement, those who were the objects of Christ's personal ministrations 1900 years ago, were no better off than we of today, to whom the same divine help comes from Him through others: He was to be, and actually is, "Jesus Christ yesterday, today, and the same forever."

I'll have to make the instruction brief this evening, so let us get back to where we left off in our last instruction. You asked if all denominations today were in some sense *The Church*.

Mr. J. I was only declaring what I have often heard and wanted you to tell me on what plea Protestant sects gain so many followers, and on what they base their claims.

Father S. Although Catholics are agreed that the Church is made up of all baptized persons united in the same true faith, the same sacrifice or worship, and using the same sacraments, under the Authority of the Successor of St. Peter, the Pope, and the bishops in communion with him, the term "Church" has a very vague meaning for most non-Catholics. A simple trust that Jesus' merits will save them if they lead a decent life—especially, if they publicly profess that they want Jesus to be their Savior—they think, makes them Christians. Many hold that they need not affiliate with a religious denomination, though if they will, so much the better. They think that they may select the Methodist, Baptist, Presbyterian, or any of the hundreds of other forms of religion. Most denominations are all united in one thing—in directing their members to read the Bible for guidance in the development of the Christian life. They teach that the individual is responsible to God *directly;* that to require him to believe certain things, to impose a creed, is to restrict his liberty of thought; that to impose certain observances is to interfere with his liberty of action. They see only a two-fold commission to the Church, viz., to baptize and to preach; and "to preach" means to announce Christ as the Savior and to stimulate people to lead good lives. Little attention is paid to "Teach them to carry out everything I have commanded you."

They contend that Christ gave us the command to "search the Scriptures." As a matter of fact, He was telling the Jews that they read the Scriptures wherein He was prophesied. But He was stating a fact, not issuing a command. Even if He actually told them to "search the Scriptures," He could have meant only the Old Testament. These people never saw the New Testament, which had to do with His Church, nor did the Apostles themselves ever see the whole New Testament, nor did people for 400 years after Christ, though the Church had enjoyed her golden era—the days when people died for their faith by the thousands. And during the next one thousand years, the generality of Christians could not read the Bible, not because the Church kept it from them, but because the art of printing, by which books are now multiplied, was not invented until the year 1438. We wonder how, in "searching the Scriptures," our separated brethren do not feel the force of such statements of Our Lord as "if he ignores even the Church" (Matt. 18:17); "I will build my church" (Matt. 16:18); "there shall be one flock then and one shepherd" (John 10:16). We wonder why they do not admit that the true Church can be identified and distinguished from others, when it is compared to one "body" with one head, to "a kingdom," to "a city on a mountain," to "a house," to "a sheepfold," and so on.

Mr. J. Doesn't it resolve itself into what I have said: they have a wholly erroneous idea of God's plan of salvation?

Father S. Yes, and "searching the Scriptures" independently of a divinely protected Church, to which difficult passages should be referred for correct interpretation, has produced the hundreds of contradictory sects which make Christianity ridiculed by the pagans. The Catholic Church cherishes the Bible, supports its teachings by it, and offers special favors to the laity who read it every day; but like St. Peter, it reminds its people that: "Paul, our beloved brother, wrote you this in the spirit of wisdom that is his, dealing with these matters as he does in all his letters. There are certain passages in them hard to understand. The ignorant and the unstable distort them (just as they do the rest of Scripture) to their own ruin" (2 Peter 3:15-16).

Mr. J. A friend of mine is a great Bible reader, and when a few days ago, I asked him if he was sure that he understood its difficult passages, he answered: "Yes, the Holy Spirit assists the reader to understand its true meaning."

Father S. And you should have asked another question; you should have asked: "If that be true, how is it that such assistance of the Holy Spirit does not lead all Bible readers to understand the same passages in the same way?" There are several other questions which would be pertinent: "How do you know that the book you are reading is actually the Word of God?" "Since it is a translation, how do you know that it is a reliable version?" "Since it was translated only from a *copy* of the original, how do you know that even the copy is correct, or that something was not omitted or changed?" On the authority of the Catholic Church alone, can he be assured that the Bible contains the Word of God; and without any warrant from the book itself, he assumes that the Bible *only* decides and contains what he is to believe.

Mr. J. Is the Catholic Bible the same, in all respects, as the one used by Protestants?

Father S. The New Testament is usually quite the same, but ours contains seven more books in the Old Testament. Non-Catholics are not consistent in rejecting these as uninspired, because the same authority, on which they believe any of the books to be the Word of God, also declared these seven to have been inspired by God. Christ recognized these books, which non-Catholics frequently call "apocrypha," because He frequently quoted from the Old Testament version which contained them. You must remember, Mr. Jackson, that at His time there were two versions of the Old Testament, the one in Greek, containing these seven books, and the other in Hebrew not containing them. Out of about 350 quotations from the Old Testament which are found in the New Testament, 300 are taken from the Greek version which the Catholic Church uses and about 50 from both the Greek and the Hebrew versions.

Perhaps we can best close this instruction with this thought and two quotations from Vatican II:

*The magisterium alone gives us the proper meaning of
the Bible.*

Revelation (10): "The task of authentically interpreting
the Word of God whether written or handed down has been
entrusted exclusively to the living teaching office of the
Church, whose authority is exercised in the name of Jesus
Christ."

Revelation (25): "It devolves on sacred bishops 'who
have the apostolic teaching' (St. Irenaeus) to give the Faithful
entrusted to them suitable instruction in the right use of the
divine books, especially the New Testament, and above all the
Gospels, through translations of the sacred texts. Such translations are to be provided with necessary and fully adequate explanations so that the children of the Church can safely and
profitably grow familiar with the Sacred Scriptures and be
penetrated with their spirit."

'One Fold under One Shepherd'

Hence the mission of the Church is not only to bring to men the message of Christ and the grace of Christ but also to penetrate and perfect the temporal sphere with the spirit of the Gospel. — *The Laity, 5.*

For it is through Christ's Catholic Church alone, which is the all embracing means of salvation, that the fullness of the means of salvation can be obtained. . . . our separated brethren whether considered as individuals or as communities or churches are not blessed with that unity which Jesus Christ willed to bestow on all those whom He has regenerated and vivified into one body and newness of life. —*Ecumenism, 3.*

Father S. Knowing what you now do concerning the nature of Christ's Church, what kind of an institution would you look for today, were you not already convinced that the Catholic Church is that one?

Mr. J. At this late day, I would expect to find that Church spread throughout the world, all her members believing exactly the same, the successors of the Apostles teaching with unmistakable certainty, applying divine helps for man's spiritual advancement, forgiving their sins, marks like that.

Father S. You would therefore eliminate any religious denomination which made its appearance as a separate body after the first century?

Mr. J. Yes, Father; for how could such a one claim Christ directly as its Founder?

Father S. That's right. And you would give no hearing to a church, which points to Mr. or Rev. So and So as its founder?

Mr. J. Surely not; for how could anyone but God establish a Church which could lead to Heaven? If Heaven belongs to God, only God could offer it to man on His terms.

Father S. Good. I might promise you the court house in this town on certain conditions laid down by me, but no matter how well you fulfilled such conditions, you would never get the reward promised, since "no one can give what is not his own." I presume that you would also set aside a Church whose teachers do not agree among themselves on every point of belief?

Mr. J. Yes, Father; because if they received their teaching from a divine Church, from the same source, they would have to agree.

Father S. Then, you would have to eliminate from your consideration all Churches but one.

Mr. J. Surely. Even if Christ never stated that His Church would be one and the same for everybody, everywhere, at all times, I could not conceive of God establishing two or three Churches much less several hundred and each contradicting the other.

Father S. You have not yet read the Bible sufficiently to quote any passages which tell that the Church should be one?

Mr. J. No, Father, but I remember the substance of a few passages which you have already quoted: Christ spoke of *The* Church and of building *My* Church, not Churches. Then, didn't He say there would be *one* flock and *one* shepherd?

Father S. Yes; and the Apostle affirms that if there is only one Lord, there should be only *one* faith, and one baptism (Eph. 4:5). Jesus declared that "A kingdom torn by strife is headed for its downfall. A town or household split into factions cannot last for long." (Matt. 12:25). Christ prayed that all His followers "may be one even as we are" (John 17:11).

Some people might argue that the men who were the founders of other Churches were moved by God to do so, but St. Paul says that "even if an angel from Heaven" made such a claim, he should not be listened to (Gal. 1:8); "He who is not with Me is against Me" (Matt. 12:30).

Mr. J. Oh, you need not go farther. To me nothing is more plain than that Almighty God would want no division among His children. There is such harmony in all the lesser works of God, and He surely would want it in His human family, when there is question of knowing and serving Him.

Father S. Well now, Mr. Jackson, outside the Catholic Church, there is no united Christianity. In our own country alone, according to the latest figures there are about 250 denominations among which the 94 million Protestants of North America are divided, and they differ woefully. Only in a very few points could they agree to teach the same. Each of the larger denominations is rent by many divisions, so that separately any one of them has a very limited membership here, and only a small following in other nations. Contrasted with them is the Catholic Church, which has at least 725 million members, and is represented everywhere on earth. Its followers are many in all civilized countries, and though differing in race, color, language, habits, and so on, are "one flock and one shepherd" (John 10:16). According to the will of Christ, all its members profess the same faith, have the same worship and Sacraments, and are united under one and the same visible head, the Pope. Vatican II stated it in this fashion:

"This Church, constituted and organized in the world as a society, is the Catholic Church, which is governed by the successor of Peter and those Bishops who are in union with that successor.

"Christ the sole mediator established and ceaselessly sustains here on earth His holy Church, the community of faith and hope and charity, as a visible structure. . . . This is the unique (only) Church of Christ. . . . which in the Creed we avow as one, holy, catholic, apostolic" (The Church 8).

Mr. J. It is strange that this marvelous oneness of Catholics in belief and the lack of it among non-Catholic religions is not considered by learned Protestants, for it is surely the plainest argument in favor of the Catholic and against the other Churches. But I have heard Protestants say they are apostolic, that they are only a reformation of a corrupted church.

Father S. What they say is quite apart from the facts. Only the Catholic Church continues the apostolic succession in the Popes. The facts are that when the various groups broke away from the Catholic Church, they denied papal authority, reinterpreted the Eucharistic sacrifice into a symbol, deliberately rejected Catholic sacraments and their forms, invented new dogma and doctrine; in short, they reflected what moderns would call "the hang-ups" of their founders.

Mr. J. It is clear to me from the history I have been reading that what you say is correct. But was there need for a reformation in the Church?

Father S. There was and it was done by the Church itself in the Council of Trent. The Church constantly updates itself. After Trent there was Vatican Council I, and in our own day, Vatican II. If the so-called protesters had stayed within the Church and worked for reformation, there would have been no schism and heresy. They chose to throw the baby out with the bathwater and created an inheritance of confusion and disagreement even among themselves.

Mr. J. I appreciate your honesty, Father. It also seems to me that the fact that the Catholic Church could survive so many vicissitudes over the centuries is but one more proof of its divine foundation.

Father S. It is. Because Christ said that it was by the unity of His followers that man would know that He was God. But they fail to see its force because of their erroneous concept of what God's Church was to be. Students of history are aware that for centuries the Catholic Church was the only Christian Church on earth, and that the oldest Protestant church is only slightly over 400 years old.

Mr. J. This ought to be another telling argument; because if the Catholic was the first Christian body, it must have been the one Christ established. And a Church that had no existence for a thousand years or more after the Apostles could not be the same Church that the Apostles propagated.

Father S. You will make a good defender of the Church you are embracing, Mr. Jackson. On the basis of what you asked previously and what we have been discussing, how would you answer a sincere Protestant who should contend that, while the Catholic Church was once the true Church, it fell into error and became quite corrupt, and that men like Luther, Calvin and Henry VIII, left it to re-establish the pure Christianity of the first centuries?

Mr. J. I would say that either Christ or these men are deceivers, for Christ declared that He would be with His Church all days, and that the Spirit of Truth would keep it in truth. If Christ was God, He must keep His promise to preserve His Church from error. In fact, I know He would, even if He made no such promise.

Father S. Good answer.

Mr. J. Then I would ask if those men they speak of, Luther, Calvin, Henry VIII, etc., agreed among themselves. If they did not, which of the three was right? And since you say that other denominations are constantly changing and subdividing, they are the ones in need of a reform to make them what the parent body originally was.

Father S. Very good. There never could be a reformation of the Creed of the Church. An individual might fall into error, even a priest, or a number of bishops, but not the Church as a Church. Granting that people's lives needed reforming, it would be no argument against the divine origin of the religion which they confessed. Even the successors of the Apostles could break the Ten Commandments, but to believe that they as a body could teach error would be to lose all faith in God, to discredit the promise of Jesus, to blaspheme the Holy Spirit, Who was sent by Christ to protect the Church from falling into error and to preserve it, as Christ founded it, until the end of time (John 14:17-26).

The true Church of God must be characterized not only by "oneness," but it must be holy; it must be Catholic or universal; it must be apostolic. These are *marks* of the true Church by which is meant clear signs by which all men can recognize it as the true Church founded by Christ. No other Church possesses these marks.

Mr. J. This does not mean that every member of the Church must be holy does it?

Father S. No, it means that the Institution, often referred to as the Mystical Body of Christ, must be holy both because its Founder was God, and because it is guided and directed by the Holy Spirit; and also because it was furnished by Christ with means to make people holy. If all its members are not holy, it is their fault and not that of the Church, because all members of the Church could become saints if they strove to.

The Church is divine, therefore, in itself, but its members are human. Christ compared His Church to a field in which both wheat and cockle grow, to a net which contains both good and bad fishes, to five wise and five foolish virgins. Sinners have their place in the Church because the chief mission of the Church is to sanctify and save them.

Mr. J. Is the Church truly universal?

Father S. Yes, universal and "Catholic" mean the same thing. We distinguish between universality in time, in teaching, in place. I hardly need to tell you that the Catholic Church has existed from the time of Christ down to our own. Neither do I need to tell you that it has taught the same doctrine from the beginning. It could not have been universal in place until opportunity was given for the Apostles and missionaries to extend it to all nations.

On the very day it was born, namely, on Pentecost, people representing nearly every nation were received into it by St. Peter himself. The Roman Empire governed most of the world outside the Orient until it collapsed through the invasion of barbarians, but in the year 342 the religion of Christ was officially recognized as the religion of the Roman Empire. Before the year 1000 practically every nation in Europe was converted to the Catholic Church. It was Catholic missionaries who brought this faith to the Indians of North, Central and South America.

Mr. J. This description is very interesting and I know that no other single Church is as widespread as the Catholic, and that in most countries separate denominations have only a scant following.

Father S. In instructions you have already received you have learned that the Catholic Church is apostolic, which means that it goes back to the time of the Apostles, has today successors of the Apostles, and that these successors are empowered, as the Apostles were, to offer up the Holy Sacrifice of the Mass, to forgive sin in God's name, etc.

Mr. J. All this is very clear and logical to me. I know that the major Christian sects are losing members while certain fundamentalist groups such as the Mormons and Jehovah's Witnesses are experiencing growth. Both of these groups have had missionaries come to my home. What should I say to them?

Father S. It is better not to get into discussions with them at all. Their members get a few biblical texts and use them. Mormons preach one religion but have another for initiates. They believe that Christ preached to the American Indians and that an angel appeared to Joseph Smith in New York State and gave him the book of Mormon to reestablish the church in America. They hold all Christian churches, to be false. There is not one God but many gods for many worlds. After death man may become a god for his own planet. The Mormons have had many schisms of their own. They are wealthy and have great power but their teachings are nonsense.

The same thing can be said about Jehovah's Witnesses whose aggressive missionary tactics have won many converts, ill-informed about their own religions. The Witnesses were founded by scandal-ridden Charles Russell, who was strongly influenced by the Adventists. They believe that we are in the last days before Armageddon; bad experiences with predictions in the past have now led them not to set any dates. They seem to be against everything: blood transfusions, Catholics, Christmas trees, saluting the flag, liquor, Protestants, movies, tobacco, voting, women's rights, and an almost endless list. They would have died of their own silliness except "Judge" Joseph Rutherford came along and reorganized them. Rutherford spent time in prison for sedition. Nathan Knorr succeeded Rutherford, established sound business methods, and has built the Witnesses to their present numbers.

I think the relevance of these two sects speaks for itself. They are hardly Christian.

Mr. J. If we know our own beliefs, we need not worry about these groups.

True Church Must Be Infallible

We believe in the infallibility enjoyed by the Successor of Peter when he teaches ex cathedra as Pastor and Teacher of all the Faithful, and which is assured also to the Episcopal Body when it exercises with him the supreme magisterium.
—*Credo of the People of God.*

This infallibility with which the divine Redeemer willed His Church to be endowed in defining a doctrine of faith and morals extends as far as extends the deposit of divine revelation, which must be religiously guarded and faithfully expounded. This is the infallibility which the Roman Pontiff, the head of the college of bishops, enjoys in virtue of his office, when, as the supreme shepherd and teacher of all the faithful, who confirms his brethren in their faith (cf. Lk. 22:32), he proclaims by a definitive act some doctrine of faith or morals. Therefore his definitions, of themselves, and not from the consent of the Church, are justly styled irreformable, for they are pronounced with the assistance of the Holy Spirit, an assistance promised to him in blessed Peter. Therefore they need no approval of others, nor do they allow an appeal to any other judgment. For then the Roman Pontiff is not pronouncing judgment as a private person. Rather, as the supreme teacher of the universal Church, as one in whom the charism of the infallibility of the Church herself is individually present, he is expounding or defending a doctrine of Catholic faith. . . . This religious submission of will and of mind must be shown in a special way to the authentic teaching authority of the Roman Pontiff, even when he is not speaking ex cathedra. That is, it must be shown in such a way that his supreme magisterium is acknowledged with reverence, the judgments made by him are sincerely adhered to, according to his manifest mind and will. His mind and will in the matter may be known chiefly either from the character of the documents, from his frequent repetition of the same doctrine, or from his manner of speaking.

The infallibility promised to the Church resides also in the body of bishops when that body exercises supreme teaching authority with the successor of Peter. To the resultant definitions the assent of the Church can never be wanting, on account of the activity of that same Holy Spirit, whereby the whole flock of Christ is preserved and progresses in unity of faith. — *The Church, 25.*

Father S. In our last instruction we referred to the harmony of belief among Catholics. Now, this is made possible by an *infallible* authority behind the teaching of the Church. If there be a "Church of the living God" upon earth; if it has been commissioned "to teach the nations"; if the Church is nothing less than Christ continued through the centuries, then it must be able to speak with infallible authority. The Church's voice must be God's voice, her teachings must be His teaching, her authority must be His authority; this means that the Church is infallible. Thus we can see how belief in the infallibility of the Church is rooted in our belief in God's infallibility. Since He knows all things, He cannot err, and since He is all good, He cannot wilfully deceive us.

It is hardly necessary to prove that God is infallible, because if He could err, He would not be God. Since Christ was God, He must also be incapable of teaching error, then the Church, too, must be infallible when it teaches those things concerning which Christ promised protection from error.

Mr. J. Is that what the word "infallible" means?

Father S. Yes, but most non-Catholics think it means something else. When we say that the Pope, who speaks officially for the Church, is "infallible," they surmise that we regard him as a kind of God, who cannot sin, nor make a mistake. But we merely mean that when he speaks for the Church on matters that God has revealed pertaining to what must be believed or done for salvation, he is protected by the Holy Spirit from teaching error. We claim no such protection for him when he speaks on other matters, nor in his personal or private life.

Mr. J. That seems to me to be self-evident truth. If the spokesman for the Church taught all the members error, Christ's mission to spread God's truth would have been in vain.

Father S. That's right. How could one really believe that the Church was *commissioned* to teach the nations, and still could err in matters pertaining to faith and morals? Can you conceive of God commanding men to hear the Church, and yet allowing that Church to teach them wrong? Our non-Catholic brethren do not see the necessary connection between an infallible Church and some living voice to speak for her. They think of an infallible *book,* not considering that the Bible could have no weight unless an infallible authority had declared it to be inspired, and then protected readers from misunderstanding or misinterpreting it. While they reject the infallibility of one representative of Christ in the Church, they go to the extreme of ascribing infallibility to every Bible reader.

Mr. J. Yes. As I told you before, a friend of mine contends that the Holy Spirit protects him from misunderstanding the Bible. If this were true, he would be infallible, at least for the moment, would he not?

Father S. Yes. Applied to the Pope, infallibility is nothing more than freedom from error when he exercises his authority as a divinely appointed and divinely protected teacher, when, in the name of God, he makes clear to the people of the whole world what the precise revelation of God has been. Infallibility is not for the *Pope* alone, it is nothing that the Church glories in for her own sake; it is for the people. The whole Church benefits by the infallibility of the Pope.

Mr. J. Plain as all this is to me, I am interested in having Bible proof, if there be any.

Father S. Exactly. Different passages of Scripture would prove the infallibility of Christ's Apostles; in fact, no non-Catholic could attach weight to New Testament teaching and deny to the Apostles the power to teach, to rule and to sanctify their fellow men.

"Full authority has been given to me both in heaven and on earth; go, therefore, and make disciples of all the nations. Baptize them in the name of the Father, and of the Son, and of the Holy Spirit. Teach them to carry out everything I have commanded you. And know that I am with you always, until the end of the world!" (Matt. 28:18-20).

Thus did Christ give to His Apostles and their lawful successors, the authority to teach the faithful and to govern them in spiritual matters until the end of the world. Thus we are assured that the Church will always do the will of its divine Founder, who remains forever its invisible Head.

Yet they were not to go to work independently, but were to constitute the teaching body of the primitive Church under the leadership of one who would be spokesman for the Church. Christ addressed Himself to His Apostles as a unit, but He addressed Himself more emphatically to the one whom He constituted the first visible Head of His Church.

In the Scriptures we learn that Jesus selected one of the Twelve and changed his name from "Simon" to "Rock" (Peter) because, in representing Christ on earth as the foundation of His Church, he (and his successors, because the Church would go on after his death) would be the source of stability and unity in this body, a living spokesman and a divinely guided arbiter in disputes.

In Mark 1:16 and in Luke 5:3-5, it is noted that this Apostle's name was "Simon" when he was selected by Jesus. But in Matthew 16:17-19, you will observe that Christ conferred on him a new name—after he, speaking for all the Apostles, made a profound profession of faith in the divinity of

Jesus. The change of Simon's name to Peter is noted in Matthew 4:18; 10:2; Mark 3:16; Luke 6:14; John 1:42.

In John 1:42, we are told that Andrew brought his brother Simon to Jesus: Jesus, who looked at him and said, "You are Simon, son of John; your name shall be Cephas (which is rendered Peter)."

The word "Cephas" is the word for "Rock" in the language which Jesus spoke; "Peter" is the Greek word for "Rock." The Gospel of St. John was written in Greek, and that is why John gives the meaning in Greek of the Cephas. Christ's clear meaning becomes evident if we observe Him as saying: "Thou art Cephas, and upon this cephas I will build My Church." Such was His actual language, such was his actual declaration in the language in which He spoke. To no other Apostle did Christ ever address such words as these:

"I for my part declare to you, you are 'Rock,' and on this rock I will build my church, and the jaws of death shall not prevail against it. I will entrust to you the keys of the kingdom of heaven. Whatever you declare bound on earth shall be bound in heaven; whatever you declare loosed on earth shall be loosed in heaven" (Matt. 16:18-19).

Mr. J. Those are indeed strong and very significant words.

Father S. To Peter alone Christ addressed other words which leave no doubt about his selection as the *universal* pastor and teacher of all in the name of Christ. According to John 21:15-17, after receiving from Peter a threefold profession of love in atonement of his threefold denial of Christ during His passion, Christ committed to him the feeding of His entire flock in these words: "Feed My lambs; feed My sheep."

Christ loved to call Himself the Good *Shepherd,* and to refer to His followers as His *flock.* His flock, containing lambs and sheep, needed a shepherd after His return to Heaven, and that office was committed to Peter.

Mr. J. Lambs and sheep *do* constitute the whole flock.

Father S. Equally significant are the words of Luke

22:31-32. Addressing Peter, Christ reminded him that Satan was conspiring against all the Apostles: "But I have prayed for you that your faith may never fail. You in turn must strengthen you brothers."

The words in Matt. 16:19, and in Luke 22:32, also in John 21:15-17 have opened the eyes of millions to the place of Peter in the Church.

Mr. J. Was Peter the *acknowledged head* of the infant Church?

Father S. Most assuredly. Those who claim he was not, use this strange argument. They say Paul was a greater Apostle; Paul worked harder than Peter; Paul resisted him to his face; Peter denied Christ. The dispute of Peter and Paul was not about a question of faith (Gal. 2:11-15), nor was Peter speaking in his official capacity, when alone his verdict would be held as infallible. Peter had repented of his denial before he was actually told to be the Shepherd. St. Paul might just as well be accused, for he was a persecutor of the Church before his conversion.

Mr. J. If I understand it right, the personal, private life of the Head of the Church is not to be identified with his representative character?

Father S. Surely not. The President's signature to a bill would be official no matter what his private life might be.

In listing the Apostles, the evangelists give the names of all others without order, but are careful to head the list with Peter. After the reception of the Holy Spirit on Pentecost, Peter is the first to address the people. Peter works the first miracle. In the first 12 chapters of the "Acts of the Apostles" Peter's name occurs 53 times, far oftener than all the other Apostles taken together. Peter presided at the Council of Jerusalem, which was evidence of his acknowledged position as head. When Peter was imprisoned, all prayed for him. From the very first centuries, the Primacy and Supremacy of the Bishop of Rome have been recognized, but whether Peter or his successors lived at Rome is a matter of no consequence. Of course, he did live there and died a martyr there. Deny a Supreme Ruler in the Church here below, and how are disputes to be settled? Our country needs a Supreme Court, and so does the Church. Deny infallibility to the head of the Church on earth, and there is no possibility of a man knowing whether he believes right or wrong. If you and I disputed about the meaning of a certain word, we would consult a dictionary, and would regard it as a final authority. Deny divine protection to the voice that speaks in God's name, and the Church has no right to command submission.

Mr. J. It is so plain that if I were a member of no church, and wanted to know the truth, none but an infallible Church would have any attraction for me, for how else would I be sure that the Church would not mislead me? Not to claim infallibility would be equivalent to the admission that the Church might teach me wrong.

'Bible Only' Theory a Failure

The task of authentically interpreting the Word of God whether written or handed down has been entrusted exclusively to the living teaching office of the Church, whose authority is exercised in the name of Jesus Christ. — *Revelation, 10.*

It devolves on sacred bishops 'who have the apostolic teaching' (St. Irenaeus) to give the Faithful entrusted to them suitable instruction in the right use of the divine books, especially the New Testament, and above all the Gospels, through translations of the sacred texts. Such translations are to be provided with necessary and fully adequate explanations so that the children of the Church can safely and profitably grow familiar with the Sacred Scriptures and be penetrated with their spirit. — *Revelation, 25.*

Father S. Did you go to Mass yesterday, Mr. Jackson?

Mr. J. Yes, Father; there is my main difficulty. I find it harder to understand your services than to grasp the Church's teachings.

Father S. No need to hurry. Before long you will understand the Mass, too.

Mr. J. I hope so.

Father S. We have seen, Mr. Jackson, that the Church's last word, when determining a matter pertaining to faith or morals, must be infallible, otherwise the millions who would follow Christ's command to "hear the Church" might be led into error. The need of this seemed very plain to you, did it not?

Mr. J. Yes, Father; if the Church's word were not final and infallible, it would surely be impossible to keep all the nations united in the identical belief. In the State we have a supreme tribunal, to which people may submit disputed questions for a final decision, and by whose judgment the litigants must abide. And I see a greater need of such a tribunal in the Church, because there is so much more at stake.

Father S. That's right. What if there were no Supreme Court to determine the precise meaning of obscure passages in the Constitution? What if the general government placed copies of this Constitution in every home and expected each person to read it and apply it as he should understand it? What if hundreds of divergent opinions existed concerning some of its clauses, and the state permitted all lawyers and others to sustain and act on such opinions? It would never do. We would have no *United States*, but the most disturbing confusion in the land.

Mr. J. Do other Churches defend such a principle in religion?

Father S. Most do. The Orthodox (Greek) Church and the High Church (Anglican) defend most of their beliefs — which agree with the Catholic—by appealing to the first six General Councils. But the Pope or his representative presided even over these Councils. Lutherans believe in the "Bible only" theory, but most of them have reduced their faith to a *system* taught definitely in parochial schools. Others believe in placing the Bible in every home and permit all readers to interpret it in their own way. This unreasonable theory is still advocated even though it has split up Christianity into a thousand divisions. Acting on this theory not even the minister is *sure* that he is right. Some time ago I attended a meeting of a ministerial association and explained the attitude of the Catholic Church toward the Bible. Then I asked the reverend gentlemen some questions. I picked up the Bible and asked them if they all believed it to be the Word of God. Ministers representing nine different denominations, *said:* "Yes, we do." Then I replied: "I believe it to be the Word of God from cover to cover, but I do not understand how any of you can consistently believe that." They asked: "Why not?" To which I responded: "Well, prove to me that the contents of this book are inspired in any other manner than on the authority of the Catholic Church. Now, the Catholic Church either was infallible when it said so, or it was not. If it was not, it might have been mistaken; and in such case you do not know whether the book contains the Word of God or not."

Mr. J. What did they reply to that argument?

Father S. One of them said: "Why, the writings bear upon their face plain marks of their inspired character." To this I replied by opening the book and reading something from the Old Testament which had rather the appearance of the devil's authorship. Then I told them that the Koran, which the Mohammedans regard as inspired, contains some most edifying reading. So do Smith's revelations, which the Mormons revere, but that they would never concede that these writings were the "Word of God."

They were silent. But one of them, to change the subject, and probably to get me in a corner, asked if we did not have the "apocrypha" in our canon.

Mr. J. I believe you referred to that portion of the Bible before, Father. What do you mean by "apocrypha" and "canon"?

Father S. By "apocrypha" Protestants understand certain writings contained in the Old Testament which they regard as *doubtfully* inspired. And by "canon" is meant the Church's official list or collection of writings which constitute the Bible.

Mr. J. And what answer did you give?

Father S. I told him that if they deny the infallibility of the Catholic Church their whole Bible contained apocrypha, for the same voice which declared to be the Word of God the books they accept as inspired, also declared the other seven books, which we have, to be inspired. To be consistent, they would have to accept all.

Mr. J. Were they convinced?

Father S. First, I asked if they really believe the "Bible only" to be the rule of faith; and three of them answered "Yes." Then I asked why they do not observe the Saturday instead of the Sunday; why they do not believe in the absolute necessity of baptism for salvation; why they do not anoint the sick with oil; why they permit remarriage after divorce; what St. Peter meant when he declared against *private interpretation* of the Scriptures (2 Pet.1:20); what about the things which St. Paul said should be observed though he did not deliver the same in writing (2 Thess. 2:14, and 3:6); what Christ meant by the words "hear the Church" (Matt. 18:17); "he who rejects you, rejects Me" (Luke 10:16); what St. Paul meant by condemning even an angel from Heaven who would differ from his teaching (Gal. 1:8); how they could hold that the Church fell into error, against the plain promises of Christ to protect it from error (Matt. 18:20; Matt. 16:18; John 14:16; 16:13; 1 Tim. 3:15); how they deny to any the power to forgive sins in God's name (Matt. 9:6; John 20:23; Matt. 18:18); why they do not regard marriage as a sacrament, (Eph. 5:32), and others.

Mr. J. I should say you did show where they do not follow the Bible.

Father S. Then I said to them: "Your presence here as ministers of nine different denominations shows that you do not all understand the Bible alike; your discussions prove that you are not *sure* that your particular belief is correct."

Mr. J. What did they say to that?

Father S. One of them stated: "No, but we are sincere and honest in our inquiries; we meet to exchange views on obscure things." I smiled and rejoined: "Then of what use is an inspired book, if you are not sure of its meaning? Christ declared: 'You shall *know* (not search for) the truth.' " I told them that they sorely needed a Pope, even if they gave him another name; I asked each to tell me his precise understanding of Christ's few words: "This is My body." There were four views quite conflicting among the nine. I reminded them that the correct belief on this point was surely essential, for what if Christ actually meant what He said? Before leaving I declared: "Gentlemen, your 'Bible only and private interpretation' theory is certainly weak and a creator of dissensions; you had better weigh the 'Hear the Church, divinely protected from error' theory, and see if it is not safer."

If One Cannot Decide, None Can

We believe that the Church founded by Jesus Christ and for which He prayed is indefectibly one in faith, worship and the bond of hierarchical communion.

In the bosom of this Church, the rich variety of liturgical rites and the legitimate diversity of theological and spiritual heritages and special disciplines, far from injuring her unity, make it more manifest.

Recognizing also the existence, outside the organism of the Church of Christ, of numerous elements of truth and sanctification which belong to her as her own and tend to Catholic unity, and believing in the action of the Holy Spirit who stirs up in the heart of the disciples of Christ love of this unity, We entertain the hope that the Christians who are not yet in the full communion of the one and only Church will one day be reunited in one Flock with one only Shepherd. — *Credo of the People of God.*

Father S. Well, where did we leave off with the last instruction?

Mr. J. We were discussing what you termed the "Bible only" theory and the infallibility of the Pope. What about the contention that St. Peter was never in Rome?

Father S. It is absurd. No historian pretended to make such a charge until this last century, not even the Church's greatest enemies; and even now, reputable historians all agree that St. Peter was bishop of Rome, and with St. Paul suffered martyrdom there. But even if it were true (which it is not) that he was not bishop of Rome, what would it prove? The point at issue is: Was he appointed visible head of the Church of Christ? Whether he resided in Jerusalem or Rome would not matter. If years after his death his successor moved to Rome, future bishops of Rome would be his successors.

The seat of the United States government was transferred from Philadelphia to Washington, yet succeeding Presidents living in Washington have been successors of George Washington.

Mr. J. Of course, the place of residence is not essential. But is it true some Popes were not good men?

Father S. So few, that it is remarkable, especially when one takes into account that in the middle ages wicked kings and emperors did their utmost to have men elected Pope who would not disturb them. Forty popes died martyrs for the faith, and about 90 are canonized saints. Even if every twelfth one had been privately bad, the proportion would be no greater than among the twelve Apostles chosen and schooled by Christ Himself. Moses, whom God chose to be the leader of His people in the Old Law, with whom God conversed personally, through whom He gave His commandments to the world, committed a sin for which he was punished by being denied his ambition to reach the "Promised Land." But nevertheless he continued to be God's representative in the world (Exod. 18:15); even Caiphas, who participated in the execution of Jesus, was God's representative among the Jews (John 11:49-50); Our Lord condemned the failings of the Scribes and Pharisees but He told the people to listen to their teaching because "they have sat on the chair of Moses" (Matt. 23:2-3).

While the Church must be holy, because it is the work of God, because Christ has promised to be with it until the end of the world, and because the Holy Spirit is its principle of supernatural life, still its members are men, whose wills are not forced to keep God's commandments.

Mr. J. What did you say about the Holy Spirit and the Church?

Father S. I said that the Holy Spirit, that is Christ's Spirit, and His Heavenly Father's Spirit, the Third Person of the Trinity, gives supernatural life to the Church, as He did since the first Pentecost Sunday and will continue to do until the end of time.

Mr. J. But since the members of the Church are free, could not many of them sin despite the grace of God?

Father S. Yes. Christ compared His Church to a field in which the wheat and cockle would exist together until the harvest; to a net, which contains both good and bad fishes. The Church, as a whole, is holy; the popes, as a body, have been the world's holiest men. Why do some people judge the representatives of Christ by the three or four unholy ones, instead of by the 260 holy ones? They do not condemn the twelve Apostles because of the sins of two or three of them. They would not refuse to accept a decision of the Supreme Court if the private life of one of its members were not commendable.

Mr. J. That point is clear to me. But I have been wanting to ask another question: If I grasp the situation correctly, Christ did not formulate a creed; how, is it, then, that the Church's teachings are put together in a systematic way.

Father S. It is true that Christ did not do that personally. But He certainly taught definite truths to the Apostles, and ordered them to teach others to observe all things whatsoever He had taught them (Matt. 28:20). Morever, the Savior told them that He had not instructed them fully: "When he comes, however, being the Spirit of truth he will guide you to all truth" (John 16:13). What the Church has crystallized in a creed has been taught from the beginning, but was definitely defined only when someone in the world preached doctrines that were at variance with what the Church taught. In nearly every century from the time of Christ, successors of the Apostles, the bishops of the world, were summoned together to meet in a General Council as the Apostles themselves met at the Council of Jerusalem to express the mind of the Church for the people of their day. If some false teacher had been propagating a dangerous error, it was condemned and the precise truth concerning the matter stated.

For instance, in the beginning of the fourth century, a man who had a considerable following denied that Christ was truly God. Then the Pope convened the Council of Nicea, in the year 325, and authoritatively declared that Christ was as truly God as the Father. In the same century, to counteract another heresy, and to state the truth officially, the Council of Constantinople was held; and so on through the centuries. Even as late as the last century other truths of faith were solemnly defined — that of the Immaculate Conception of the Blessed Virgin, and the infallibility of the Pope. In 1950 Pope Pius XII infallibly proclaimed the dogma of the Assumption of Mary. There was no occasion for the Church to express these truths explicitly before, because no Catholic had openly denied them.

Mr. J. Have the Church's infallible decisions always been given through such General Councils? I thought that the Pope was divinely protected, so that he could make such a decision without convoking a council of all other bishops.

Father S. You have correct understanding. As I just mentioned, Pope Pius XII proclaimed dogma on his own. But greater external solemnity is given the Church's decree when all her bishops, jointly with the Pope, make the decision. Then this mode of procedure is more conformable with that of the Apostles, who met at the Council of Jerusalem in the same way, in the year 51. Moreover, it is certainly beneficial to all the bishops to meet in such a convention. The written records of such Councils from the earliest centuries are a great treasure, and with them, how easy is it for the Church today to determine whether the prevalent belief is identical with that of the remote ages! These records constitute the Church's diary, and make her authority in matters of faith. During these instructions I have continually referred to Vatican Council II which was held from 1962 to 1965. This is the most recent example of the Church as Church teaching. This Council commanded the attention of all the world and was even open to non-Catholic observers. Is the infallibility of the Church sufficiently plain to you now, Mr. Jackson?

Mr. J. The plainest of all I have learned about the Church: for, if man must accept certain truths, is it not absurd to suppose that God would leave to each individual to determine what these truths are? How could doubts or disputes be settled, if there was no divinely constituted authority outside the Bible — since people can make the Bible mean anything and prove anything? If the Catholic Church fell into error, how am I to be sure that any of the reformed religions is correct, because only infallible authority could determine that, and none of them claim such authority?

Father S. There is nothing shaky about your faith, Mr. Jackson.

Mr. J. Not any longer, Father. There is only one other matter I want a little light on at this juncture. I have heard that the Catholic Church bases some of her teaching on *Tradition.* Isn't there danger of error creeping into circulation when teaching is passed from one generation to another *by word of mouth?*

Father S. There would be, (1) if the Church did not have the guidance of the Holy Spirit and, (2) if Tradition were principally *oral*, as you understand it. But the Church's Tradition is chiefly "written." She has preserved the *writings* of learned saints of all centuries from the time of the Apostles. Then, as we have already seen, she possesses the decrees of General Councils beginning immediately after the age of martyrs. Remember that the Tradition which we believe contains the Word of God is *Divine* Tradition, not human. Divine Tradition is the divinely revealed truth taught orally by Christ and His Apostles which is not found in the Bible, though recorded for all time by churchmen in the early age of the Church.

Heaven a Reward

We believe that the multitude of those gathered around Jesus and Mary in Paradise forms the Church of Heaven, where in eternal beatitude they see God as He is, and where they also, in different degrees, are associated with the Holy Angels in the divine rule exercised by Christ in glory, interceding for us and helping our weakness by their brotherly care. — *Credo of the People of God.*

Father S. Now, Mr. Jackson, since you have a clear understanding of the Church's nature, organization and mission, we shall take up one by one, those teachings of the Church which we have not already touched on: You know that we believe in God, in whom there are three Persons; that the Son, the second Person became man to atone for mankind's sins and to establish in the world a spiritual kingdom, through which people would be both properly taught and supernaturally assisted in the business of saving souls. Incidentally we have referred to the reward which is in store for those who faithfully observe God's commandments and "hear His Church," and to the punishment which awaits those who disregard either. Now let us take up the several doctrines of the Church specifically.

Mr. J. Very well, Father, I am ready for them. Let us begin with Heaven.

Father S. Yes, I presume you are most ready to believe that there exists a place of eternal happiness?

Mr. J. I am ready for the pleasant and unpleasant. You only need to tell me what Christ's Church, taught by God Himself, teaches.

Father S. Well, concerning Heaven, the Church teaches that it is God's own home, where the saved see God face to face, are associated with the angels, and enjoy a happiness beyond the conception of any human being, and that will never end.

Mr. J. That's worth working for, Father.

Father S. Indeed it is. If happiness, such as the almighty power of God can prepare, were to be only of one or ten years' duration, it would be worth a lifelong struggle, but considering that it will last as long as God Himself will endure—eternally—its attainment should be the one great concern of every human being. No one should be willing to run even the remotest risk of losing it.

Mr. J. But no one who dies in grievous sin can attain the joy of seeing God, can he?

Father S. No, because by serious sin he rejects that happiness and makes himself incapable and unworthy of enjoying it.

Mr. J. It does not seem to me that any man could be worthy of such a reward as you describe Heaven to be.

Father S. Surely no man without God's grace could be *worthy* of it, but God chose thus to reward those who love and serve Him here on earth. I am glad that you are not so presumptuous as some people, who believe that whether a man does God's will or not, he will be saved.

Mr. J. That would be unreasonable. It would be against all justice to reward the wicked. Think of a person being rewarded for ever and ever for breaking God's laws throughout a long life, and not even seriously repenting!

Father S. I see that it will be easy to prove to you the existence of Hell; you are touching upon it already.

Mr. J. Well, isn't Heaven to be a *reward* for virtue and the service of God?

Father S. Yes, except for infants who die in their baptismal grace; they receive it as a gift. But those who come to the use of reason *earn* Heaven by complying with God's requirements.

Mr. J. That seems just and right. Since God does not owe Heaven to anybody, it surely rests with Him to dictate the terms on which it is to be attained, and man has no one to blame but himself if he refuses to comply with such terms.

Father S. Exactly.

Mr. J. On this same principle, I presume that there are degrees of reward in Heaven, for surely some deserve more than others?

Father S. Oh, yes; the person who gives his best years to the devil, but repents before death, will receive less reward than those who were devoted friends and lovers of God throughout life. Speaking of Heaven, did not our Lord say: "In My Father's house there are many dwelling places" (John 14:2)? Our heavenly reward will be proportioned to our works: "For the Son of Man . . . will repay each man according to his conduct" (Matt. 16:27). And St. Paul wrote: "Even among the stars, one differs from another in brightness. So it is with the resurrection of the dead" (1 Cor. 15:41-42).

Mr. J. But all are called saints, are they not?

Father S. Yes, all the saved are called saints; but they came into possession of Heaven by different claims. Some, in days of persecution, gave up their lives, rather than betray Christ; they are called martyrs. Thousands won Heaven in this way during the first three centuries. Others consecrated themselves, soul and body, to Christ; they sacrificed chances to marry, in order that they might expend all their heart's love on Jesus; they would have been ready to die a thousand times rather than offend God by the slightest sin; many of them went to the desert to live amid privations and to devote their whole lives to prayer and quiet meditation. But still others lived like the majority of us, in a world of sin, subject to thousands of temptations. They cared for their families, attended to their work, but did not neglect their souls. They prayed, submitted to Christ's easy yoke, and employed the means of salvation placed by God's Church at their disposal.

Mr. J. But only the *spirits* of the good go to Heaven?

Father S. Yes, until the general resurrection day, at the end of the world. In the Apostles' Creed we say: "I believe in the resurrection of the body." By His almighty power God will cause the body of every human being to rise from the earth and to be reunited to and revivified by his soul which was in Heaven, Hell or Purgatory (John 5:29). Then the whole assemblage of human beings will be judged by God (cf. Matt. 25:31-46); and thereafter, as human beings—*body and soul united*—they will be welcomed into Heaven, or sentenced everlastingly to Hell. There will be no Purgatory after the last judgment. The bodies of the saved will be like unto Christ's risen body, glorious, radiant with heavenly beauty, spiritualized, and no longer capable of the slightest suffering; but the bodies of the wicked will reflect the sinful state of their souls. As the body participates in many good works, and in many evil deeds, it is fitting that it should share the reward or punishment.

Mr. J. Is not the soul judged at death and its fate settled?

Father S. Yes. This is called the *particular* judgment (Heb. 9:27).

Mr. J. Why, then, another judgment at the end of the world?

Father S. For several reasons, two of which are: (1) To glorify Christ before the whole world. On earth He was unjustly judged by men and sentenced to death. (2) To vindicate the justice of God. On earth people frequently accuse God of being unjust and criticize His Providence, which they do not understand. Here we frequently see poverty and trials, sickness and misfortune associated with virtue and holiness, while the wicked often prosper. God will show that He was a *just* God nevertheless.

Mr. J. Does anybody know when the end of the world will be, Father?

Father S. No; so don't be alarmed at the prophecies on which many new religions are thriving.

Mr. J. What do you mean by that?

Father S. By the sale of prophetic books, by interpreting the Book of Daniel or Revelations to fit current events, certain preachers and self-proclaimed seers are making lots of money and well-meaning people are their victims. Simply remember that Christ told us that we do not know the day or the hour of His coming.

Mr. J. Will relatives and friends know each other in Heaven?

Father S. Assuredly; anything which would conduce to the greater happiness of the blessed will be granted by God.

Mr. J. Don't you think that the ones whose happiness is inferior will envy those who are rewarded more?

Father S. No; those who have the least reward in Heaven, possess all that they could contain. Each saint has a certain capacity for heavenly joy, and is filled to overflowing. A bucket running over with water would not envy the barrel, which contains more; it has all it can hold.

Doctrine of Hell Is Reasonable

For a monumental struggle against the powers of darkness pervades the whole history of man. The battle was joined from the very origins of the world and will continue until the last day, as the Lord has attested. — *The Church Today, 36.*

Father S. In our last instruction, Mr. Jackson, we considered Heaven the final reward of those who die in the state of grace, now we must deal with the punishment of those who die in the state of mortal sin. The more you appreciate the justice of God and the true character of mortal sin, the more you will see the truth of the words of the Bible: "The beginning of wisdom is fear of the Lord" (Proverbs 9:10).

Mr. J. The Catholic Church, then, does not believe that any are "sanctified" in the sense that they cannot be lost — as some Churches hold?

Father S. No. St. Paul tells us that even he was not absolutely certain of his salvation: "I am not conscious to myself of anything (any sin), but in this I am not justified"; and in another place the Bible says that no one is certain whether he be worthy of love or hatred. We are not sure how we shall correspond with God's graces in the future. But the Bible tells us that "he who perseveres to the end (in living right) will be saved."

Mr. J. Now, Father, what does the Catholic Church teach about Hell?

Father S. She teaches: (1) That there is a hell; (2) That it will last forever; and (3) That those detained therein endure a dreadful twofold punishment: — they are deprived of the vision of God and suffer torments.

Mr. J. I suppose Hell is quite opposite from Heaven.

Father S. Exactly; the blessed in Heaven see God, are free from every form of pain and anxiety, have their every reasonable desire satisfied, and have no fear of losing their happiness; the lost do not see God, endure acute suffering and have no hope of ever being liberated therefrom.

Mr. J. If I did not believe in the infallibility of the Church, Father, this teaching concerning everlasting punishment would be most difficult to accept; up to this point God has always appeared to me as the *good* and *merciful* God.

Father S. Well, express your objections, and see if they can be squared with right reason and common sense.

Mr. J. Now, first of all, it seems repugnant to believe that God would punish a man so dreadfully.

Father S. Let us keep our facts straight. Remember Our Lord plainly tells us that in the final judgment, He will say: "Come. You have my Father's blessing! Inherit the kingdom prepared for you from the creation of the world. . . . Out of my sight, you condemned, into that everlasting fire prepared for the devil and his angels!" (Matt. 25:34, 41). You will agree that if the reward of which He speaks is everlasting, so also must be the punishment. It does not seem repugnant to believe that God would reward so munificently, does it?

Mr. J. No, Father, because I had known Him to be such a good God — by Creation, and especially by the Incarnation and Redemption.

Father S. Certainly God is merciful. Most of the Church's teaching is a record of His mercy. But why so many warnings to unrepentant sinners — why did He go out of His way to tell us what to do in order to be good — why did the

Son of God become man — why did He suffer and offer His life as He did? These are all mysteries of His infinite mercy toward us; but why these manifestations of infinite mercy if not to save us from infinite justice? He rewards the very good eternally, because His goodness is infinite, or without limit. Isn't that true?

Mr. J. Yes, Father.

Father S. Then He should punish the very wicked eternally, because His justice is infinite, or without limit. All His attributes must be equally infinite. God cannot be any more indifferent toward evil than toward virtue.

Mr. J. That seems very logical.

Father S. Let us suppose a case which is quite common: A highway robber holds up a man by pointing a revolver at his head, and demands his money: robbery and murder (if necessary) are in his heart, but the man whom he "holds up" bests him, and shoots him, killing him instantly. This man, guilty before God of robbery and murder, goes into eternity without the slightest repentance. Surely he will not be "rewarded" forever?

Mr. J. Impossible.

Father S. Then there is no alternative but Hell. Exclusion from Heaven is the worst kind of Hell. And if the exclusion were not eternal, that man would one day be saved. If Hell's punishment were not eternal, the sinner could, to use a homely expression, "put one over" on God; for God could say in a hundred commandments: "You shall do this; you shall not do that," and the sinner could reply: "I shall not do this, I shall do that throughout my life, and You must save me, because my soul is immortal and Hell is not eternal." Thousands of sinners by their acts do defy God in this manner.

Mr. J. You are right, Father.

Father S. People are led more by sentiment than by reason when considering this subject. They allow themselves to think only of God's mercy and shut their eyes to His justice because it doesn't fit in with an irresponsible life of easy indulgence. If these same people were dealing with offenders against themselves, they would not disregard justice. What if a man assaulted your daughter? How often do you hear people call for stronger law and punishment to cut down on street crime, drug pushers, and the like? According to human justice a person who has committed murder is cut off from his fellow man forever. Human justice exacts a punishment as everlasting as it can make it. The law punishes some criminals as long as it can punish them. People are often so impatient to mete out justice rather than mercy, that they take the law in their own hands, and "lynch" the criminal. Now since we are made for God alone, are placed here to serve Him, are aided by God's grace to avoid sin, are called to Heaven, which we can attain if we will—is it not reasonable that if we chose to do everything else but "the one thing necessary," we should be cast aside as "worthless servants"?

Mr. J. It is, Father.

Father S. God would be cruel and eternal Hell would be unreasonable if we could not escape it. But remember, if the sinner be lost, it is wholly his own fault. Just as the criminal puts himself in the penitentiary by his crime, so the lost put themselves in Hell by their sins. A person who dies in the state of sin puts himself in an everlasting state of refusing God's mercy. God has done more than His part to save the sinner. He underwent a cruel death to bring salvation to the sinner, but He will not rob him of his free will. Good people are not afraid of Hell, because they have firmly decided to escape it; just as you and I would not care if this State had a thousand penitentiaries, because we intend to stay out of them. Hell exists for the violators of God's laws, just as the penitentiary exists for the violators of man's laws. Both can be avoided—so where is the injustice unless it be man's injustice to himself?

Mr. J. I don't see that there is any.

Father S. Now, let us repeat what the Bible has to say on this matter. Matthew 25:41, records the words which Christ Himself will address to the wicked in the General judgment:

"Out of my sight, you condemned, into that everlasting fire."
This sentence expresses the three points which I declared the
Church to teach about Hell: *"Out of my sight,"* expresses the
worst of hell's punishment—separation from God; *"that fire,"*
the torture; *"everlasting,"* the eternity of the punishment. The
same truths are clearly contained in the parable of the "Rich
Man and Lazarus" (Luke 16:19-31). Our Savior tells us that
the rich man died and was buried in Hell; there he pleads for a
drop of water from Abraham, "for I am tortured in these
flames." But Abraham answers: "Between you and us there is
fixed a great abyss, so that those who might wish to cross from
here to you cannot do so, nor can anyone cross from your side
to us." This parable, therefore, emphasizes the existence of
Hell, its torments, its eternity.

Mr. J. So the Catholic Church really believes that there is
fire in Hell?

Father S. She has never defined as an article of faith that
there is actual material fire, such as we have on earth. The
New Testament speaks of "fire" 30 times as the cause of suffering in Hell; it speaks of "everlasting fire" (Matt. 25:41);
"unquenchable fire" (Mark 9:43); a "fiery furnace" (Matt.
13:42); "as in a limekiln," "consuming fire" (Isai. 33:11-12),
etc. But what if our Savior meant *imaginery* fire? I cannot see
that the slightest consolation would be afforded the sinner;
because the figure would have to convey the meaning that
Hell's torments are as terrible as fire. If you told me that your
tooth pains like fire, would you have relief, if I tried to console
you by saying: "But it isn't fire"?

Mr. J. No, Father; I would be just as miserable.

Father S. The means of punishment depend on God's free
will. If He decided on fire, no number of protests from man
will affect it. But don't forget that, no matter how fearful the
suffering from fire may be, that cannot be compared with the
suffering which results from the loss of the vision of God due to
one's sins.

Purgatory, Plain Church Teaching

We believe in the life eternal. We believe that the souls of all who die in the grace of Christ, whether they must still be purified in Purgatory, or whether from the moment they leave their bodies Jesus takes them to Paradise as He did the Good Thief, are the People of God in the eternity beyond death, which will be finally conquered on the day of the Resurrection when these souls will be reunited with their bodies. — *Credo of the People of God.*

Mr. J. Father, I haven't the faintest idea of your teaching on Purgatory, but I know it comes in for severe and sarcastic condemnation.

Father S. That is because our real teaching is not understood. Purgatory is a most reasonable and consoling doctrine, and it is demanded by God's justice. God Himself tells us that nothing imperfect can enter heaven. You have conceded that only the *very good* can expect to go to Heaven *immediately* after death, and that the *very bad* deserve Hell, have you not?

Mr. J. That's right.

Father S. Well, then, how about the great multitude, which you would class neither with the *very* good nor the *very* bad; where will their souls go right after death?

Mr. J. I never thought of that. Surely they go somewhere.

Father S. Precisely. To Purgatory.

Mr. J. That fits in with my way of thinking, for I believe that the majority of people are neither so free from all sin as to merit immediate entrance into Heaven, nor so bad as to be punished forever in Hell.

Father S. You grasp the idea, and will understand it better if you compare the exercise of human justice with that of divine justice. Human justice would not deserve the name unless it were modeled after the divine. Yet human justice recognizes little criminals and big criminals, and punishes them accordingly. It has a jail for those whom it punishes for one, ten, or 30 days, and a penitentiary where it punishes many for life. What if in our town two men are arrested, one for murder and the other for driving a car faster than the speed ordinance allows; both are tried and sentenced to the penitentiary for life?

Mr. J. Why, the people would denounce such a manifest injustice.

Father S. Deny Purgatory, and you are accusing God of dealing in that unjust manner with His disobedient creatures.

Mr. J. Is Purgatory, then, where those who die with small sins unatoned are punished for a time?

Father S. Yes, but remember that those who go to Purgatory, die in the state of grace. They are the friends of God, who, before death, were guilty of venial or easily pardonable sins, or they failed to do sufficient penance for sins which had been forgiven.

Mr. J. Any man with a little reason must see the propriety of such a place.

Father S. And he would see it if he removed the mists of prejudice from his mental vision, for at heart every Christian believes in Purgatory, no matter how vehemently he might denounce it by word. This is evident from the prayers he says almost unconsciously, for his deceased friends and relatives. There is scarcely a Christian funeral without prayer; it is a case of actions speaking louder than words — for if there be no Purgatory, of what avail is prayer? If the soul of the deceased be in Heaven, it needs no prayer; if it be in Hell, prayer cannot help it.

Mr. J. Well, doesn't the Bible mention Purgatory?

Father S. It refers to the place, but does not call it by that name. This is the shallowest of all objections. You might as well deny that there is a book called the Bible, because no such name is found in the inspired writings. On the same grounds, deny the Trinity, Incarnation, etc., because these words cannot be found in the Bible. The name does not make the place; the place must exist first, then we give it a name. Call the place of temporary punishment any other name you please; Catholics call it Purgatory, which means a cleansing place, because therein souls are purged from the small stains of sin, which prevent their entrance into the holy presence of God.

Mr. J. You say that the Bible speaks of the place; would you tell me where?

Father S. St. Matthew (5:26) speaks of a prison house in the other world, from which the soul will not be released "until you have paid the last penny." Now, no last penny needs to be paid in Heaven, and from Hell there is no liberation at all; hence the reference must apply to a third place. The same evangelist in Chapter 12:32, speaks of a sin against the Holy Spirit: "it will not be forgiven him either in this age or in the age to come." The implication is that some sins can be forgiven *in the world to come.* But not in Hell, from which there is no liberation; nor in Heaven, for there "nothing profane shall enter it" (Revelation 21:27). Then the Bible *clearly implies* a place for temporary punishment after death in the many passages which tell that God will reward or punish *according to man's works.* Let us suppose, Mr. Jackson, that there is no Purgatory. Then what will become of you and me? On the one hand, the Bible declares that nothing defiled can enter Heaven, and on the other that an idle word (little faults) defiles the soul (Matt. 12:36); if there be no place of temporary punishment, the one guilty of little sins would be consigned to Hell. Who would be saved?

Mr. J. That's so, Father. But you spoke of a common custom of praying for the dead. Do you mean that we can assist those in Purgatory by prayer?

Father S. Yes; by prayers, good works, indulgences and especially by the Church's divinely instituted sacrifice, called the Mass. We shall talk later about Indulgences and the Mass.

Mr. J. This is surely a consoling teaching — that we can be of help to our dead.

Father S. Yes, it is. This teaching alone has converted many to the Catholic faith. Just as I can pay your food and utility debt, so I can offer up my good works to be applied towards the payment of the last penny of satisfaction which a soul in Purgatory might owe to the Almighty. Christ Himself says that what we do for the least of His brethren, we do for Him, and the souls in Purgatory are, in a sense, the least of Christ's brethren, because though they can help others by prayer, they cannot help themselves. You see, death ended the time of repentance and mercy for them; after death God exercises justice only; that is why the last penny must be paid.

Mr. J. Does the Bible tell us that prayer helps the dead?

Father S. Yes. In the second book of the Machabees, 12:46, we have both Scriptural proof for the existence of Purgatory itself and evidence that the Jews had sacrifices offered for those of their brethren who had lost their lives in battle: "Thus he made atonement for the dead that they might be freed of their sin." Why pray for the dead in Heaven or Hell? That they prayed for them shows they believed in a place where they could be helped (we call it Purgatory) and that the prayers of the living could help them. These words were so plain in favor of the Catholic custom, that the whole book containing them was removed from the Protestant Bible. But this does not help their case, because the book, even if not inspired, would still tell us what was the practice among God's chosen people. Even today, Jews pray for the dead.

Mr. J. But why should non-Catholics desire to reject a teaching so full of consolation?

Father S. Well, they want to believe that the merits of Christ applied to the sinner who trusts in Him, will remove all sin; and hence the believer will go at once to Heaven. This is un-Scriptural, since Christ tells us that to enter into life we must keep the commandments, hear the Church, do the will of His Father, and much more.

Mr. J. How long must people who go to Purgatory remain there?

Father S. We do not know; all depends on the state of their souls. Probably you have heard non-Catholics say that the priest pretends to know, and that for a certain amount of money "he will pray their souls out of Purgatory"?

Mr. J. Yes, I have, Father.

Father S. It's another silly absurdity. No priest knows who is in Purgatory and who is not, nor what length of time they might be detained there. God in His infinite justice must sentence each individual soul to the punishment it deserves. Only God knows what that punishment shall be both as to its severity and duration. But we are certain that by our prayers, we can aid the souls in Purgatory and hurry their entrance into Heaven.

PART II

The Commandments of God

"If you wish to enter into life, keep the commandments."
Matt. 19:17.

I am the Lord your God.

1. *You shall not have strange gods before Me.*
2. *You shall not take the name of the Lord your God in vain.*
3. *Remember to keep holy the Lord's day.*
4. *Honor your father and mother.*
5. *You shall not kill.*
6. *You shall not commit adultery.*
7. *You shall not steal.*
8. *You shall not bear false witness against your neighbor.*
9. *You shall not covet your neighbor's wife.*
10. *You shall not covet your neighbor's goods.*

Exodus 20:1-17; Deut. 5:6-21.

Precepts of the Church

1. *To rest from servile work and assist at Mass on all Sundays and holydays of obligation.*
2. *To fast and abstain on certain days specified by the Church.*
3. *To confess one's sins at least once a year.*
4. *To receive Holy Communion once a year during Eastertime.*
5. *To contribute towards the support of religion.*
6. *Not to marry persons who are blood-relations down to the third degree, nor to solemnize marriage during what are called "forbidden times."*

INSTRUCTION 15

Actual Sin

The highest norm of human conduct is the law of God; it is objective, universal, eternal. By this law God directs the entire universe and all the ways of mankind according to a plan conceived in wisdom and love. — *Religious Freedom, 3.*

In the depths of his conscience man detects a law which he does not impose upon himself but which holds him to obedience. Always summoning him to do good and avoid evil, the voice of conscience can, when necessary, speak to his heart more specifically; do this, shun that. For man has in his heart a law written by God. To obey it is the very dignity of man; according to it he will be judged. — *The Church Today, 16.*

Father S. Before beginning our series of instructions on the Commandments, I feel that we should talk about that which is the purpose of the Commandments to prevent, namely, sin. You have learned what Original Sin is, but it is more important to know how Almighty God regards the sins, serious and lesser, which we commit ourselves by the violation of His Commandments. Those sins of wilful thought, word, deed, or omission, are known as "actual" sins, because they result from our failure to do good "acts" or to avoid the evil "acts" proscribed or forbidden by the law of God.

Mr. J. What would be a good definition of Actual Sin?

Father S. Probably the best definition is this: Actual Sin is the *wilful* violation of a Law of God.

Mr. J. *Unwilful* violations of the Law of God would, therefore, not be sins.

Father S. No, although those whose business it is to administer *human* laws will not accept the plea of "ignorance," Almighty God does. Human laws deal only with *external* acts, while God sees the heart, and when there is no knowledge of His law and no willingness to offend God, He does not take offense.

Mr. J. I presume some sins are much more serious than others.

Father S. That is very clear. We call grievous offenses against the Divine Law *"mortal"* sins, and lesser offenses *"venial"* sins.

Mr. J. Will you kindly explain the meaning of those words?

Father S. The word "mortal" means "deadly," and serious sins are deadly to the supernatural life of the soul and to our friendship with God. The word "venial" means "pardonable," i.e., they are more easily pardoned, because by these sins we do not cease to be friends of God. They are pardonable not only through the Sacrament of Penance, as are all sins, but even by our acts of sorrow and love, and by the reception of the Holy Eucharist.

Mr. J. Just when is a sin mortal?

Father S. It is mortal when the thing done or omitted is serious matter, and when the sinner acts with full deliberation and full consent of the will.

Mr. J. Does this mean that if one should do something which is very seriously wrong, but not do it fully conscious of its wrong, or not give full consent of the will to it, it would not be mortal?

Father S. You are right. *All three* conditions must be fulfilled before the act done or omitted becomes a "mortal" sin.

This will become more clear to you as we take up the Commandments one by one, and consider the sins which offend against each. However, I must offer a caution. We hear a great deal today about following one's conscience. Vatican II made it very clear that a person must follow conscience and cannot be coerced to the contrary. This doctrine comes from St. Thomas Aquinas who teaches that man is always culpable if he does not do what his conscience tells him to do. Unfortunately, many people use this argument to commit sin and violate God's law. They fail to read the succeeding part of St. Thomas where he declares man has an obligation to form a correct conscience. From the Nazis down in our own time we have heard the excuse, "But I only did what I thought was right." St. Thomas does not accept this argument saying: "Your wickedness is greater that you would not recognize the evil of your acts." When conscience tells us to act contrary to Church law or the teaching of the Pope, it is a clear indication that we should determine with certitude whether our conscience is right or not. The presumption should always be in favor of the law.

Mr. J. That is a thoughtful argument. It makes mortal sin clear to me. What makes a sin venial?

Father S. A sin can be venial in two ways: (1) when the evil done is not seriously wrong, (2) when the evil done is seriously wrong, but the sinner sincerely believes it is only slightly wrong or does not give full consent to it. Such sin makes us less fervent in the service of God.

Mr. J. Do not some people make light of the violation of all God's laws on the score that God is too great to be concerned about what *we* do, who are so far beneath Him?

Father S. Yes, they do, but it does not mean that they reason rightly. Not all of us choose to be children of God; all of us are, however, creatures responsible to God. We belong to Him absolutely; we were made for the purpose of serving Him. It is precisely *because God is infinitely great and perfect* that He cannot look with indifference on sin. You will recall that when the angels rebelled against God they were immediately punished, and have been suffering the consequences of their sin ever since.

We measure the malice of sin by the greatness of the one Whom it offends. Since we cannot measure the greatness of God we cannot measure the malice of mortal sin.

Mr. J. You call sin "rebellion." Is it always that?

Father S. It is in a sense, because God is present wherever we are, and when we deliberately act contrary to His will in His presence, our act takes on the nature of rebellion. This is especially true of mortal sin because of its deliberateness.

Mr. J. I take it that if mortal sin destroys the supernatural life of the soul and, in addition, offends God seriously, the guilty one makes himself deserving of punishment in Hell.

Father S. That has been Christian teaching from the very beginning, and it is also the teaching of common sense. The person who commits a mortal sin acts like a man who would deliberately throw himself into a pit from which he knew he could never extricate himself. If the soul of man lives forever, and if it leaves the body refusing grace and, in addition, willing to be separated from God, it evidently cannot enter Heaven, a place of *reward*. You have already learned that the worst punishment of Hell is the loss of Heaven and the vision of God, of which the unrepentant sinner makes himself unworthy. It is because of the serious consequences of sin that we should avoid even the near occasions of sin; that is: all persons, places, or things that may easily lead us into sin.

Life with God is a life of grace and when we deliberately commit serious sin we cut the channel of grace and are spiritually dead. Your telephone works as long as it is connected to a central terminal. If the line carrying power from the terminal is cut, your telephone is dead. Committing mortal sin is like cutting that line.

Mr. J. If one who dies unrepentant of mortal sin deserves Hell, does the one who dies unrepentant of venial sin deserve Purgatory?

Father S. Your inference is correct. Mortal sins are punished in Hell; and those who die in venial sin, or who did not make full satisfaction for forgiven mortal sin, go to Purgatory.

In closing this instruction I might note that by mortal sin we relinquish all past merit, but when mortal sin is forgiven through the Sacrament of Penance, merit revives in proportion to the sincere and loving sorrow with which the sinner receives that sacrament.

First Commandment

"You shall not have strange gods before Me."

Father S. We have covered the lessons dealing with the basic truths of faith. But faith alone will not save a person. When St. Paul tells us that we must live by faith, he means that we must live *according to the teachings* of faith, and if there be one thing emphasized by Christ it is that we must observe the Commandments—the ten Commandments given by God through Moses which He came "not to abolish them, but to fulfill them" (Matt. 5:17); and His two great Commandments.

Mr. J. I never heard of Christ's two Commandments.

Father S. Our Lord's Commandments are the Ten Commandments, the whole law of God, in a nutshell. They are in the words of Jesus: " 'You shall love the Lord your God with your whole heart, with your whole soul, and with all your mind.' This is the greatest and first Commandment. The second is like it; 'You shall love your neighbor as yourself.' On these two Commandments the whole law is based, and the prophets as well" (Matt. 22:37-40). Thus He gave us a short cut to the observance of the Ten Commandments. St. Paul tells us this, when he says: "Love, is the fulfillment of the Law" (Rom. 13:10)—the love of God and the love of neighbor as oneself.

Mr. J. That makes it all rather simple, doesn't it?

Father S. Yes, simply stated, but not so easy when put into practice. However, don't get the idea that we should be satisfied with doing merely what we are commanded. We should be ready to do good deeds even when they are not commanded.

Mr. J. For example?

Father S. Although not strictly commanded by the law of God, Our Lord especially recommended voluntary poverty, lifelong chastity and perfect obedience. But let us get back to the Ten Commandments. What is the First Commandment?

Mr. J. I am the Lord, your God, Who brought you out of the land of—

Father S. You need not include that explanatory clause. The brief way is: "I am the Lord, your God, you shall not have strange gods before Me." By those other words, God would relate the favor He showed to the Israelites in leading them in a miraculous way out of the slavery of Egypt.

Mr. J. But the other words are important, are they not— "You shall not carve idols for yourselves"?

Father S. Well, yes; but the words, "You shall not have strange gods before Me," include that prohibition. However, I am glad that you brought this up since it suggests that I tell you that Catholics and some non-Catholics differ in determining where the first ends and the second begins. You see, in giving the Commandments, God did not say first, second, third, etc.; neither did Moses thus number them; this was done centuries after they were listed in the Bible. Catholics argue that God forbids the making of graven *things* (such as statues), and the likeness of things (such as pictures) for the purpose of false worship, and that this is implied by what we regard as the closing words of the First Commandment, namely: "You shall not bow down before them nor worship them." Some non-Catholics, on the other hand, contend that the *making* of statues and pictures, etc., is forbidden by the First Commandment, and that the words "thou shalt not bow down before them or worship them constitute the Second Commandment.

Mr. J. Then non-Catholics must have eleven Commandments?

Father S. No; they combine our ninth and tenth as one, thus getting ten.

Mr. J. But surely non-Catholics would not contend that it is a sin to make a statue or picture. It would mean to condemn all works of art, all monumental work, all photography, history itself.

Father S. To be consistent they would have to condemn all that; but they modify the meaning of the Commandment, referring it to the making of statues and images for use in churches. This view is untenable, because there were no churches at the time God gave the Commandments, nor for many years later. The Jews worshipped before the Ark of the Covenant, which itself was sheltered between graven things, made by God's own direction.

And when God did give instructions concerning the first grand church or temple, He required that figures representing angels be near the very "Holy of Holies," and that the walls of the whole temple be "carved with diverse figures and carvings . . ." and diverse representations as it were standing out . . . (1 Kings 6:22-29).

Mr. J. It does seem to me that religious representations belong in the church, for they remind the worshipper that he is in a holy place.

Father S. Surely. Just as we have pictures of our friends in our homes, so it is fitting that we should have the pictures of God's friends in His house. That they are great aids to reverence and devotion is recognized by many non-Catholics, who would never think of speaking loudly in a Catholic church, even outside of religious services.

Mr. J. I have frequently heard that Catholics pray to statues and pictures. Would not that be wrong?

Father S. It would be if it were true. Non-Catholic missionaries write from other lands telling how Catholics worship the image of saints, how they honor Mary more than Christ; and here in our country we are similarly accused, even though every Catholic catechism in use anywhere tells that it would be idolatry, a grievous sin against the First Commandment, to worship anyone or anything that is not God.

Mr. J. I suppose people conclude that, because Catholics have images and statues in their churches, they worship them?

Father S. Yes, they sometimes see Catholics kneeling in prayer before a statue, or see out-of-door processions in which a banner or an image of the Blessed Virgin is carried and they hastily conclude that we are image-worshippers. It never occurs to them that one could kneel before a crucifix in prayer and not pray to the crucifix. You could hardly pray at all if you had a comic representation before you; you could pray better if it were removed; you could pray still better if a crucifix were substituted, a representation of Jesus bleeding and dying for you, calling for your repentance and love. Nothing brings home a truth more than pictures; that is why magazine articles are illustrated with them, why school books are filled with them, why motion picture houses are patronized, why television has such a cultural impact. At patriotic celebrations, when speeches are given before statues of famous men, when the hat is lifted to the flag as a mark of respect, when statues of generals or statesmen are unveiled, no one accuses the participants of worshipping the statues. No one accuses the non-Catholic of worshipping his chair or his bed because he says his prayers before them. Then why should Catholics be accused of worshipping statues because they might say their prayers before them? Catholics teach that the First Commandment forbids the worshipping and not the making of images. We pray, not to the images, but to the persons they represent.

Catholic Devotion to Saints

We believe in the communion of all the faithful of Christ, those who are pilgrims on earth, the dead who are attaining their purification, and the blessed in Heaven, all together forming one Church; and We believe that in this communion the merciful love of God and His Saints is ever listening to our prayers, as Jesus told us: Ask and you will receive. — *Credo of the People of God.*

Father S. What did we dwell on in our last instruction?

Mr. J. On the use of images and statues.

Father S. Oh, yes; we saw that the First Commandment could not forbid the *making* of images even for the adornment of churches. However, the First Commandment, not the second, does strictly forbid giving *divine* worship to any person or thing that is not God. Idolatry, or idol worship, as practiced by pagan people, is wrong; so would be the *worship* of a saint or any other creature.

Mr. J. Then Catholics do not worship the Virgin Mary?

Father S. No, that would be *idolatry.* We *honor* her more than we do any other holy *creature* of God, because she was the greatest saint, because Almightly God Himself honored her first and more than any other creature.

Mr. J. I have heard people say that to honor a saint lessens the honor we pay to God; and that Catholics honor Mary more than Christ. Can you show that it's just another one of their many false impressions?

Father S. Yes, they misunderstand us. By honoring a saint we honor God; we honor the saint only because he or she was so dear to God and led so virtuous a life on earth. Would the President of the United States feel slighted if you honored his mother, who is very dear to him? Would he not know that you were honoring her principally because she is *his* mother? When you praise a painting, do you not thereby honor the artist? You will find that Catholics are encouraged to honor the saints by imitating their holy lives, by asking them to pray to God for us, and by showing respect for their remains, their images, and the like.

Mr. J. I see that the critics of Catholics are wrong again. But does the *Bible* mention Mary very prominently?

Father S. More prominently than anyone else outside of Christ. I do not mean that the Bible devotes more chapters or pages to her. It would be foolish to attempt to determine the greatness of a person by the number of words expended on him or her by the eulogist. It would be like appraising the value of a painting by the number of square feet of canvas used for it. One single sentence might contain a greater message than a whole book. If the Bible contained no more than this sentence: "It was of her that Jesus who is called the Messiah was born" (Matt. 1:16), it would be saying as much as if the whole book treated of her. And since, as St. Gregory says, "Christ's example is a commandment," we have a very forceful argument in favor of honoring Mary. Christ honored her by taking His human nature from her, by living with her for 30 years, by being "subject to her," by working His first miracle, "before the time had come," at her request, by bequeathing her to us as a mother with His dying words on the Cross, "Behold your Mother." The angel *sent by God* honored her when he announced that she was to be the mother of God. Should we do less? The words of St. Luke (1:26-35) record an incident of honor paid Mary by God, which takes our breath away.

Mr. J. But Catholic also *pray* to Mary, do they not?

Father S. We rather ask her to join us in prayer to God. Christ said He more readily hears our prayers when two or more are gathered together in His name. The prayers of the Church are all addressed to God "through Christ, our Lord"; so are the prayers which we place in Mary's pure hands; they are offered by her to God, through Christ, her Son, Our Lord. We pray to Mary not in the same manner we pray to God. We do not ask her to *grant* us favors, but to obtain them for us by her intercession. Does not the Bible tell us to pray for one another? I can pray for you, and you for me; then why cannot the saints, God's best friends, pray to Him for us? And if Christ heeded Mary's prayers on earth, will He not still heed them in Heaven?

Mr. J. It seems reasonable.

Father S. I think we have said sufficient on this subject. Let's now see what else the First Commandment forbids. It forbids all practices which are equivalent to idolatry, such as attributing to persons or things, powers which only God has.

Mr. J. For instance, Father?

Father S. Consulting fortune tellers for certain information about the future. Only God knows the future. Believing in signs, dreams, going to spiritists, etc.; ascribing sure protection from Heaven to charms, stones, medals, etc. Astrology is a modern superstition that has many followers. Millions read their horoscopes each day. That is superstition: attributing to creatures powers that belong to God alone.

Mr. J. I thought Catholics believed in wearing medals, and something else they wear around their neck?

Father S. They believe that by the devout use of blessed articles they may seek the protection of Heaven, but they do not expect it infallibly, nor do they expect the help directly from the medals or scapulars—that "something else" you mention—they wear, but from God.

Mr. J. Why are medals worn?

Father S. To ask the protection of the saint in whose

honor they are worn. There are medals worn in honor of the Sacred Heart of Jesus, of the Blessed Virgin, St. Benedict, and others. They are blessed by the priest and worn out of devotion to the ones in whose honor they are carried.

Mr. J. Catholics are not superstitious, then?

Father S. Not as much so as any other class of our American people; they do not believe that a horseshoe hanging over the door—or anyone but God—can send them good luck; nor do they believe travel on Friday, or eating with twelve others at table brings bad luck. Other people might perceive the folly of such superstition, but the Catholic Church tells her people that *it is wrong* to look to any thing or any person for what God alone can give or withhold.

Likewise, since Catholics are taught to revere persons, places and things that are consecrated to God, we look upon the mistreatment of such persons, places and things as the sin of *sacrilege.*

Mr. J. That is clear enough.

Father S. We have been talking about the things *forbidden* by the First Commandment; now a word about what it *requires* of us. It demands that we offer God the supreme worship that is His due—(1) adoration of God; (2) prayer, by which we acknowledge our dependence on the Almighty; (3) acceptance of His revelation, or in other words, *faith;* (4) a trust in His promises, or *hope;* (5) the *love* of Him as our Father.

Mr. J. It is a sin not to pray?

Father S. Surely.

Mr. J. How often should a person pray?

Father S. It is difficult to determine when one sins by neglecting his prayers, but the least people can do is to pray morning and night, and in time of temptation. St. Paul tells us that we should pray *always;* and he means that besides saying actual prayers, we should perform our work, enjoy our recreation, take our meals, etc., in the name of God: "The fact is that whether you eat or drink — whatever you do — you should do all for the glory of God" (1 Cor. 10:31). This constant union with God is so easy to enjoy, and it takes away bitterness from our work and sorrows or hardships.

Mr. J. It is a practical idea, too.

Father S. Let me explain briefly the meaning of faith, hope and charity. Faith is an act of the mind whereby we accept as certain what God has revealed for us to know and to do in order to be saved. The fact that God has condescended to make this known to us, obliges us to believe firmly and to profess our faith openly whenever this is necessary. Likewise we should make serious effort to find out what God has revealed and to understand it as far as possible. God gives us the inspiration and the help to believe, so we must safeguard this grace by making acts of faith in Him frequently, by praying that He increases our faith, by studying Christ's teaching, by good reading and by avoiding whatever might harm our faith, such as people and literature that are hostile to our faith.

Remember that it is possible to sin against faith. To refuse to accept the teachings of Christ after acquiring sufficient knowledge of them is *infidelity*. When a person is baptized and professes to be a Christian, but rejects certain teachings of the Church which Catholics must accept on the authority of God's revelation, he is guilty of *heresy*. Were such a one to reject all Christian teaching, he would be guilty of *apostasy*. Likewise I should mention the sin of *indifferentism,* which is the assertion that all religions are equally good and true.

Mr. J. What about attending non-Catholic church services?

Father S. There is nothing wrong in being present at a non-Catholic service, but we should not take active part in it. Truth is not divisible or contradictory, and we must avoid giving the impression that one religion is as good as another. Ecumenism is not the watering down of one's own beliefs. It is the respect given to the religious beliefs of another as being honest beliefs. Participation in the religious service of non-Catholics would give a false impression. However, when obliged by reason of his office, or out of friendship for one whose funeral or marriage is being held in a non-Catholic church, a Catholic might be present without taking active part in the service.

I don't want to keep you too late this evening, but I would like to mention hope and charity.

Mr. J. That's all right, Father.

Father S. Christian hope is important because we must trust firmly that God will give us everlasting life in Heaven and the means to obtain it. A person can lose Christian hope by either of two grave sins. He may reject God's help and rely entirely on his own efforts to be saved or he may rely on God's help without giving any personal effort or cooperation. This would be the sin of *presumption*. Secondly, he might positively refuse to trust God and His help. This would be *despair*.

I have already explained that *any grave sin is contrary* to the love we owe God, but we must also love our fellowmen — our neighbors. We can fail against this love chiefly by any word or deed that is calculated to lead our neighbor to commit sin — for example by passing around bad books or obscene pictures, using blasphemous or impure language, especially in the presence of the young. This is known as *scandal.*

Since we must love our neighbor as *ourselves,* we can fail in the love of self by *sloth.* This is not so much physical laziness as an indifferent negligence with regard to our own salvation and the necessary means of insuring it.

One last thought before you go home. One of the marks of true love is in wanting good for the person loved. Thus if we love our fellowman we will want him to have enough to eat, decent shelter, security for himself and his family. Love has many religious, social and economic applications. Then we want for him the greatest good of all — the true Faith, namely the Catholic Church.

All of this will give you plenty to think about until our next meeting. It really all comes down to the Golden Rule in action.

Second Commandment

"You shall not take the name of the Lord your God in vain."

Father S. What is the Second Commandment?

Mr. J. "You shall not take the name of the Lord your God in vain."

Father S. I presume the meaning of those words is sufficiently plain. But since every Commandment requires and forbids more than the mere words indicate, we shall devote some minutes to its consideration. It enjoins respect and reverence for God's and Jesus' names, and for the personality suggested by these names. Out of reverence, the Jews of old never uttered the holy name of God, and Catholics bow their heads when the name of Jesus is pronounced. Our disposition should be like that of David: "I will bless the Lord at all times; His praise shall be ever in my mouth" (Ps. 34:2). "From the rising to the setting of the sun is the name of the Lord to be praised" (Ps. 113:3). In some Catholic countries the greetings of people, in place of our "How do you do?" is "Praised be Jesus Christ." Our "good-bye" stands for "God be with you." In our country there are over 5,000,000 Catholic men, who are pledged not to misuse God's name, not to curse. They belong to the Holy Name Society.

Mr. J. That's a real expression of manliness, Father.

Father S. Yes, what a contrast it is to the shocking profanation of God's and our blessed Savior's names, which we hear every day in our country — on the street, at work, in the home! To my mind, there is no greater evidence of the existence of the evil spirit, than this prevalent profanity. It is bad enough for people not to bless God's name; but deliberately to abuse it, curse it, to blaspheme Him, to Whom they owe everything, is diabolical and wicked.

Mr. J. I am not familiar with the exact meaning of "taking God's name in vain."

Father S. It simply means the deliberate use of the name of God or Jesus without reverence: for example to express emphasis, surprise, or anger. Ordinarily it is a venial sin.

Mr. J. Is cursing one of the sins against the Second Commandment?

Father S. Yes, because in cursing, the name of God is usually used or implied. Cursing means the wishing of evil to persons or things. Some people commit this sin when they are angry, others do it from habit; even children are guilty of it. For example, the curse, "God damn it!" is heard frequently.

Mr. J. Yes, I hear it every day, Father; and I'm sorry to say, have often been guilty myself.

Father S. Leaving aside the wickedness of cursing, have you ever stopped to reflect how foolish the habit is? It is not gentlemanly — people do not do it before ladies. It is disrespectful. It reveals a stunted vocabulary. It shows exceedingly bad taste. It never brings the slightest benefit to the one who curses, but on the contrary, God's displeasure: "He loved cursing; may it come upon him" (Ps. 109:18). Hence, why are people guilty of it? Cursing is the language of Hell; the lost ones, who hate God, are ever cursing Him. This has led many saints to believe that the curser is greatly under the influence of the devil. Cursing can be a mortal sin, but ordinarily it is not because most people who curse do not really wish the evil to others which their words express. Likewise the emphatic use of "damn!" and "hell!" which is so common, is only improper, not sinful. Unfortunately, it becomes a habit.

Mr. J. It really does appear foolish and wicked to curse. Are any other sins forbidden by the Second Commandment?

Father S. Blasphemy, irreverent words or actions dishonoring God, violates the Second Commandment because by it God is insulted, or is spoken of contemptuously. In the Old Law it was punishable by death. Deliberate blasphemy is a mortal sin.

Mr. J. Is the Commandment violated in other ways?

Father S. Yes, by swearing. Since, in taking an oath, God is called on to witness the truth of the statement or promise, unnecessary oaths are forbidden by this Commandment and especially *perjury,* by which one deliberately associates God in his lie and which is a serious sin.

Mr. J. When is one allowed to swear or take an oath?

Father S. When it is very important that the truth concerning a matter be known, such as in court, when legal documents are to be signed. In an oath, we ask God to sustain our statement; and because it would show little reverence for God to call on Him unnecessarily as a witness, we must not take oaths without good reason. Hence, it is not right to use such expressions as, "God knows I tell the truth"; "May God strike me dead, if it be not true." However, oaths are lawful when there is a good reason for them, when we are convinced that what we say under oath is true and we are not swearing or taking an oath to do what is wrong.

Mr. J. Do not many societies of men require their members to take an oath of secrecy? And is the reason sufficient in these cases?

Father S. The Church does not regard the reason as sufficient. Hence, she does not approve of such secret societies as require an oath from their members. But even from other points of view, such oaths are wrong. A man is swearing blindly; he is not sure that everything that will take place in a meeting of the society may conscientiously be kept a secret. Then see how it lowers the dignity of men who are in authority. For instance, some of the Presidents of this great country have

joined such secret orders while in office. How improper it is
for those who rule over many people, solemnly to swear to
obey the rules and orders of some society! Much trouble has
ensued in France, Spain, Portugal, Italy, and other countries
in the past because of this.

Mr. J. The Catholic Church, then, has no oath-bound
secret societies?

Father S. No.

Mr. J. I had supposed that the order of "Knights of
Columbus" was one.

Father S. No; this order exacts only a promise, but no
oath; and the promise is not valid in case it conflicts with the
dictates of conscience, or with one's duty as a citizen.

Mr. J. Then, the Masonic Lodge to which I belong, is
forbidden?

Father S. Are you a Mason?

Mr. J. Yes, Father, and I really have always thought that
its influence on its members was for good.

Father S. Of course, these societies have many good fea-
tures; their charity, benevolence and brotherly spirit are to be
commended, but the Catholic Church disapproves of them,
especially for two reasons: (1) they require this blind oath, and
(2) they become a substitute for the Church to many members
because of their ritual, burial services, chaplain, etc. In the
proportion that men interest themselves in the lodge, they lose
interest in the Church. Many men say: "I don't go to church, I
get religion in the lodge."

Mr. J. That's true, Father.

Father S. Well, you see, on principle, the Catholic
Church could not approve of that. The Church is a divine institution, and no matter what excellent help and encouragement for good a man might get from a secret order, it is only a
human organization. The lodges should leave the Bible, and
burial services to the Church where they belong; then they
might not have the tendency to wean people away from the supernatural divinely-founded religion.

Mr. J. What is that "Knights of Columbus" document so much talked of as the K. of C. oath?

Father S. It is a forgery, pure and simple, just as the "Jesuit Oath" and the "Layman's Oath" are forgeries. Years ago, when anti-Catholicism was rampant, the K. of C. was forced to prosecute those who published this false oath. Cases were brought in practically every state and in each instance the K. of C. obtained a judgment against the user. If the printing press had been in existence at the time of Christ, all kinds of untrue and wicked things would have been printed concerning Him.

Mr. J. Is a promise the same as a vow?

Father S. No, a vow is more than a promise because, by a vow, a person binds himself to God *under penalty of sin* to do something that is especially pleasing to God.

Mr. J. I had not known that distinction.

Father S. Well, Mr. Jackson, this will suffice for this instruction. But remember: By the Second Commandment God requires reverence for His own person and name, as also reverence for persons and things dedicated to God. Then this law of God forbids cursing, unnecessary and false oaths, blasphemy, profane language, the unholy use of God's or the Savior's name or of sacred objects.

Third Commandment

"Remember to keep holy the Lord's Day."

Father S. Well, have you been trying to overcome that bad habit of cursing?

Mr. J. I have been trying my best.

Father S. Fine. Now, let us take up the Third Commandment: "Remember to keep holy the Lord's Day."

Mr. J. You stated once before that if we followed the Bible only, we would keep holy the Saturday. Isn't the "Sabbath" Sunday?

Father S. No, the word "Sabbath" means "rest," the seventh day of the week, or Saturday.

Mr. J. Well, did Christ change the day?

Father S. We have no record that He did, but we have evidence that the Church did shortly after Christ returned to Heaven (Acts 20:7; I Cor. 16:1-2).

Mr. J. It isn't plain to me that the Church is empowered to change a law of God.

Father S. The law of God was not changed. The substance of the law remained the same, namely, that man must cease from servile work and give God public worship once a week, every seventh day. The Church only transferred the obligation from Saturday to Sunday. As far as the law of God designated a certain day, it was ceremonial; and all the ceremonial laws of the Jews ended with the coming of Christ; the moral laws, besides being positively given by the Almighty, were also founded on the natural law; these the Church could not change.

Mr. J. Would you kindly tell me, Father, why the Church changed the day of worship?

Father S. Certainly. The first reason was, that even after they became converts to the Church, many Jews thought they had still to keep the ceremonial law of Moses, such as circumcision, abstinence from certain meats, the scrupulous observance of Jewish sacrifice on the Sabbath. To remove such impressions was difficult, because their ancestors for 2,000 years had thus acted. Hence the Apostles deemed it advisable to abolish Saturday public service altogether, and have the converted Jews conform to the requirements of the Christian Church. The day was changed from Saturday to Sunday. It was by far the best method of convincing the Jews that the Old Dispensation was at an end and a new era, a more perfect religion, substituted.

Mr. J. I see; and I suppose there were reasons for choosing the first day of the week rather than any other?

Father S. Yes. It was on Sunday that Jesus rose from the dead, and on Sunday that the Holy Spirit descended on the Apostles. It was particularly by the Resurrection that Christ proved Himself, and therefore His Church, to be divine, and on Pentecost that the Holy Spirit entered the Church, as its soul, the source of its divine life — and both these great events occurred on Sunday.

Mr. J. The Third Commandment does not define in what particular way the Sunday must be kept holy, does it?

Father S. The words of the Commandment do not, but in giving the Commandment to Moses, God specified that no work should be done on the Sabbath, and it must be sanctified (by divine worship) (Exod. 20:10-11). This is a serious obligation. Hence one thing we must *not* do, and another thing we *must* do. We must *not* do any hard, unnecessary work, and we *must* worship God in a public way according to the requirements of the Church.

Mr. J. Necessary work is allowed, therefore.

Father S. Surely: "Necessity knows no law." For instance, if your house were burning, the fire department could and should try to put it out, even though it required the men to work hard.

Mr. J. But one's ordinary daily work is forbidden, if not necessary?

Father S. The Church distinguishes between servile and intellectual work. The former refers to physical, bodily work, the latter to work which is principally mental. While it would be wrong for a farmer to work on a Sunday unless it was absolutely necessary, it would not be wrong for an office worker to garden as a form of relaxation or recreation. But, broadly speaking, the Church urges you to honor God by resting from your daily occupation on Sunday so that you can better honor God on His one day in seven. Today, unfortunately, many industries and services must operate on Sunday. If people could not retain their jobs unless they worked on Sunday or are needed to maintain necessary services the reason would be sufficient to justify work. More and more entire shopping centers are open on Sunday. Individual merchants justify their acts as necessary to be competitive, and unfortunately this is true. It is just as unfortunate that God's law is being ignored. People are mainly to blame. They could just as well shop on Saturday or some weekday evening. But it is one more indication of the secularization of our world and the eternal quest for the dollar.

Mr. J. Are all forms of amusements and games forbidden on Sunday?

Father S. No; rest does not mean idleness. God intended that the Sunday should also be a day of relaxation and rest from the work and cares of the week. What would be innocent and harmless recreation on week days could not become sinful on Sundays.

Mr. J. Is it wrong for taverns and nightclubs to keep open on Sunday?

Father S. As the tavern is in this country, yes. Why should it be favored more than any other store? The liquor dispenser's work is not intellectual nor necessary, and his place of business does not contribute to the honor and glory of God. It is purely lucrative. Restaurants are legitimate business to operate on Sundays. They give families a chance to be together and mother a welcome relief from the kitchen. The serving of liquor should be accidental to the business. But where liquor is the primary business, then there is a violation of the Sunday observance of God's day of rest.

Mr. J. I suppose charitable work is allowed?

Father S. Yes, and it is recommended; light efforts which relieve poverty, help the sick, or even benefit the animal are recommended. We have Christ's own example (Luke 14:4).

Mr. J. You say that public worship is enjoined. Would it not suffice for people to keep Sunday sacredly at home?

Father S. No. On Sunday God wants every one to unite with all the rest of the human family and worship Him publicly as the Heavenly Father. Worship of God has community aspects. This was true in the Old Covenant and is equally true in the new. The Mass is seen by the Church as a community at worship and sacrifice and not primarily as an act of individual worship as many made it in the past. The Church of Christ has a form of worship which is of divine institution, one capable of honoring God as He deserves to be honored, and it requires all who have attained the use of reason to come out for that on Sunday, if it be at all possible. This, too, is a serious obligation.

Mr. J. Is that the Mass to which you just referred?

Father S. Yes.

Mr. J. I go every Sunday, but I do not grasp its full meaning yet.

Father S. You will, after I shall have explained it. In the meantime, offer up the Mass which you assist for the intention of the priest, and pray in your own way to Almighty God during Mass. You might get a Sunday missal to follow. It will help you. Although, ideally, there are parts of the Mass to be listened to rather than read, unfortunately the acoustics in many churches are far from perfect and some lectors have better intentions than accomplishments.

In our next instruction we shall take up the Fourth Commandment. You have probably noticed that the three Commandments already covered were concerned directly with our duties to God. The remaining seven point out the duties by which we prove our love for our fellowmen, beginning with those near to us — our parents.

Our Lord made love of our fellowmen the distinctive feature of Christians: "This is how all will know you for my disciples: your love for one another" (John 13:35). Christian charity must include all — even our enemies, those who hate us, wish us evil or positively injure us (Matt. 5:44). Charity, to be true, must find practical expression in deeds of kindness in which we must take into account the fact that the soul is more important than the body. Remember that Christians are obliged to perform works of mercy according to their own ability and the need of the neighbor.

Mr. J. What are these "works" of which you speak?

Father S. They are many. And I'll give you the principal ones. The *Corporal* works of mercy are: To give food, drink, clothing, and shelter to those in extreme need; to visit people who are sick or in prison; and to assist in burying the dead. The chief *Spiritual* works of mercy are: To admonish sinners, to instruct the ignorant and to advise the doubtful, to comfort the sorrowful, to bear wrongs patiently, to forgive all injuries, and to pray for the living and the dead.

Mr. J. It looks as though every good deed or act of kindness would be a work of mercy.

Father S. Yes, if done in a sincere Christian spirit, any ordinary deed which relieves the corporal or spiritual needs of your neighbor is a true work of mercy.

Mr. J. And who is our neighbor, someone who lives close to us?

Father S. It is interesting that you should ask that question because the very same question in almost your exact words was put to Christ. He replied with the Parable of the Good Samaritan (Luke 10:29-37) which indicated that the name of our neighbor is everyman. In the parable the Samaritan, an enemy of the Jews, was the only one who would help the injured Jew.

Vatican II (The Church Today 27) speaks out very forcefully on this subject: "This Council lays stress on reverence for man; everyone must consider his every neighbor without exception as another self. . . . In our times a special obligation binds us to make ourselves the neighbor of absolutely every person and of actively helping him when he comes across our path, whether he be an old person abandoned by all, a foreign laborer unjustly looked down upon, a refugee, a child born of an unlawful union and wrongly suffering for a sin he did not commit, or a hungry person who disturbs our conscience."

Mr. J. Yet I have always heard that charity begins at home.

Father S. Perhaps, but it doesn't end there.

Mr. J. I am amazed at how clear, concise and universal is the teaching of the Church.

Father S. I notice you said "the Church" and not "your Church." There is hope for you yet.

Mr. J. More than hope, Father; expectation.

Fourth Commandment

"Honor your father and mother."

Father S. Are your parents living, Mr. Jackson?

Mr. J. My mother is not; she died four years ago.

Father S. You had a mother long enough, then, to appreciate what one owes to a parent.

Mr. J. Yes, Father: I had a good mother, and I often think how little I appreciated her care and sacrifices for me. I have often wished that I had only been able to repay her slightly before her death.

Father S. Then you see the reasonableness of God's law as expressed in the Fourth Commandment: "Honor your father and mother"?

Mr. J. I see the propriety, surely.

Father S. By the Fourth Commandment God requires children to love, honor, and obey their parents in all that is not sinful, and to support them if necessary. You see, parents hold God's place with reference to their children. To their parents young children must look for food, shelter, clothing, education, care in sickness; also for a training in virtue. For these benefits parents surely merit their children's gratitude and love; and they deserve in return material assistance should they be in need, when their children are able to work.

Mr. J. These demands of the Commandment are certainly just.

Father S. But in our country they seem to be little recognized. Foreign-born children are often more considerate of their parents than American-born. Too many of our young people seem to think that they sin against the Fourth Commandment only by disobedience. In many countries, children, even after they are married, show the greatest reverence and respect for their parents. Here, the parents, if they must depend on their child for comfort and support, are regarded as an almost intolerable burden. American youths wrongly suppose that when they become of age, parental authority and parents' rights end. But this is not true; nothing ends but strict obedience to parents. Love must remain, respect must continue, necessary assistance must still be rendered. It is one of the tragedies of the times and our circumstances that parents when old are shunted off to nursing homes where they are seldom visited.

Mr. J. I suppose obedience is required by the very authority which God vests in parents, if, as you say, they represent God?

Father S. Exactly. Children must obey parents in all things lawful. Sometimes parents do not represent God; as for instance, those unscrupulous ones who often ask children to do what God or His Church forbids. In this case, obedience would be wrong, because as St. Peter exclaimed: "Better for us to obey God than men!" (Acts 5:29).

Mr. J. And if parents should die, I presume that any others who might hold the place of parents, represent Almighty God's authority?

Father S. Yes. Teachers and guardians, hold this place with reference to children; and God exacts reasonable respect not only from children, but from all people towards those in authority; workmen should respect their contract with their employer, citizens should be loyal to their rulers. "Give to Caesar what is Caesar's . . ." (Matt. 22:23). Then there is a spiritual authority, representing God, which all Catholics should cheerfully honor and obey; the Pope, as Vicar of Christ, and ruler over the whole Church; the bishop in his diocese, the priest in his parish. "He who hears you, hears Me, he who rejects you, rejects Me" (Luke 10:16).

Mr. J. Since parents hold God's place in regard to their children, do not they sin, too, if they do not fulfill the duties of their station?

Father S. Surely. Children have a God-given right to know God, and hence, parents are obliged to teach them about God, about the love of God in becoming man; they are obliged to teach children their prayers, send them to a school where a Christian education may be received. But remember always that parents have the primary responsibility for the religious education of their children. It is not one that they can unquestioningly shunt off to teachers or catechists. Besides providing for their bodily needs, parents are obliged to set the child good example; they must go to church themselves, to the sacraments, must pray, must guard their language, and so on.

Mr. J. I suppose many parents are responsible for the impiety of children?

Father S. Unfortunately, yes. Many parents expect the school to take over their responsibility, and then will not cooperate with the school. Today parents often obey children better than children obey their parents.

The Fourth Commandment dictates that children love their parents, that they never grieve them wilfully, never strike or curse them; that they cheerfully obey any reasonable request they make; cheer them up in their old age; never be ashamed of them. Almighty God promises to reward, even here, those children who are good to their parents, and to punish the undutiful ones. Then we must ever show proper respect to all legitimate authority, civil, as well as spiritual, "for there is no authority except from God" (Rom. 13:1). Unfortunately, civil authority often shows little respect for the constitution according to which it is expected to rule.

Mr. J. To what extent are citizens obliged to obey civil authorities?

Father S. Generally speaking every citizen must obey civil rulers, because their authority to rule, after election, comes from God, the Source of all authority. Citizens should be glad to support the local, state, and federal governments both by their taxes and by doing what is in their power to promote a healthy moral state of society. Hence, they should vote honestly and unselfishly, and defend the country's rights when necessary. And if citizens are thus obliged, certainly those who hold public office are obliged to be just to all in exercising their authority and to promote the welfare of all.

Vatican II (The Church Today 74, 75) considered the complexities of this problem. It stated: "the political community exists for that common good in which the community finds its full justification and meaning. . . . It also follows that political authority . . . must always be exercised within the limits of morality and on behalf of the dynamically conceived common good. . . . When such is the case citizens are conscience-bound to obey. This fact clearly reveals the responsibility, dignity, and importance of those who govern. . . . Authorities must beware of hindering family, social or cultural groups. . . . For their part, citizens both as individuals and in association should be on guard against granting government too much authority and inappropriately seeking from it excessive conveniences and advantages."

Fifth Commandment

"You shall not kill."

Father S. What is the Fifth Commandment, Mr. Jackson?

Mr. J. "You shall not kill."

Father S. I presume you think that you need no instruction on this law of God, for who would believe that any person may kill his neighbor?

Mr. J. I was thinking that, but possibly it forbids more than killing.

Father S. You are right. This commandment compels reverence for the human person (The Church Today 27). By it certain obligations are imposed on us with regard to the proper care of our own health and that of our neighbor; and it forbids all those things which often lead to murder.

Mr. J. I presume it forbids those things which injure a person's health?

Father S. It does. It forbids practices which shorten life, such as intemperance in food and drink, exposure, daring unnecessary risks, and similar acts. But first of all it forbids actual killing, whether of oneself or another. Our own lives belong to God. He did not consult us about our birth, He does not ask when or where or how we wish to die. We are His creatures, belong to Him, and hence have no right to take our own lives. That suicide results largely, if not from a deranged mind, from a lack of faith is plain from figures which show that the number of suicides is greatest in countries where there is little religion.

Mr. J. Is killing ever justifiable?

Father S. It is, if it be committed purely in self-defense when one is attacked by an unjust aggressor. However, one must be content to *wound* the assailant, if that would suffice to save one's life.

Mr. J. What do you think of hanging or other forms of capital punishment?

Father S. Personally, I am opposed to capital punishment because after working in prisons and on Death Row, I do not see it as a deterrent. However, it is an arguable opinion. The Church does allow capital punishment for a sufficient reason on the principle that society has the right to protect itself. The Bible tolerates it (Gen. 9:6): "If anyone sheds the blood of man, by man shall his blood be shed." However, no individual, no mob, is permitted to hang or lynch a criminal but the civil authority, representing God, may inflict such punishment as an extreme measure and a last resort. Individuals are members of society, just as our arms or feet are parts of our body. And as a diseased limb may be amputated for the good of the whole body, so may criminal members of society be executed by public officials, when this is necessary for the good of the whole society.

Mr. J. Murder and suicide seem to be terrible deeds.

Father S. They are, and the suicide is a coward. Real heroism is displayed by bravely bearing our miseries, privations or sufferings. Such trials, if borne for love of God or in the spirit of atonement, are most meritorious. The murderer can not be happy after his deed. As a rule, he himself dies a violent death; murder is called a sin which cries to heaven for vengeance.

Mr. J. I presume that killing a man in war is all right?

Father S. Well, I hate to say "all right." But the answer is yes, if the war itself be a just war. But there have been few just wars. Catholics moralists teach that for a war to be just, four conditions must be fulfilled: (1)The State which declares war must be morally certain that its rights are being actually violated or are in certain and imminent danger; (2) That the cause of the war is in proportion to the evils of the war itself; (3) That every peaceful method of settlement has proved inadequate; (4) That there be a well-grounded hope of bettering conditions by the conflict. If these conditions were observed in the declaration of war — they rarely have been in history — there would be very few wars.

Mr. J. I once heard a priest who was called in to arbitrate in a strike tell some workmen that practically those same requirements were necessary for the strike to be just.

Father S. Yes, a strike is an industrial warfare. The conditions which justify a strike are quite similar to those which justify war. But just strikes occur far more frequently than do just wars.

Mr. J. But did not the martyrs surrender their lives without necessity?

Father S. Absolutely not! They had the alternative of giving up their faith or their heads, and were obliged to choose the latter. "If anyone . . . is ashamed of me and my doctrine, the Son of Man will be ashamed of him when he comes with the Holy Angels in his Father's glory" (Mark 8:38). The martyrs gave up their lives rather than sin and betray their God. This was so laudable an act that Jesus Himself promised Heaven for it: "Whoever loses his life *for My sake,* will save it" (Luke 9:24; Matt. 10:39).

Mr. J. Is it wrong for one to risk his life in charity or to save others?

Father S. No, it is praiseworthy. Thousands of missioners have done this, Sisters of the Catholic Church have done it during the many wars, working in plague-ridden slums, say, or nursing those who are afflicted with infectious disease. In these various instances, death is not sought directly.

Mr. J. Now, what are some of the sins which often lead to murder, and which, therefore, are forbidden by the Fifth Commandment?

Father S. Anger, hatred, the desire for revenge, envy, quarreling, fighting, drunkenness, dueling, abuse of drugs.

Mr. J. Why do you speak of drink and drugs in connection with this Commandment?

Father S. Because drunkenness opens the door to many different evils, often sins against the Fifth Commandment. What is more, it may be contrary to the proper care one should take of one's health. It is always a sin to get drunk and a mortal sin to get so drunk as to be unable to distinguish right from wrong. What is said about the abuse of alcohol applies equally, if not stronger, to drugs. I am not talking solely about the hard drugs of the street, everyone knows the ruin they cause. But the drugs used in the home, the uppers, the downers, the sleeping pills, all these can be the subject of abuse and therefore sinful. God alone knows how many have died from drug overdose.

Mr. J. Is anger a very grievous sin? I know that it is very common.

Father S. It depends on the intensity of it, and whether one tries to subdue it. The common, daily outbursts of people are not mortal sins, but those who have a bad temper habitually must strive to keep it in check.

Mr. J. What about abortion?

Father S. It is a murderous attack on the unborn child. From the very first moment of its conception the child is a human being with a right to life given by the Creator who alone has the right to take that life when He wills. The physician who assists in it and the party who consents to it are equally guilty. Even those who suggest or recommend it are participants in this cowardly crime to the commission of which the Church attaches the penalty of excommunication. Today, the proponents of abortion color the issue with words like "fetus" for child, "viability" for existence outside the womb, "women's right" without consideration for the right of unborn life.

Vatican Council II (The Church Today 27) clearly stated Catholic doctrine regarding this commandment: "Furthermore, whatever is opposed to life itself, such as any type of murder, genocide, abortion, euthanasia, or wilful self-destruction; whatever violates the integrity of the human person, such as mutilation, torments inflicted on body or mind, attempts to coerce the will itself; . . . all these things and others of their like are infamies indeed."

I would call your attention to the word mutilation in the quote I just read. This particularly refers to sterilization and vasectomies which are gaining in popularity as birth control methods. Such acts are seriously and intrinsically wrong.

Mr. J. Since you touched the subject, how about birth control?

Father S. That is rather a sin against the Sixth Commandment, although those who unsuccessfully practice artificial birth control are sometimes led to commit abortion. You see, the use of contraceptives aims sinfully to *prevent* life. Abortion *destroys* human life after conception has taken place.

Mr. J. Then is "planned parenthood" wrong?

Father S. It depends on what you mean by "planned parenthood." Those words are used with various meanings. If you mean family planning, it is not wrong. But if by planned parenthood is meant the use of contraceptive measures or devices in marriage relations, it is mortally sinful. In this case planned parenthood is made a respectable title which masks a degenerate vice.

Mr. J. It is no sin to kill animals which belong to us, is it?

Father S. No; animals exist for the service and needs of man, but it would be wrong to treat them with wanton cruelty.

Mr. J. Is anything else forbidden by this Commandment?

Father S. Well, under this head we usually include what is known as scandal, or bad example; because by this sin, the supernatural life of another's soul is hurt, which, before God, is a more serious injury than any which could be inflicted on the body.

Now, I presume that it will be plain to you, that when it is possible for the one who injures or wrongs another to repair the injury, he must. For instance, if you unjustly did another a bodily injury, which demanded the service of a physician and incapacitated the person for work, you would be obliged to pay his doctor bills and would be liable for the money he lost. Moreover, if, by your example you scandalized another, you would at least owe him an apology, and should tell him not to imitate the deed for which you are sorry.

We must practice the Golden Rule by being kind, not provoking others, not showing a revengeful or hateful disposition. We must forgive others and treat them as we should like to be treated. St. Paul's advice is excellent and, carried out, would endear us to our fellowmen as well as to God: "See that no one returns evil to any other; always seek one another's good and, for that matter, the good of all" (1 Thes. 5:15).

Mr. J. That is good advice, but, I fancy, very difficult to carry out.

Father S. Not so difficult, if an effort be made. No one ever becomes angry without regretting it afterwards. Nothing is gained by it. We make ourselves as unhappy as we make others. A cheerful, agreeable, forgiving disposition is enviable. It is always more difficult to renew friendship with one after we have been angry towards him, than to have kept back the unkind words at the beginning.

Mr. J. I believe you are right, Father.

Sixth and Ninth Commandments

"You shall not commit adultery."
"You shall not covet your neighbor's wife."

Father S. We shall take up two Commandments this evening that are closely related. Can you tell me the Sixth and Ninth Commandments, Mr. Jackson?

Mr. J. The sixth is: "You shall not commit adultery" and the ninth is: "You shall not covet your neighbor's wife."

Father S. Do you see the close relationship between the two? The ninth expressly forbids the *desire* and the sixth the *act* of adultery.

Mr. J. Are these two Commandments concerned only with adultery?

Father S. No, they forbid all kinds of impurity and immodesty; and forbidding impurity, they command purity and chastity.

Mr. J. I have heard these words and seen them in print, but their meaning isn't at all clear to me.

Father S. For practical purposes, we give purity and chastity the same meaning, although there is a shade of difference between them. They mean the proper control of sex pleasure in thoughts, desires, words and actions. For the unmarried, chastity or purity means the abstaining from such pleasure, while for the married it means using such pleasure naturally and reasonably, in marriage.

Mr. J. Then impurity is the unlawful enjoyment of sex pleasure.

Father S. Yes. Whether this be from thoughts upon which one deliberately dwells for this purpose, from wilful desires, words or actions performed alone or with another.

You see, the Creator has endowed human nature with two natural appetites — to nourish oneself and to reproduce oneself. Into the satisfaction of these appetites, He has wisely woven pleasure, for these functions are necessary for the preservation of oneself and the propagation of the race. Thus one finds pleasure in taking food and drink and in sex, but the primary purpose of both is not the pleasure, but rather self-nourishment, and the generation of offspring and the expression of marital love, respectively. When the primary purpose is excluded, one acts contrary to nature and to the will of God, the Author of nature. God meant the pleasure of eating to serve the nourishment of the body and sex pleasure to serve the propagation of the race and as a sign of love between husband and wife.

The earliest command given to humanity was "Be fertile and multiply; fill the earth and subdue it" (Gen. 1:28). Our Lord said: "At the beginning of creation God made them male and female; for this reason a man shall leave his father and mother and the two shall become as one. They are no longer two but one flesh. Therefore let no man separate what God has joined" (Mark 10:6-9). I wish many of our Protestant brothers who place so much emphasis on the Bible would heed this text and Christ's quotation which follows: "Whoever divorces his wife and marries another commits adultery against her; and the woman who divorces her husband and marries another commits adultery" (Mark 10:11-12). The Catholic Church is accused of being antiquated in its position on divorce but I challenge anyone to show me any clearer texts in the Bible.

Sex relations between married and unmarried persons, or between married who are not married to each other are called adultery; between the unmarried they are called fornication. Both are mortal sins (Ephes. 5:5).

Mr. J. Are the other sins against chastity mortal, too?

Father S. Nearly every sin against chastity or purity is grievous. Sins against purity cause the loss of more souls than any other sin; the Almighty has sent many severe temporal punishments on its account. The great deluge was provoked by sins of impurity; the cities of Sodom and Gomorrah were destroyed by fire on account of it; whole nations have become extinguished by it. This truth must be retaught to the world because so many factors are today contributing to the destruction of that moral sense, which had for centuries been almost an instinct in Christians. The movies, TV, magazines, even pictures and advertisements in newspapers make light of things strictly forbidden by Almighty God.

Mr. J. I presume that, while all such sins are grievous, some are more so than others?

Father S. Oh, yes. Immodest deeds are worse than words, for instance; and deeds differ in malice, according as they are committed by the unmarried (Deut. 22:21), by the married (Lev. 20:20), by persons related to one another (1 Cor. 5:1), or alone (Rom. 1:24-26). But St. Paul tells us that all these exclude from Heaven. You see, each of us stands between the angels and the lower animals, part spirit and part animal. The Bible says we were created only a little less than the angels, and that God destined us for the same happiness as the angels. The human body is the dwelling place of that spirit made according to God's own image. In fact, when a person's soul possesses God's grace, God is united to it, so that the Bible calls our bodies a "temple of the Holy Spirit" (1 Cor. 6:19). Hence to defile the body, or to yield to its lusts and evil inclinations, degrades a person.

Mr. J. I see. God expects us to raise ourselves up nearer the angels, rather than become more like the animals.

Father S. Precisely. Each is gifted with a mind, with reason, which must always rule over the animal inclinations.

Mr. J. But people excuse such indulgences by saying that they are natural.

Father S. It is *not* according to nature, as the punishments inflicted by nature itself for such abuses clearly show. This inclination to evil is a consequence of original sin, but it can and must be subdued by one's higher self—by one's reason and will. People who minimize such sins do not take into account the fact that our life on earth is a warfare; that Heaven is to be a reward for victories won, both over the devil and over self. Every temptation is an invitation to fight, for which, St. Paul says, God will always supply the necessary grace and strength. Hence, in permitting us to be tempted, Almighty God is ever good; He wants us to have abundant opportunity for earning new reward in Heaven.

The social diseases, known as syphilis and gonorrhea, so prevalent in our day, make clear one of nature's ways of punishing those who live impurely. So, too, are the side effects from contraceptives and the mental turmoil of an unwanted pregnancy. God asks us to seek purity, and He does not command the impossible. When we go against God's laws we suffer the consequences here on earth and hereafter.

Mr. J. I never thought of that, but it is plain. If Almighty God required us to avoid what we cannot, it would not be just. But if He asks only sacrifices and self-denials and victories over temptations, in order that He may reward us the more, He is good; especially if He presents us with the weapons needed to fight temptations. I presume, then, that the only lawful indulgence is what belongs to marriage?

Father S. That is all. Now let us briefly sum up. The Sixth Commandment forbids immodest conversations, suggestive jokes or remarks, immoral reading; it forbids us to attend theatricals which are obscene, or wilfully to look upon anything which sullies purity; hence, it forbids women to dress immodestly, or in such a way as to be the occasion of temptation for others (1 Tim. 2:9). Then the *ninth* forbids one wilfully to dwell in thought on, or to desire, the things which the

Sixth Commandment forbids. Christ says (Matt. 5:28) that to look upon a woman with a lustful desire is as bad as the unclean deed itself.

In recent years, numerous magazines have come into being which are excessively "sexy." Those who read them co-operate with the publisher in a sinful enterprise, deliberately provoke their passions, feed their minds on things lewd, corrupt their hearts.

Mr. J. But merely having impure imaginations is not a sin?

Father S. No. You do not know what will run through your mind ten minutes from now. Things you hear or read or see occasion unclean thoughts. If they are not wanted and an effort is made to dismiss them, they even become sources of merit.

The best people are sometimes annoyed with unclean thoughts, but they need not worry if they do not wilfully permit them to tarry as they pass through the mind.

Mr. J. Unclean talk is very prevalent, isn't it?

Father S. Yes; despite the fact that it advertises the person so unfavorably. "Out of the abundance of the heart the mouth speaks." When you hear a person indulge in such conversation, you have a reason to conclude that his or her thoughts are unclean; because one must think first before speaking. Everyone must at heart respect the person who blushes at the immodest remark. Purity is called the angelic virtue. No more precious thing could be possessed by anyone. Parents should do all they can to plant this virtue in their children. People should be ashamed to be seen at a show that is suggestive. Just as a young man would wish to have the purity of his sister respected, so all young people should encourage the virtue of purity in a boyfriend or girlfriend.

Mr. J. What you are really saying is that we should teach and practice self-control.

Father S. Exactly! Unless we teach young people morality and self-control, in our words and in our example, and instill in them a dread of sin, we will never "solve" such problems as teenage pregnancy and abortion.

Mr. J. What if one had never been taught what you tell me in explaining the Commandments of God, and, because of ignorance, was guilty of many violations of them: would such a one have cause to worry?

Father S. No, because knowledge you receive today does not affect what you did before you had that knowledge. What you did in the past was no worse before God than your conscience considered it at the time.

Mr. J. I imagine that most young people in the United States have never had the Commandments interpreted for them.

Father S. You are probably right. The New York *Times* once took a survey among 50,000 students at New York high schools, and found that 37,000 of them declared that they had not the faintest idea what the Ten Commandments were.

Seventh and Tenth Commandments

"You shall not steal."
"You shall not covet your neighbor's goods."

Father S. As we combined the Sixth and Ninth Commandments in our last instruction, because of their close relationship, so today we shall treat the Seventh and Tenth together, and for the same reason.

Mr. J. How are they related?

Father S. Well, the tenth forbids us to desire to do what the seventh absolutely forbids us to do. Some people don't steal only because they do not get the chance. What are the Seventh and the Tenth Commandments?

Mr. J. "You shall not steal," and "You shall not covet your neighbor's goods."

Father S. Do you know what the word "covet" means?

Mr. J. "To desire."

Father S. The Seventh Commandment forbids stealing or anything equivalent to stealing: theft, robbery, cheating, refusal to pay honest debts, not living up to business agreements, keeping things which belong to another, the exaction of exorbitant interest from a man who must have money, the acceptance of bribes by public officials, paying an unjust wage, modern serfdom, in short, anything against the virtue of justice.

Mr. J. In giving this Commandment, Almighty God approves of the possession of private property?

Father S. Certainly. He even commands us to respect what belongs to others.

Mr. J. Then Socialists must repudiate the Commandment?

Father S. Some do. Although it was not God's will that a few should own almost everything and the majority possess nothing, God sanctions the ownership by people of property on which they can support themselves and those dependent upon them. If all man's time were consumed by a struggle to exist, his eternal interests would be neglected. From the time man was created, he had private property; Cain and Abel sacrificed their separate possessions; the patriarchs bequeathed their property to their eldest sons by a solemn benediction.

There are many persons today who see in socialism the answer for all the world's injustices but they do not face the problem in the light of history and in the recognition of the natural rapaciousness of man. Utopia is always an unrealizable ideal and will be until the Kingdom of God is established. One need only to look at the uneven class structure in the Soviet Union and China to realize that the ideal is never accomplished. Rather, we should view the social problems of the world through God's eyes as expressed in Luke 6:20-25. This does not mean that we should be fatalistic and not try to improve man's lot but we should realize that given man's fallen nature there will always be inequities that will have eventually to be set right by God in His judgment.

Mr. J. Violations of the Seventh Commandment are very common, I think; especially by cheating, misrepresenting goods, and by neglecting to pay debts.

Father S. That's true enough. Shop-lifting by young children seems to be growing; it is due to lack of conscience-training in the home and the schools. Juvenile crime consists largely of theft and robbery. But theft on a large scale, known as swindling, is also on the increase. The penitentiaries contain some of the thieves, but only a small portion of them.

Mr. J. Can the sin of theft be forgiven if the guilty one refuses to make good his injustice?

Father S. No, restitution must be one's sincere intention. The thief must return the article or its equivalent in money to the rightful owner or to the latter's heirs.

Mr. J. What if the rightful owner or heirs cannot be found?

Father S. Then restitution is made by contributing to the poor or to charity. One cannot rightly benefit from dishonesty.

Mr. J. Must the thief go to the owner in person and acknowledge the theft?

Father S. No. One may return what was stolen, or its equivalent, by mail or in another anonymous way. The thief is obliged only to restore to the owner what was stolen. The same principle holds for unjust damage to another's property. The damage should be repaired or compensated for as far as possible.

Mr. J. I presume that a merchant who has cheated his customers may make right the wrong by giving over-weight to these same people in the future?

Father S. That would be all right; and clerks in stores, who have helped themselves at the money drawer, may return their stealings, little by little, until all is returned.

Mr. J. What if the thief has become impoverished, and cannot restore what he or she has stolen?

Father S. Of course, no one is obliged to do the impossible; the thief must resolve to restore what was stolen as soon as possible, and must economize so as to be able to meet this obligation.

Mr. J. Must a person return something found?

Father S. Surely, if its owner can be identified and located.

Mr. J. What if I should unknowingly buy an article that was stolen?

Father S. Even in such a case, you could not keep the article if its lawful owner were known. You would have to bear a loss, true, but no more of a loss than the person from whom the article was stolen. The item remains the property of its owner until the latter decides to relinquish his or her claim to it.

Mr. J. So "honesty is the best policy" is a good rule to follow.

Eighth Commandment

"You shall not bear false witness against your neighbor."

Father S. We have seen, Mr. Jackson, that it is sinful to rob others of any things that belong to them. However, it is even more seriously sinful to rob others of their good name (Prov. 22:1); this is what the Eighth Commandment primarily forbids. It commands us to speak the truth at all times and forbids all kinds of false witness, such as common lying, but more especially such falsehoods which blacken our neighbor's character or injure his or her good name.

Mr. J. What do we call this kind of falsehood?

Father S. Calumny, slander, or libel.

Mr. J. I have always regarded it as wrong to talk injuriously about another, even if I were telling the truth, but I did not know against which Commandment the sin would be.

Father S. Against this Eighth Commandment; for it injures your neighbor's reputation and is called "detraction." I intended to remind you of this. Now let us get order into our instruction: (1) We are obliged to respect the name and character of another; (2) It is wrong even to suspect wrong of another without good grounds because this would be a rash judgment; (3) We are never allowed to tell a wilful falsehood; (4) There is such a thing as lying by action as well as by words; (5) If we have seriously hurt our neighbor's reputation, we must make it right; (6) We are obliged to keep a secret when we have promised to do so, when our office requires it, or when the good of another demands it.

Mr. J. Is it always a sin of detraction to speak of the faults of another?

Father S. Not if they be already publicly known, or known to the people with whom we converse; though, even then, it is a failing against charity. The one who has fallen may rise, and become better than we are; and we, against whom there is no evil report, may fall some future day. Disclosing another's mistakes or expressing our suspicion about another are faults all too common.

Mr. J. Yes, I hardly believe that a day passes in which we do not fail at least slightly in this matter.

Father S. That is true.

Mr. J. Is it allowed to tell a lie to keep a person from being punished?

Father S. No, not even to save ourselves from severe punishment. You see, to lie is intrinsically wrong; that is, it is an evil in itself which no circumstance can ever make right, and hence God, Who is Truth itself, must abhor it.

Mr. J. According to that, it must be wrong to lie even in jest?

Father S. It would be, if you saw that the person with whom you joke were actually deceived. Of course, if what you told were wholly incredible, or you supposed the person knew you to be joking, it would be different. A good definition of a lie is "the intention to deceive," whether by word or by act; in the latter case it is called hypocrisy or dissimulation. The Pharisees spoken of in the Gospels were denounced severely by Christ because of "acting" lies (Matt. 23).

Mr. J. Of course, some falsehoods are much more sinful than others?

Father S. Yes, according as great or little harm is done by them.

Mr. J. We are, then, obliged to tell our business to everyone who inquires about it?

Father S. Not necessarily. There is a difference between telling a lie and evading the question. We are under no obligation to answer a question which another has no right to ask. We may decline to answer, or give an evasive reply.

Mr. J. You said that if we injure our neighbor, we must repay the injury. What is to be said when what we say is true? It seems to me that it would often be impossible to repair such an injury, for we could not deny what we had said. This would be a lie, and always evil.

Father S. You are perfectly right, for detraction is just that: injuring the character of the neighbor by telling the truth about that person. You might be able to correct the matter as far as the one you told it to is concerned by admitting the detraction. But what if this person has already passed what you said on to others, and they to still others? You are obliged to correct the evil so far as you can, but you cannot deny what you had originally said. This is a difficult, often impossible, obligation to fulfill. If what you said was not known to many, you should report something good about the injured person, hoping thereby to offset your earlier detraction.

Mr. J. Detraction seems much the same as calumny.

Father S. Actually, there is an important difference. Calumny and detraction both injure a person's reputation — calumny by saying something *false* about the person, detraction by saying something *true* about the person.

Mr. J. This appears to be so serious that a fellow should certainly think twice before he speaks.

Father S. That's right. Now, I would not want to make you scrupulous on this subject; that is, I would not want you to worry about how you might correct mistakes made under this head. If you can recall having *seriously* injured another by calumny or detraction, follow the directions just given in trying to correct it. In minor matters, do not worry; only resolve to be a little more careful in the future.

Lying often arises from jealousy. People see the mote in the eye of those they do not like and make a beam out of it. They exaggerate, and even invent charges against their enemy; they would be only too pleased if their enemy's good name were injured. This is a bad passion with which to be possessed. It was jealousy or envy which prompted the devil to lie to our first parents.

If lying could be tolerated, there would be no public confidence, which is so necessary for the welfare of human society. How grand it would be if we could place perfect reliance on every utterance of our fellow citizen! "Lying lips are an abomination to the Lord" (Prov. 12:22).

Sundays and Holydays

In very fact Christ works through His ministers to achieve
unceasingly in the world that same will of the Father by
means of the Church . . . For loyalty toward Christ can
never be divorced from loyalty to His Church. — *Priests, 14.*

Father S. We are now about to bring to a close the second
part of your instruction. You are well acquainted with most of
the truths of faith, with all those which are contained in what
is known as the *Apostles' Creed;* and you have learned what
God requires you to do and to avoid, as outlined in the Commandments. However, God's Church has found it necessary to
make a few laws to promote Christian life, and they are contained in the "Precepts or Commandments of the Church."

Mr. J. Are the laws of the Church so binding on the conscience that a member actually sins if he does not obey its
laws?

Father S. Yes. Christ said to the first teaching and governing body of His Church: "He who hears you, hears Me.
He who rejects you, rejects Me" (Luke 10:16); again, He said
to the first Pope, Peter: "Whatever you declare bound on
earth shall be bound in heaven" (Matt. 16:19). The right to
make laws is exercised by the bishops, the successors of the
Apostles, and especially by the Pope, who, as the successor of
St. Peter, has the right to make laws in spiritual matters for

the whole Church. Hence, the Church's laws are God's laws, and equally binding. There is this difference, however, that the Church can dispense from obedience to its own laws, but cannot dispense from obedience to the laws given directly by God.

Mr. J. How many precepts has the Church made?

Father S. There are six, which may be briefly stated as follows: Catholics are required (1) To rest from servile work and hear Mass on all Sundays and holydays of obligation; (2) To fast and abstain on certain days specified by the Church; (3) To confess their sins at least once a year; (4) To receive Holy Communion once a year during Eastertime; (5) To contribute toward the support of religion; (6) The sixth forbids blood-relations down to the third degree to marry, and forbids a solemn marriage during what are called "forbidden times."

I presume you have observed the similarity between the first commandment of the Church and the Third Commandment of God?

Mr. J. Yes, I was going to mention it.

Father S. You see, the Third Commandment of God does not declare explicitly *how* the Sabbath day should be kept holy; hence the Church determines it. She tells us that we must assist at that form of worship which honors God more than any other, the Mass. Then the Church has instituted some festivals, called holydays, which must be observed, if possible, the very same as the Sundays.

Mr. J. Why these holydays?

Father S. They are to commemorate and keep fresh in our memories the great events or truths in the lives of Christ and of His Blessed Mother, which have meant so much to God's people. Holydays in the Church are kept for much the same purpose as holidays in the State. You know why the Fourth of July, Memorial Day, Washington's Birthday, Thanksgiving Day, are kept, and what they commemorate?

Mr. J. Yes, Father.

Father S. Well, in the Church we have Christ's Birthday (December 25th), Christmas; the octave of Christmas on which we honor Mary, the Mother of God, coinciding with our New Year's Day (January 1st); the day on which Christ returned to His heavenly glory, after having sojourned here for 33 years, called Ascension Day (40 days after Easter). Then we keep two other feasts of Christ's Mother, that of her Assumption into Heaven (August 15th) and that of the Immaculate Conception (December 8th). I explained, when speaking of Original Sin and the Incarnation, the significance of the "Immaculate Conception." It honors Mary's highly prized sanctity, and holds up her sinlessness, purity and virtue for the imitation of her spiritual children. The "Assumption" honors the reward paid to Mary's pure, virginal body by being preserved from corruption and taken to heaven.

Mr. J. So Catholics believe that Mary's body has already been taken into heaven?

Father S. Yes. Reunited to her soul, it was taken up soon after her death. There is no express mention of this fact in the Bible, but from the earliest times this was believed by the Universal Church. Records of its belief are found in the catacombs. It was celebrated as a feast for 1,500 years before finally being defined as a dogma, or infallible truth that must be believed, by Pope Pius XII in 1950. Does this belief surprise you?

Mr. J. Not exactly, though I was not aware of it. No, I would not be surprised to hear that Jesus did anything for her, who was His mother, and who was so loved by God.

Father S. Since St. Paul assures us that death is a consequence of original sin, which Mary did not inherit, we would not even be surprised if she had been taken to heaven without dying. Her Son died, so she, who was so closely associated with Him in His work, did not expect exemption from death. But as her Son's body did not see corruption, neither should hers have, which gave that Son His human body, and the very blood with which He redeemed mankind. Then, could you believe that Christ would permit the pure body of His good mother to be buried and then decompose in the grave?

Mr. J. It would be repugnant to our religious sense to think it.

Father S. Just as the Redemption was anticipated for the preservation of her soul from Original Sin, so was the Resurrection of the Dead anticipated for the reward of her body.

Mr. J. Nothing seems more fitting.

Father S. Then one holyday is kept in memory of all God's saints. It is the Church's "Decoration" or Memorial Day. Just as once a year all patriotic Americans honor the memory and love to extol the valiant deeds of our soldier-dead, so does the Church ask her people to honor the memory of and praise God for the grand and holy lives of those heroes of Christ, the saints and martyrs of almost 2,000 years; this occurs on November 1st. It is called All Saints Day and is intended to commemorate all those in heaven who have lived on earth.

Mr. J. There are then six holydays of obligation?

Father S. Yes.

Mr. J. Are there more or fewer in other countries?

Father S. Both. In countries which are nearly wholly Catholic, there are more holydays kept. You see, these are of ecclesiastical institution, and hence the Church adapts herself to the conditions which obtain in different countries.

Mr. J. The Church is surely thoughtful. Does the law requiring attendance at Mass on Sundays and holydays obligate all Catholics?

Father S. All who are seven years of age and older. Of course, it does not obligate those who cannot go because of sickness, or who live a great distance from a church, or those who absolutely can't attend because of work on those days. However, a Catholic who through his own fault misses Mass on a Sunday or holyday of obligation commits a mortal sin. Besides with Masses allowed the evening before and on the evening of the feast, there are very few who can't attend services if they really try.

Penance in the Church

Penance should not only be internal and individual but also external and social. The practice of penance should be fostered according to the possibilities of the present day and of a given area, as well as individual circumstances. — *Liturgy, 110.*

Father S. I imagine you have heard how Catholics used to never eat meat on Fridays.

Mr. J. Yes, and I wonder why this practice was stopped.

Father S. It has not stopped completely, as I will explain in a moment because Catholics are still required to fast and abstain on certain days appointed by the Church. But on most Fridays of the year Catholics may now eat meat, although many families still observe the traditional abstinence. It was the opinion of authorities in the Church that while the form of Friday abstinence was being observed, the reason behind the law was being lost. Therefore, while Friday would remain a day of penance, or reparation for sin, the manner in which this would be exercised was left to each individual Catholic. It was hoped that these freely chosen penances would be a means of advancement in the spiritual life.

Mr. J. Then penance is still a requirement of the Church.

Father S. Yes. This is a requirement of the second precept of the Church and is based on reasons found in the Bible and dictated by common sense. Everyone who has sinned must do penance. The 13th Chapter of St. Luke presents this fact in a dramatic manner. Now, there are different ways of doing penance. "To chastise one's body and bring it under subjection," as St. Paul did, is the surest way to cure its evil tendencies. The very first law given by Almighty God was one of abstinence. Then the Jews were forbidden altogether to eat certain meats. Christ, our Divine Model, fasted rigorously for 40 days; so had the great Moses, and the holy prophet Elias; St. John Baptist set this kind of example to the people to whom he preached penance. Christ declared that His followers would fast, and gave good advice on the manner of fasting (Matt. 9:15; 6:16). The Church wisely sees to it that her members follow the directions of Christ. Hence, we fast and abstain in order to make satisfaction for our past sins; likewise, that we may strengthen our wills to control our bodily appetites and thus be able to raise our minds more freely to God.

Mr. J. I see that the reasons behind the Church law are as strong as could be.

Father S. Now the particular reason why every Friday is a day of penance is that Christ died for the world on that day. Could you conceive of a more praiseworthy practice than that, according to which Catholics show their gratitude every Friday to their divine Savior for the Redemption He brought to the world?

Mr. J. No, indeed, Father; it is a wonder that the Christians of all denominations do not do that much for Jesus.

Father S. By specific law, Catholics are obliged to abstain on all Fridays of Lent and to fast and abstain on Ash Wednesday and Good Friday. By general law, they are obliged to some personal penance on other Fridays.

Now I shall explain the Church's regulations in this matter of fast and abstinence. These regulations have been made uniform throughout the United States.

First of all, everyone over 21 and under 59 years of age is bound to observe the law of fasting, unless injurious to health.

Mr. J. I don't quite see the difference between fasting and abstinence.

Father S. On the two days of fast, only one *full* meal is allowed. Two other meatless meals, sufficient to maintain strength, may be taken according to each one's needs; but together they should not equal another *full* meal. So, you see, fasting has to do with the amount of food one takes. Abstinence, on the other hand, concerns the refraining from the use of meat.

Mr. J. Who are bound by the laws of abstinence?

Father S. Every Catholic fourteen years of age or older is bound to observe the laws pertaining to abstinence.

Complete abstinence means that meat, soup, or gravy made from meat cannot be used at all.

Mr. J. What are the people to do in place of abstinence when they are not obliged by law?

Father S. They are urged to substitute other good works, such as attendance at weekday Mass or extra prayers; to deny themselves delicacies, luxuries, to practice some forms of self-denial; for instance, the men can give up the use of tobacco, abstain from hard drinks, say the rosary; women can abstain from tea and coffee, from fruits and pastries. Many could attend weekday Mass, or make the "Way of the Cross."

Well, I believe we have gone over the whole ground covered by the Church's second commandment. We shall pass over the third and fourth precepts, since they will be treated in connection with the Sacraments of Penance and the Holy Eucharist. Hence in our next lesson, we shall take up the fifth commandment of the Church.

Support of Religion

With the possible help from experienced laymen, priests should manage those goods which are, strictly speaking, ecclesiastical as the norms of Church law and the nature of the goods require. They should always direct them towards the goals in pursuit of which it is lawful for the Church to possess temporal goods. Such are: the arrangement of divine worship, the procuring of an honest living for the clergy, and the exercise of works of the sacred apostolate or of charity, especially towards the needy. — *Priests, 17.*

Father S. In this instruction we are to deal with a subject, Mr. Jackson, which I should prefer to pass over. It's the fifth precept of the Church, by which Catholics are obligated to bear their fair share of the financial burden of the Pope, their bishop and their parish.

Mr. J. Why don't you like to treat it?

Father S. Because I dislike to talk about money in connection with religion.

Mr. J. I do not see why you should feel that way, since any sane man knows that churches and schools have to be built and maintained and that priests must eat and clothe themselves.

Father S. That is true, and as a matter of fact, God Himself gave laws governing the support of religion. He required the Hebrew people to pay a tax toward church-support, and He required their first earnings.

Mr. J. How much did He require?

Father S. One-tenth of their income.

Mr. J. That was more than one's month's salary.

Father S. It was not always salary, but the equivalent. For instance, He required the *first* olive oil and fruits and grain of the farmer: "All the best of the new oil and of the new wine and grain that they give to the Lord as their first fruits" (Numbers 18:12).

Mr. J. Was such a heavy tax necessary for the support of their religion? All the people belonged to the same religion, and hence a community had only one place of worship to support, instead of a dozen as now, when many different religions are represented in a community.

Father S. It is not likely that one-tenth of their products was necessary, but the Almighty was emphasizing an important principle, namely, that the greatest value must be placed on the benefits of religion.

Mr. J. That reason appears to have been a good one.

Father S. For about the same reason: He wanted them to deeply realize their dependence on Him for the good crops they reaped.

Mr. J. Despite the fact that a debt hangs over most churches, I am inclined to believe that people do not give one-tenth of their earnings to the support of religion today.

Father S. Some people give quite generously, but the average wage-earner does not give three per cent.

Mr. J. Shouldn't we fear that if we slighted the cause in which the Almighty is more interested than anything else, He would not be so generous to us with His blessings?

Father S. That is common sense. We have so many requests to make to Almighty God, and He has an ever-standing one with us to interest ourselves in the furtherance of the great cause for which His Divine Son came to earth, and for which He died.

Mr. J. What are some of the items of regular expenses which the average parish must meet?

Father S. There is the first heavy expense of purchasing property and erecting buildings, which are usually four: the church, pastor's house, school, and Sisters' house. Then the furnishings of these buildings. Seldom is a parish started with funds to pay for more than one-third of the initial outlay. Hence every year the interest must be met, also insurance. Then there are fuel and light, always a heavy bill. To this add the allowances to pastor and school teachers, school supplies, the things needed for divine services, etc.

Mr. J. One can readily see that the parish cannot be well run, and debt reduced unless all people contribute their proper share. I know that the salaries of pastors and Sisters are small.

Father S. Yes, and it takes 12 years to become a priest, during which time the student expends more than the average priest saves during his lifetime.

Mr. J. So no one would become a priest for what "there is in it"?

Father S. No indeed. If the young man were after money, he could turn his education, resulting from eight years of study beyond high school, into far more lucrative channels.

Mr. J. How do you get by?

Father S. Well, you see, in the first place, we do not need so much as married ministers; and secondly, our people make offerings when they direct Masses for a special intention, or when they get married. Of course, the priest does not pay house rent, and the congregation supplies the heat and light.

Mr. J. But offerings made cannot amount to much in small parishes. I have heard friends say that the Mass was a source of very large income.

Father S. That's simply not true. The ordinary parish priest says one parish Mass a day. If he is not saying Mass for his own intention, he can accept a stipend that averages about $5 for the accepted intention. Yet if it were not for Mass offerings, the priest's salary would have to be larger.

Mr. J. Father, you priests are terribly misrepresented.

Father S. We know it. And while we have no wives and children for whom we must pay doctor's bills, buy hats and shoes, etc., we must dress respectably ourselves, buy books for our library, pay our medical expenses, set the good example of assisting the poor and foster works of charity.

Mr. J. That's a good argument in favor of celibacy of the clergy.

Father S. It is.

Mr. J. And how can the Sisters get along with so little?

Father S. Well, they have their house rent and fuel free. Then they are under a vow of poverty. They deliberately choose to be poor and to deny themselves everything except what is necessary for their food and clothing. Several Sisters live together and their simple table fare is the main item of expense.

Mr. J. I had always heard that they kept house for the priest.

Father S. Another mistaken idea! They seldom visit the priest's house, nor he theirs.

Mr. J. In what manner is the church usually supported?

Father S. In most places by a Sunday envelope collection.

Marriage Regulations

The Church's descipline with regard to mixed marriages . . .
takes the form of two impediments to marriage: mixed religion and disparity of worship. The first of these forbids
marriage between a Catholic and a baptized non-Catholic,
while not taking from the validity of such a marriage. The
second renders invalid a marriage between a Catholic and a
non-baptized person. — *Instruction on Mixed Marriages.*

Father S. We are now at the sixth or last precept of the
Church, whose provisions you would understand more readily
had we already discussed Christian marriage as one of the sev-
en Sacraments instituted by Jesus Christ. We will take up that
subject later. For the present, let's discuss the laws of the
Church concerning marriage.

Mr. J. Are there many such laws to be learned?

Father S. There are many Church laws related to marriage, but most of them are technical. The two that we might
best discuss at this point are these: (1) The Church expects a
Catholic to marry a Catholic in the Catholic rite of marriage,
witnessed by an authorized minister (priest or deacon) and
two other witnesses. (2) Marriage with a second cousin or
anyone in closer blood-relationship is forbidden.

Mr. J. But I know of Catholics married to non-Catholics.

Father S. Those marriages we call mixed marriages, in
which the Catholic spouse has obtained a dispensation from
the bishop. One thing that must be remembered about Church
law is that, for a sufficient reason, the Church can grant a dis-

pensation from its own regulations. The same is *not* true of divine law. The Church can dispense even from the requirement that the marriage take place according to the Catholic ritual, if there is a sufficiently weighty reason.

Mr. J. I knew that most States forbid first cousins to marry, but I didn't know that the Church extends the prohibition one degree farther.

Father S. Yes, it does, the statistics are at hand to show the wisdom of the Church's attitude. Of course, the law is not so absolute that it admits of no exception. A dispensation may be obtained to make a marriage between cousins allowable, but the children of such unions quite frequently suffer physically or mentally.

Mr. J. May a man marry his sister-in-law after his wife dies?

Father S. No, the impediment of affinity is in the way.

Mr. J. What is meant by affinity?

Father S. Affinity designates a relationship arising from marriage. Such a relationship exists only between a husband and the blood relations of his wife, and between a wife and her husband's blood relations. The degrees of affinity are counted like the degrees of blood relationship. Thus a wife's sister becomes the husband's sister-in-law.

Mr. J. Why does the Church prohibit a man, whose wife is dead, to marry his sister-in-law?

Father S. When a man marries into a family, this fact brings him into frequent and intimate association with the members of that family. There may be daily contact or even the necessity of living under the same roof. If marriage with his wife's sisters is out of the question, there is less danger that he will allow affection for her sisters to develop or will indulge in forbidden familiarities. If he is not free to marry, he is not free to indulge in such approaches to marriage. Thus the best interests of Christian marriage and morality are safeguarded.

Mr. J. May two brothers marry two sisters?

Father S. Yes.

Mr. J. Now Father, I hardly need any explanation on the subject of mixed marriages. Since I have become acquainted with the nature of the Catholic Church, her teaching, and the plan of God to lead people to Heaven through this Church, it is plain to me that a Catholic should have a marriage partner who would be one with him in religion.

Father S. I am pleased that this fact is so clear to you. If husband and wife are to be one in everything else, they surely should be one in the faith, which is paramount. They work together to get a home, to educate their children for this world, etc. Surely they should work together for a heavenly home and to have their children trained in certainty, and not in doubt, about the eternal things. The office of teacher which parents fill is a most important one; and how could either teach with any authority, if they differed in their teaching relating to God, the soul, the child's obligation, etc.? Or it would be just as bad if one parent insisted on the child following him or her in religion, and the other parent were indifferent. God Himself cannot look favorably upon indifference towards the religion He came to earth to introduce any more than He can look favorably upon erroneous teaching. In a mixed marriage you are sure to have one or the other situation in one parent.

Mr. J. That's true.

Father S. Yet there are Catholics, otherwise seemingly good, who are afraid to let their non-Catholic friends know that they are deeply interested in the religion they profess. It is bad enough that the non-Catholic does not care to know anything about the religion of his Catholic friend — if he or she were interested in anything else very much, the other would want to know all about it — but it is worse for the Catholic to hide what he or she should be most proud of, and of what means more to God than all else, His religion.

Mr. J. That's right, Father. Without any attempt at boasting, I am not hiding from my friends the religion I am adopting. I have handed Catholic literature to a dozen Protestant friends, and I give away several copies of *Our Sunday*

Visitor every week. If we are convinced that we possess something so good, and that our friends haven't it because it has never been offered to them with all its attractions, why shouldn't we acquaint them with it? That's what St. Paul did. He fought the Christian Church until Christ proved to him that he had been taught wrong; then he fought harder the other way.

Father S. You have the right spirit, Mr. Jackson.

Mr. J. Of course, you would not recommend that the Catholic who is keeping company with a non-Catholic requires him or her to join the Catholic Church whether he or she could believe that way or not?

Father S. Indeed not. We would not even accept into the Church one who could not truthfully and of his own accord say after a course of instruction: "I believe the Catholic Church to be *the* Church which Christ founded, and accept all that it teaches in His name." But if the non-Catholic wishes to act fairly, he should be willing to become acquainted with the religion which is professed by the one whom he would like to have as his marriage-partner, and embrace it if its claims convince him.

Mr. J. Did the Almighty Himself ever express His will against mixed-marriages?

Father S. Yes. He never permitted one of his chosen people in the Old Law to marry one who did not profess the Jewish religion: "Neither shall you take their (unbelievers) daughters as wives for your sons" (Exod. 34:16). And if in the Old Law, when marriage was not a Sacrament, mixed-alliances were forbidden, how much stronger is the reason against them now!

Mr. J. Since the duty of a Catholic parent is to bring up his children in the faith he regards as the true one, I was just wondering what a risk there might be, should the Catholic parent die and leave little children for the non-Catholic to raise.

Father S. Another good reason against mixed-marriages.

Mr. J. But I understand that there are promises exacted of the non-Catholic in this respect.

Father S. No, while both parties must undergo a series of instructions on the Church's views on marriage, the declaration and promise to live the Catholic faith and share it with the children is made only by the Catholic. Before a dispensation can be sought for the marriage, this promise must be made to one delegated by the Church.

Mr. J. Is that a fair demand to make?

Father S. Yes, inasmuch as the Catholic should be convinced that his or her religion alone is the true one, while the average non-Catholic usually believes on principle that one religion is as good as another. Hence, the non-Catholic does not sacrifice a religious principle.

Mr. J. May I ask what is the fee required for a marriage by a priest?

Father S. There is no fee required. The priest is never allowed to demand a fee, although it is customary to make an offering.

Mr. J. Have you ever heard a charge that the fee for a marriage is so high in South American countries that many people refuse to go through the marriage ceremony?

Father S. Yes. But we are accustomed to hearing many untrue reports about conditions far enough away to prevent immediate investigation. The priest who would put a price on a Sacrament would, if reported, be punished. But Catholics are fair enough to recognize that an offering should be made to the priest who inconveniences himself considerably to prepare them for a happy marriage. The Church expects the priest to devote several hours to the instruction of the parties who are to be married; he offers the Mass for them, and must pay the organist for his services.

Mr. J. Hence the priest would actually be losing money if he received no fee?

Father S. He would be; but even then he would not be allowed to *put a price* on the Mass and the Sacrament. It might, however, be said that custom has occasioned a sort of established offering in a diocese; and hence, if a priest should ever be asked what the "marriage fee" is, he might tell what is usually given, but he could not *exact* it.

Mr. J. I am asking you these questions, Father, in order to have the correct answers when necessary.

Father S. I understand; and the more information you ask for, the better I am pleased, because we have nothing to hide, and our practice is always supported by sensible reason.

PART III

The Means of Grace

"I solemnly assure you, no one can enter into God's kingdom without being begotten of water and Spirit." — John 3:5

Peter and John *"upon arriving imposed hands on them and they received the Holy Spirit."* — Acts 8:17

"Take this and eat it; this is My body." — Matt. 26:26

"If you forgive men's sins, they are forgiven them; if you hold them bound, they are held bound." — John 20:23

"Is there anyone sick among you? He should ask for the presbyters of the church. They in turn are to pray over him, anointing him with oil in the Name of the Lord." — James 5:14

"As the Father has sent me, so I send you." — John 20:21

"Every high priest is taken from among men and made their representative before God, to offer gifts and sacrifices for sins." — Hebr. 5:1

"This is great foreshadowing; I mean that it refers to Christ and the church." — Eph. 5:32

Sanctifying Grace

In order that the sacred liturgy may produce its full effect, it is necessary that the Faithful come to it with proper dispositions, that their thoughts match their words, and that they cooperate with divine grace lest they receive it in vain (cf. 2 Cor. 6:1).—*Liturgy, 11.*

Father S. We're now ready to begin the third division of our instructions, which deals with what are usually called "The Means of Grace." We've seen what are the different points of Catholic belief, and what the laws of Almighty God and His Church enjoin and forbid. Now our instructions will be on the very pleasant subject of the divine helps which Jesus Christ has instituted to make the way of salvation easy.

Mr. J. You've mentioned these Heaven-given helps quite often, and I am already convinced of their necessary connection with a religion of which God Himself is the author.

Father S. I have noted that you were quick to perceive the essential difference between the best religion in the power of man to establish, and any form of religion of which God might be the direct author. It should be self-evident that no man could offer Heaven to another on any terms, and that he could invent no means of themselves calculated to lead to Heaven. A man could only encourage and exhort his fellows to be good and promise that the Almighty would surely recompense them in some measure. But it rests with God to *offer* us Heaven, to reveal His wishes and requirements, *and to supply the divine helps* calculated to make His service easy and meritorious. These helps are called the *means of grace,* because they either impart grace to a person who had not possessed it, or they confer an increase of grace on one who already possesses it. Now I am going to explain what we understand by *grace.*

Mr. J. I remember that you referred to it when you told how Adam and Eve were originally created, how they lost grace for themselves and their descendants by their fall, and how the Son of God made its restoration possible.

Father S. You remember your instructions well.

Mr. J. It is not difficult, because they hang together so nicely, and because certain information received in my first lessons is alluded to over and over.

Father S. You had better tell me what your idea of grace is.

Mr. J. Well, I just imagine it as the absence of original sin.

Father S. It is that and much more. It is not merely the *absence* of something, but the most *positive* reality outside of Heaven. It is God's life shared by our soul, which unites us intimately with God. Sunshine is not merely the *absence* of darkness, but something so *positive* that life on earth could not exist without it. The higher life could not exist in the soul without grace.

Mr. J. I hope that you will go more into detail with regard to grace.

Father S. Yes, I shall. Grace in general is a *gift* which enables man to save his soul. It is *in no way due to us* and could be withheld by God without injustice to us. When it is received, it comes to us as a *favor,* not as something to which we have a right.

Besides being a gift, grace is a *means* whereby we can become capable and worthy of living the Christian life here and living in Heaven hereafter. As a *means*, it is of two kinds:

The first kind is Sanctifying Grace—which is a vitalizing

and elevating perfection of the soul. We are born with souls *deprived* of this perfection due to the sin of our First Parents. We normally regain this perfection in Baptism, which is described in the words of Christ as a *rebirth*. Although we have received natural life at birth, we need that life perfected at its very source, so that our souls may more closely resemble that of Christ and our lives resemble that of God. We are *made* at birth and *remade* in Baptism and become the adopted children of God. That which remakes us, that perfection of the soul which enables us to live a new life on the higher plane upon which God wants us all to live, and which Christ died to make possible for us, is called Sanctifying Grace. No human being lacks this grace except through the sinful will of Adam (original sin) or through his own personally committed grievous sins. Hence any person who lacks this grace is in the *state of sin*. When you possess grace, you are made holy or sanctified. So it is called "sanctifying" because of its *permanent* sanctifying effect upon us. We must possess Sanctifying Grace when we die, or we have no right to Heaven.

Mr. J. Can every Catholic possess it?

Father S. Yes. The soul is capable of receiving divine influence just as the electric light bulb is capable of receiving electric impulse. There is a vast difference between the electric bulb not in contact with the electric current and one having that contact. A greater difference exists between us when our souls are not in the state of grace and when our souls are in contact with divine life. We are capable of a higher kind of action and life.

Grace and mortal sin cannot exist together in the soul. They are opposites, like light and darkness. But turn on the light and the darkness goes; turn off the light and darkness returns. Commit mortal sin and grace must go: repent of mortal sin and grace returns. But note carefully that grace is not merely the absence of sin. We have been speaking of what is known as Sanctifying Grace, but there is also *actual* grace. This second kind of grace is after the manner of a *motion* or impulse from God which raises *our actions* to a higher plane and helps us to do good or avoid evil by enlightening our mind and strengthening our will. It is given to us when we *act* and remains only as long as the action lasts. Hence it is called *actual* grace, a gift that *comes and goes,* to distinguish it from Sanctifying Grace, which is *permanent.* Of course, we can resist God's grace, for our will is free and God does not force us to accept His grace. In every adult the gift of *actual* grace must precede the conferring of Sanctifying Grace, since the Bible assures us that we cannot even begin the work of our salvation without the help of *actual* grace (John 6:44; 1 Cor. 4:7).

Mr. J. Actual grace, then, is given to the sinner and to the unbaptized as well as to those possessing Sanctifying Grace?

Father S. Yes, it is given to everybody, and everybody is free to follow it or to reject it. It is given to those who are not in the state of grace to inspire and enable them to receive Sanctifying Grace. It is given to those in the state of grace so that they can perform meritorious actions. We can make our most ordinary actions merit reward in Heaven by doing them with a motive of love of God, and by keeping ourselves in the state of grace.

Mr. J. I believe I understand its significance now. When a person is prompted to investigate the claims of the Church, or whenever he is inwardly urged to repent, to pray, to do good, it is actual grace which stirs him.

Father S. Exactly. And when a person is tempted to do wrong, God offers an actual grace, with the help of which the temptation can be resisted.

Mr. J. I see. Therefore, no one can truthfully say that he or she can long resist the power of temptation without the help of actual grace?

Father S. That's right. The Bible says that God will not allow us to be tempted more severely than we can endure, that simultaneously with the temptation will go forth from Him an actual grace to enable us to overcome it. This will always be true unless we of our own accord provoke the temptation, and remain in the occasion of sin.

Mr. J. This is all so reasonable. If God permits me to be tempted, He will mercifully strengthen me. But if I willfully walk into danger, I do not deserve the help of Heaven. But, Father, you said something about the "means of grace" when we began. What are they?

Father S. The Sacraments and prayer. But before discussing them, I shall have something to say in our next instruction about the Church as an effect of the grace of Christ, the Head of the Church. I am going to tell you something about the "Mystical Body of Christ."

Mystical Body of Christ

As all the members of the human body, though they are many, form one body, so also are the faithful in Christ (cf. 1 Cor. 12:12) . . . The Head of this body is Christ . . . Giving the body unity through Himself and through His powers and through the internal cohesion of its members, this same Spirit produces and urges love among believers. Consequently, if one member suffers anything, all the members suffer it too, and if one member is honored, all the members rejoice together. — *The Church, 7*

Father S. Now that we have discussed Sanctifying Grace, I can point out another *essential* difference between the Catholic religion and all others. They are regarded as religious organizations merely, or organizations composed of men and women for religious purposes, and the average non-Catholic regards the Catholic Church as just another religious organization, even though it be the oldest, the most widespread, and the mother Church.

But Catholics do not like to have people regard theirs as a religious organization, because it is, in reality, a religious *organism,* or an actual living body animated by a soul. The body of the Church was formed by the Son of God and the soul infused into this Body is the Holy Spirit. Hence it is even a divine organism.

Mr. J. Will you explain further?

Father S. Yes, St. John, the Apostle, and St. Paul, in several of his epistles, refer to the Church as the "Body of Christ," and refer to all members of the Church as members of this Body, of which Christ is the head. St. Augustine, who lived in the 5th century, and St. Thomas, who lived in the 13th, elaborated considerably on this idea of the Church, and drew from it the most wonderful conclusions and lessons. The Church as "the Body of Christ" is called the "Mystical Body of Christ." For a more detailed discussion than I can give tonight, I suggest that you read the encyclical *Mystici Corporis* (Of the Mystical Body).

Mr. J. Just what is the meaning of the word "Mystical" in this connection?

Father S. The word is designed to convey the idea that the Church is *not* the "physical" or natural body of Christ, which was nailed to the Cross. You might grasp the meaning of it better if we refer to it as Christ's "social" body, spread over the world. Thus the Church is called the "Mystical Body of Christ" because its members are united with one another and with Christ our Head by the *mysterious bonds of grace and charity,* thus resembling the members and head of the living human body.

The Church is a Christian "social" body, inasmuch as it is constituted of millions of followers of Christ, but it is far more than that. Christ is the Church's head, functioning as a Teacher of God's *truth* and *law* through those who represent Him, and as a Sanctifier by giving grace and supernatural *life* through His Holy Spirit, Who *vivifies* the members. Thus Christ, our Head, *vitalizes* through the influence of His grace all the living members of His Church— His Mystical Body.

By Baptism, instituted by Christ, individuals are incorporated into His Body (1 Cor. 12:13). Christ Himself brings home the idea admirably when He says: "I am the vine; you are the branches. He who lives in Me, and I in him will produce abundantly, for apart from me you can do nothing (John 15:5).

Mr. J. Since the human body has comparatively few members and the Body of Christ has millions of them, the comparison does not seem to be so apt.

Father S. Well, every cell in your body is a member of your body. In fact, in your living body there are billions of cells, each one of them living and vibrant. The organs of your body begin to deteriorate when the cells in that organ begin to decay and die. Therefore, the comparison is very apt, although it is only a comparison. There will never be as many members of Christ's Mystical Body as there are cells in a human body, because there will never be that many people on earth. Just as cells in the human organism may die, so members incorporated into the Body of Christ may also become dead members through sin.

Since the teaching of the Church concerning the *Mystical Body* of Christ (which is another name for His Church), has been utterly unknown to you and to millions of others, I shall quote for you two passages of Holy Scripture which convey the idea in the words of St. Paul:

"He (the Father) has put all things under Christ's feet and has made Him, thus exalted, head of the Church, which is His body: the fullness of Him who fills the universe in all its parts" (Eph. 1:22-23).

"The body is one and has many members, but all the members, many though they are, are one body: and so it is with Christ. It was in one Spirit that all of us, whether Jew or Greek, slave or free, were baptized into one body. . . . You, then, are the body of Christ. Every one of you is a member of it" (1 Cor. 12:12-27).

Mr. J. Those words are certainly clear, and they seem to condemn the theories of race and blood, which have created so much trouble in the world.

Father S. They do. If we are all "one in Christ" there is no just excuse for *hatred* between *races, nations* and *classes.* Owing to the deep-seated prejudices of people there is only one cure for such antagonisms, and that is believing and living according to the doctrine of the Mystical Body of Christ. Even Catholics seldom think of themselves as actual members of a divine organism, through which they have steady contact with the Holy Spirit and divine life.

The principal office of the head is to direct the body as a whole, as well as each of its members, and we cannot conceive of life in the body, or of activity in the members, apart from the head. In a similar manner the Body of Christ, the Church, must be united to Him, its head, and each member of this body must also be united to Him if the member would partake of His divine life and become supernaturally active.

Nature is filled with examples which should make quite understandable the teaching of the Church concerning the Mystical Body. For instance, look at any tree, such as the huge oak. It has numerous branches, each of which must be connected with the main body of the tree and each branch of which when so connected produces leaves, and every leaf is recognizable as an oak leaf.

Now consider that the tree of the Church was directly fashioned by God and that the source of its life is the Holy Spirit, and you will readily grasp how the millions of members, connected with this Body as the branches of the tree are connected with the trunk and the roots, can bear fruit in keeping with the nature of the tree—in this case supernatural and divine.

Baptism

We believe in one Baptism instituted by Our Lord Jesus Christ for the remission of sins.

Baptism should be administered even to little children who have not yet been able to be guilty of any personal sin, in order that, though born deprived of supernatural grace, they may be reborn "of water and the Holy Spirit" to the divine life in Christ Jesus. — *Credo of the People of God.*

Father S. In past instructions, we discussed Sanctifying Grace and how the Redemption of the world by the Son of God made it possible for the human soul to come into possession of it, even though mankind, through Adam, had forfeited all right to it; but you have not yet learned how each person may come into possession of this grace.

Mr. J. No, Father; but you promised to treat of it after our talk on the Mystical Body.

Father S. That's right. While He was still on earth, Our Lord instituted certain means which He would use to give each and every one of us the supernatural life, made possible through Sanctifying Grace. These means are the sacraments which He left in His Church. A sacrament is a visible sign or ceremony which Christ chose and uses to give us grace that is invisible to our senses. The definition fits each of the seven sacraments. They give us grace because God uses them as His instruments. All the sacraments give us Sanctifying Grace, but each gives a special grace, called sacramental grace, which helps us to carry out the purpose of that sacrament. For example, those who receive the sacrament of Matrimony are given special graces to live a good Christian married life and fulfill their duties as parents. These sacraments always give grace if we receive them with the right dispositions.

Mr. J. How many sacraments did Christ institute?

Father S. Seven. They are Baptism, Confirmation, Holy Eucharist, Penance, Anointing of the Sick, Holy Orders and Matrimony.

Baptism was instituted to impart grace the first time; Penance to restore it, if lost by sin; and the five other sacraments to intensify the life of Sanctifying Grace already possessed.

Since Baptism and Penance give supernatural life to persons "dead" in sin, they are sometimes called sacraments of the dead. The other sacraments strengthen the supernatural life of persons already living in the state of grace, so they are called sacraments of the living. Anyone who knowingly receives a sacrament of the living while guilty of mortal sin commits a mortal sin of sacrilege, because such a person treats a sacred thing with grave irreverence. Now let me explain more about Baptism, the first of the seven sacraments.

Mr. J. Is there any reason for considering it first?

Father S. Yes, Baptism must precede the others. Since the sacraments belong to the Church and are for members of God's Church, that sacrament must be administered first which admits one into the Church or the Community of the Faithful. Then if Heaven is only for those who, as the children of God, possess Sanctifying Grace when they die, and such grace is conferred the first time by Baptism, it must be necessary for salvation. And if, when we are in possession of grace, we are worthy of Heaven, we must be dear to God.

Mr. J. Isn't every person a child of God?

Father S. Absolutely, not! No person is a child of God

until God adopts him as His child. Until that time we are only *creatures* of God. God lives in a *divine* order, and we are conceived and born in the *human* order. We remain in that human order until we are raised to the divine order by adoption, and that is what Baptism is for.

Mr. J. I certainly blew that one.

Father S. No, nearly all people thoughtlessly labor under the impression you had.

St. John tells us: "Any who did accept him he empowered to become children of God" (John 1:12); and St. Paul observes: "God sent forth his Son . . . so that we might receive our status as *adopted* sons" (Gal. 4:4-5). These texts make it clear we are *not born* sons or children of God.

Mr. J. How is Baptism received?

Father S. The one who confers it pours ordinary water on the head of the person, and says, while so doing: "I baptize you in the name of the Father, and of the Son, and of the Holy Spirit."

Mr. J. You say "the one who confers it." Who may confer it?

Father S. The priest is the usual minister of Baptism, but if there is danger that a person will die without it, anyone else may and should baptize.

Mr. J. When you say anyone, you mean, of course, any Catholic?

Father S. No; Catholic or Protestant, Jew or pagan; though if possible, it should be a Catholic.

Mr. J. But what if such a person should not believe in Baptism?

Father S. No matter, so long as the *intention* is to perform the rite that Christ instituted as necessary for salvation.

Mr. J. If that is the case, why does the Catholic priest rebaptize persons who were baptized by a Protestant minister?

Father S. A priest does not always re-baptize a person who has already been baptized by a Protestant minister. When such a person is received into the Catholic Church, he or she is not baptized again unless there is reasonable doubt about the validity of the person's previous baptism. If there is such doubt, the person is baptized *conditionally.*

Mr. J. Do you accept baptism by *immersion?*

Father S. We do, if we are sure that the proper words were employed while the water was applied, and if we are certain that the minister had the intention of doing what the Catholic Church intends when she baptizes.

Mr. J. How about the sprinkling method?

Father S. While sprinking, or aspersion, is valid, we usually re-baptize conditionally. Baptism means a washing; hence sufficient water should be used to indicate a washing. It should *flow* over the surface of the body — the head or face.

Mr. J. Some people contend that Baptism must be administered by the immersion method; that Christ was baptized thus; that Baptism signifies a "dipping" or burial.

Father S. It is by no means certain that Christ was immersed; all representations of Baptism, in paintings, show Him to be standing, while St. John *pours* water on His head. Moreover, the baptism which John the Baptist conferred was not the Christian Baptism; this was instituted by Christ a couple of years later. John's baptism was known as the baptism of penance.

St. Paul baptized people in prison (Acts 16:33) where it is not likely that they could be immersed. Since Baptism is necessary for salvation, it must be possible for the sick and dying to be baptized, and to immerse them would often be to "kill" them. The burial referred to by St. Paul is mystically represented by any form of Baptism; it signifies the burial of the sinner followed by resurrection in grace.

Mr. J. You require that even infants be baptized, do you not, Father?

Father S. Yes, as soon as possible after birth. Catholic parents who put off for a long time or entirely neglect this important matter commit grave sin. Sanctifying Grace or the supernatural life of the soul is necessary for the supernatural reward which is Heaven. Christ demands that everyone be baptized: "I solemnly assure you, no one can enter into God's kingdom without being begotten of water and Spirit" (John 3:5).

Mr. J. If I remember correctly, you told me, when speaking of Original Sin, that unbaptized infants escape positive punishment in eternity; in fact, are happy with a *natural* happiness, but that they do not enjoy the vision of God and the *supernatural* happiness of the saved.

Father S. That is correct.

Mr. J. Now, Father, may I ask a few questions that occurred to me while you were talking?

Father S. Go right ahead.

Mr. J. Well, what about the millions who do not know the necessity of Baptism? Surely God will not let them miss Heaven because of mere ignorance of His requirement?

Father S. That situation is met by the all-just and fair God; there is a substitute for Baptism by water. It is *Baptism of Desire;* that is, God will give grace to those who are heartily sorry for their sins, and who ardently long for all that is necessary for salvation — those who would apply for Baptism if they only knew its necessity.

Mr. J. May a person receive the sacrament as often as he desires?

Father S. The sacraments of Baptism, Confirmation and Holy Orders can be received only once. However, the other four can be received more than once.

Mr. J. Why is it that three can be received only once?

Father S. Because those three sacraments each give the soul an indelible spiritual character which it never loses. For example, the effects of the character we receive from Baptism are that we become members of the Church, subject to its laws and capable of receiving other sacraments.

Mr. J. Here's another question in which I am particularly interested. Does Baptism take away only Original Sin?

Father S. No, it takes away Original Sin and all other

sins which the person may have committed, also all the punishment due to them. Of course, the person must be truly sorry for these sins.

Mr. J. I hear that before a person may receive Baptism, one must select godparents. What is the reason for that?

Father S. Godparents are chosen for two reasons. First, they serve as witnesses representing the Christian community, in whose name they request baptism for their godchild. Second, after the baptism of a child, the godparents have the duty to see that the child is brought up a good Catholic, should the parents neglect or be unable for some reason to fulfill this duty. The role of godparents in the case of an infant's baptism is, of course, secondary to that of the parents.

Mr. J. How soon can I receive Baptism, Father?

Father S. I think it would be best for you to be baptized after you are fully acquainted with all the teachings of our Faith. In the meantime, I suggest that you choose some saint as your special protector, so that through the prayers of this saint, God will give you the help you need to become a zealous member of the Church and a true follower of Christ. You can take the name of this saint when you are baptized and strive to imitate his virtues. By the way, St. Paul is a great saint, and a convert, too.

Confirmation

Bound more intimately to the Church by the Sacrament of Confirmation, they are endowed by the Holy Spirit with special strength. Hence they are more strictly obliged to spread and defend the faith both by word and by deed as true witnesses of Christ. — *The Church, 11.*

Father S. Grand as it is to be a child of the Heavenly Father, He wants us to be more than *children* in the Faith; He wishes that we be mature and aggressive *soldiers,* to defend His name, to fight for His cause, to oppose His enemies. This rank and office is conferred on us by another sacrament, that of *Confirmation.*

Mr. J. Is that what Confirmation is for? Will you administer that sacrament to me immediately after Baptism?

Father S. Yes. As your pastor I am authorized to confer this sacrament in danger of death and in ceremonies of Christian initiation. However, the ordinary minister of Confirmation is the bishop, who confirms the faithful within his diocese, and he will not visit our parish until next October. He is engaged in confirming somewhere in his diocese much of his time, and is able to visit most parishes only about once in two or three years.

Mr. J. Confirmation isn't necessary for salvation, then?

Father S. Not absolutely. However, those who are not yet

confirmed would be doing wrong if they omitted to receive it, through neglect, when the bishop does come to confirm. Confirmation not only confers the indelible *character* of soldier on those who receive it, but actually imparts to them Sanctifying Grace and such strength by its sacramental grace, as enables them to be valiant Christians. You have read that the Apostles, though instructed by Christ Himself, were not sufficiently strong in faith until the Holy Spirit descended upon their souls on Pentecost. The sufferings and death of Christ were enough to shake their faith in His divinity, though, of course, it came back to them when they knew of His Resurrection from the grave. Then during the forty days preceding His return to Heaven, Jesus repeatedly promised to send the Holy Spirit, Who would complete the work of preparing them for the arduous labors of their calling, and living within them, would fill them with the love and zeal which makes martyrs.

Mr. J. The coming of the Holy Spirit to them was their Confirmation Day?

Father S. Exactly; and it wrought a wonderful change in them. They now were filled with an ardent zeal to labor for Christ, and if need be, to die for Him. They did not hesitate to go to hostile territory and preach the Christian religion, and by their preaching and saintly lives, converted thousands. As true soldiers of Christ, they fought for Him, until they lost their lives in defense of His cause.

Mr. J. Shouldn't all Christians be as loyal and zealous as they?

Father S. During the first three centuries of the Christian era, millions were equally loyal. To be a Christian meant to be a martyr, if the civil authority found it out. But the religion of Christ is now well established in most parts of the world and is well respected. Yet Catholics are still called upon to defend their faith with their lives, particularly in those countries where Communists have gained control. However, even in so-called Christian lands the Church, particularly in its social message is often attacked, as we are witnessing in Latin

America and Africa in these our own times today. The main enemy, as you know, atheistic Communism teaches that God does not exist and that "religion is the opium of the people." To succeed in their plans for world revolution, Red leaders feel Christianity must be completely overthrown. However, because many Catholics forget that they are soldiers in the army of Christ, and even give encouragement to His enemies, thousands of non-Catholics are never prompted to investigate our claims. They would be attracted to the Church especially if Catholic laity were outstandingly better and gave good example.

Mr. J. What do you mean when you speak of Catholic laity?

Father S. The laity of the Church are all its members who have not received Holy Orders. They are expected to help the Church in its work by leading lives that will reflect credit on their Faith and by cooperating with their bishops and priests. Since Vatican II the laity have been given increasingly greater responsibilities in the Church.

Mr. J. Just what is involved?

Father S. The active cooperation of lay members of the Church with the Pope, bishops and priests in the Church's mission — the saving of souls. The laity under the direction of their bishops and priests endeavor to instill the Christian spirit and principles into the social and political life around them. Moreover, the laity act as lectors, Eucharistic ministers, and commentators at Mass; some become deacons.

Mr. J. But where does Confirmation come in?

Father S. After receiving Confirmation, a person should take a more active part in the work of the Church, spreading Christ's teaching and upholding it against His enemies. Priests are *ordained*, laymen are *confirmed* for this purpose.

Mr. J. Who are the enemies of Christ that you mentioned?

Father S. The Bible classifies the principal enemies of Christ under three heads: the world, the flesh and the devil. As enemies of Christ, they are also dangers to our salvation. The worldly spirit, which leads us to seek only worldly gain and worldly pleasures, is a powerful enemy. It blinds people to the higher things and kills their taste for things of the spirit. Christ told His followers that while they must live *in* the world, they should not become part of it. Today, through mass media the world and all its blandishments are always encroaching upon our lives. "The flesh" is an enemy which we carry ever with us. It is the body, which we pamper, which is too lazy to pray and go to church, too unwilling to fast and be denied sensual pleasures, too prone to indulge its appetites and evil desires. Then the devil, God's arch-enemy, is ever tempting men and laying snares for him. Confirmation furnishes the weapons with which we can resist these enemies and win repeated victories for God and our souls. The Bible calls our life on earth a warfare; and the fight is always on. It is good that such is the case, since without winning victories we cannot obtain the eternal crown. Heaven is a reward for spiritual military service.

Mr. J. In every instruction I learn new reasons why a man-made religion could not "fill the bill." At what age may Catholics be confirmed?

Father S. At any time after Baptism, although the sacrament is seldom administered before the child has received its First Communion. It is becoming more customary to confirm in the early teens since Confirmation is a sign of adulthood in the Church.

Mr. J. What is required to receive Confirmation properly?

Father S. A person should be in the state of grace and know well the chief truths of our religion. But the study of religion should not end there. We should continue to deepen our knowledge of Christian doctrine so that we may be able to explain and defend our Faith, and thus cooperate with the graces we receive as *confirmed* Christians.

Mr. J. How is Confirmation given?

Father S. Ideally the sacrament is conferred during the Eucharistic liturgy. After the baptismal promises are renewed, the bishop prays that the Holy Spirit may descend on the persons to be confirmed to strengthen them with His seven gifts mentioned in the Bible. Then he places his hand on the head of each, while he makes the sign of the cross on the person's forehead with consecrated oil, called *chrism.* While doing this he says these words: "N., be sealed with the Holy Spirit, the Gift of the Father."

Mr. J. Kindly explain the meaning of the ceremony.

Father S. Oil (olive oil) has always been regarded as a symbol of strength and vigor. Athletes often rub their muscles and limbs with oil for greater agility and strength. The cross is the Church's banner or flag. Just as the civil soldier must be proud of his country's flag, so must the Christian soldier be proud of the standard under which he or she must fight, the cross; hence it is marked on one's forehead. The imposition of hands is the traditional form when invoking the Holy Spirit upon someone.

Mr. J. The ceremony is certainly significant. Of course, I know that Christ instituted all the sacraments, but does the Bible refer to instances when the Apostles confirmed?

Father S. Oh, yes. It is usually referred to as the "laying on of hands," which today is the most significant and the effective part of the ceremony. It is spoken of in Acts 8:14-17; 19:6, and in several other places.

Mr. J. So there is considerable difference between a merely baptized and a confirmed Catholic?

Father S. Yes, there is; and in Heaven the difference will be noticeable in the souls of the two. Confirmation leaves an indelible impress on the soul, which marks it for added glory. Confirmation completes the initiation rites into the Church begun in baptism.

Mr. J. I did not know that Confirmation was so significant.

Father S. Nor seemingly do many Catholics. They leave

the defense of the Church entirely to the clergy. What if, during a war, the soldiers left all the fighting to the higher officers! The priest is usually able to influence only those who come to his church, and they are his own parishioners. The latter live next door to people who may know little or nothing about the Church; they work in offices, factories and mills with non-Catholics; they associate with them in social life — but seldom ever talk religion or think of winning friends to Christ by their good example. Converts often are greatly surprised at the manner in which Catholics keep their religion all to themselves.

Mr. J. Evidently they do not grasp their duty as soldiers.

Father S. In your next instruction you will have the greatest treat you have yet received in your lessons. We shall deal with the Holy Eucharist.

Holy Eucharist

Taking part in the Eucharistic Sacrifice, which is the fount and apex of the whole Christian life, they offer the Divine Victim to God, and offer themselves along with it. Thus, both by the act of oblation and through Holy Communion, all perform their proper part in this liturgical service . . . Strengthened anew at the holy table by the Body of Christ, they manifest in a practical way that unity of God's People which is suitably signified and wondrously brought about by this most awesome sacrament. — *The Church, 11.*

Father S. Let me begin this important instruction by stating that the Holy Eucharist is a sacrament and a sacrifice; in it our Savior Jesus Christ, body and blood, soul and divinity, under the appearances of bread and wine, is contained, offered and received.

You recall that Christ promised to be with His Church "always, until the end of the world" (Matt 28:20). But you probably never dreamed that He devised a way of living among the people of every community in person, so that each could visit Him, and nourish his soul's Christian life with the bread that comes down from Heaven. This is made possible through the Sacrament of the Holy Eucharist.

You will understand the doctrine better after you have had an instruction on the Mass, for it is in the Mass that this sacrament is made possible. But even now you can learn all that the Holy Eucharist implies.

Mr. J. When did Christ give us the Sacrament of the Holy Eucharist?

Father S. At the Last Supper, the night before His crucifixion.

Mr. J. Who saw Him do it?

Father S. The Apostles witnessed the institution of the sacrament, received it, and were commissioned to repeat it for others.

Mr. J. Tell me how He went about it.

Father S. You can read it in the Gospels. The Son of God took some of the bread and wine used at the table, divided the same into portions, and, by His almighty power, changed the same into His own living person. He said: "Take this and eat it; this is my body . . . this is my blood" (Matt. 26:26-28). When our Lord said: "This is My body," through His almighty power the entire substance of the bread was changed into His body; and when He said: "This is My blood" the entire substance of the wine was changed into His blood.

Mr. J. Were Christ's words to be taken in their obvious sense? Wasn't he speaking figuratively?

Father S. No. A whole year before the Last Supper, He *promised* that He would give to man His *real* flesh and blood, and at that time His hearers, including the Apostles, understood that He was talking figuratively, but He insisted that His words be accepted literally (John 6).

Mr. J. What did He say on that occasion?

Father S. He said that He was the "living bread," "the bread of life," that the bread He would give would be "His flesh," for the life of the world; that His flesh would be a *real* meat, and His blood a *real* drink; that those would have "eternal life" who would eat His flesh and drink His blood, and that those who should not eat the same, would not have life in them. Of course, He meant supernatural life.

Mr. J. Those statements are surely plain; but you said

His hearers were not inclined to accept His words in their plain sense.

Father S. No; they argued the question: "How *can* He give us His real flesh to eat?"

Mr. J. Then they must have understood Him to mean what He said.

Father S. That's right, but I mean they were not disposed to believe Him. Many of them even went away because Christ insisted that His words were literally true. Now, what if Christ had referred to a figurative eating of His flesh, and these people misunderstood Him, and went away deceived?

Mr. J. As God, Christ could not have allowed that; He could not countenance deception. But how about the Apostles? How were they impressed by Christ's declaration?

Father S. Christ demanded a profession of faith from them. When He saw some of the disciples walk away, He said to the Apostles: "Will you also go away?" Then Peter made an open acknowledgment of the Savior's divinity, and, of course, of His power to do what was not really plain to them — to give His real flesh and blood as nourishment of the soul's supernatural life.

Mr. J. Were the Apostles equally surprised at the Last Supper, when the Holy Eucharist was instituted?

Father S. No. I suppose that the twelve often wondered when their Master was going to give what He had so solemnly and emphatically promised.

Mr. J. But granting that our Savior favored the Apostles in such a manner, would you mind explaining how members of the Church today can be similarly favored?

Father S. Christ empowered and commissioned the Apostles to work the same wonder; after He had given them Himself as spiritual food, He said to them: "Do this for a remembrance of Me" (Luke 22:19). Thus He made them priests.

Mr. J. Would that not explain only that the power was conferred on the Apostles? But they are no longer alive.

Father S. The power conferred on the Apostles was for

the Church for all times. They were a corporate body, which was to be continued in their successors, just as the powers conferred by the constitution on the Senate some 200 years ago are possessed by senators today. Priests exercise the ministry of Christ and change bread and wine into the body and blood of Christ by repeating at the Consecration of the Mass the words of Christ: "This is My body . . . this is My blood."

Mr. J. Why is it, then, that Protestant churches do not claim this power? Surely it is something very important?

Father S. They could not prove that their ministers are the rightful successors of the Apostles; the gap of time between the Apostles' day — the first century — and the appearance of the founders of their churches, is too big.

Mr. J. I see. My family might claim connection with Napoleon's family, but if I am in no sense a lineal descendant of Napoleon, my claim is futile.

Father S. The old example comes to my mind: I might build a beautiful home, furnish it elegantly, and have it wired for electricity, but if I am not connected with the power lines, I cannot have electric light.

Mr. J. What you have said, Father, raised some questions in my mind. May I mention them before I go?

Father S. By all means!

Mr. J. You said that in the Holy Eucharist, after the bread and wine had been changed into Our Lord's body and blood, there remained only the *appearances* of bread and wine. What is meant by that?

Father S. That simply means that the color, taste, weight and shape of bread and wine — whatever else appears to the senses — remains the same after the change of the entire *substance* of the bread and wine into the body and blood of Christ. This change is called *transubstantiation*.

Mr. J. Does that mean that Our Lord is whole and entire both under the appearances of bread and under the appearances of wine?

Father S. Yes.

Mr. J. Will you explain later why people receive Communion only under the form of bread?

Father S. Actually, Communion under both forms is given but I'll take that up when we discuss Holy Communion.

Mr. J. One last question. Why did Christ give us this sacrament?

Father S. For several reasons: that He might remain ever with us as a proof of His love for us and to be worshipped by us; to be received in Holy Communion; and to be offered as a sacrifice commemorating and renewing the Sacrifice of the Cross for all time. We'll take up the Mass in our next instruction.

The Mass

Through the hands of the Priest, in the name of the whole Church, the Sacrifice of the Lord is offered in an unbloody and sacramental manner. (*Priestly Life, 2*).

They (priests) exercise this sacred function of Christ most of all in the Eucharistic liturgy or celebration of Mass. There, acting in the person of Christ and proclaiming His mystery they join the offering of the Faithful to the sacrifice of their Head. Until the coming of the Lord (1 Cor. 11:26) they re-present and apply in the sacrifice of the Mass the one Sacrifice of Christ offering Himself once and for all a spotless victim to His Father (Heb. 9:11-28). — *The Church, 28.*

Father S. Well, Mr. Jackson, our instruction tonight will be on the Mass.

Mr. J. Very well; I'll be glad to know all about it, since I have been attending Mass for some time.

Father S. Remembering that the Almighty is a Being infinitely great, I presume it is plain to you that no form of worship could be too good for Him.

Mr. J. That's clear.

Father S. And since God is in a class by Himself, it seems that the honor due to Him should differ in kind from honor which we may bestow upon anyone else.

Mr. J. That's also plain; the worship directed to Almighty God should be the highest, both in quality and quantity.

Father S. I'm glad that you so readily perceive this. We are accustomed to bestow different marks of honor on people according to their rank. We merely bid the time of day to an acquaintance, but we clasp the hand of a friend and entertain him at our home. Should the President visit our city, we would decorate our streets, acclaim him with cheers; yet we would still be honoring a man. What homage would we bestow upon an angel of Heaven, one who is so far superior to a king or president? But even the most exalted angel and the whole assemblage of angels dwindle into insignificance when compared to their Creator, God. His majesty is *infinite,* and hence He can be honored adequately only by a worship of *infinite value;* and this no human is capable of inventing. Our best gifts and worship can never be more than finite. Hence we should surely expect that the Son of God before leaving earth would institute for His perfect religion a form of worship which would honor the Trinity as It deserves to be honored.

Mr. J. But did not Christ so honor the Trinity when He offered His life on the Cross?

Father S. Yes; but in the religion He founded He wanted the Holy Trinity to be worshipped, as It deserved, every day until the end of the world. He wanted God honored as much and as uninterruptedly on earth as in Heaven. That worship was begun, not on the Cross, but the night before His death at the Last Supper. It was the *first* Mass offered on earth by Jesus in person, and was only the beginning of many daily Masses which would be offered by Him through ministers, the Apostles, and those who would be ordained by them for that purpose.

At the Last Supper sacrifice, immediately after the Savior pronounced over the bread and wine the words which changed them into His body and blood, He said to the Apostles: "Do this." They were to be God's instruments for effecting *the presence* of Christ under the form of bread. Thereupon He

Himself would repeat the same offering He made to the Father at the Last Supper, thus rendering in our name a worship of infinite value. What more pleasing sacrifice could there be than the God-Man, the perfect victim, offering Himself to His heavenly Father?

In Genesis we read that Melchisedech (Gen. 14:18), "a priest of God Most High" was accustomed to offer a sacrifice of bread and wine. David (Ps. 110:4) foretold that Christ would be a "priest *forever* according to the order of Melchisedech," and St. Paul (Heb. 8) refers to Christ as exercising the priesthood foreshadowed by Melchisedech's sacrifice. This priesthood was inaugurated by Jesus at the Last Supper, and its continuance provided for "until He come" (namely, at the end of the world). David prophesied that Christ would be a priest "forever"; another prophet foretold that the sacrifice would be offered in every place (Mal. 1:11); St. Paul calls the attention of the people of his day to it (1 Cor. 10:16), and argues that this priesthood of Christ would be "forever" (Heb. 7:24).

Mr. J. You call this worship "sacrifice," do you not?

Father S. Yes. From the beginning of the world the form of worship known as sacrifice was the kind by which the Almighty was adored. A sacrifice is the offering of a victim by a priest to God alone, and the destruction of it in some way to acknowledge that He is the Creator and Lord of all things.

You see, sacrifice contains an acknowledgment of the creature's relationship to the Creator, as does no other form of worship. In sacrifice a visible object is offered to God, then destroyed, to denote that we owe everything to Him, and that we deserve to be destroyed because of our sins. Old Law sacrifices were instituted by God Himself, and they were to be figures or foreshadows of the great sacrifice of the New Law. Christ was called the "Lamb of God," because in the Old Law a little lamb was daily immolated after the people prayed that God might regard it as loaded with their sins, and accept its life in place of the lives of the people. God saw in this sacrifice His beloved Son, burdened with the load of mankind's sins, and offered in place of the real sinners, and hence it had value.

Mr. J. But I do not quite see how these bloody sacrifices are related to the Mass, though they seem to point clearly to the bloody death of Christ on Calvary.

Father S. You are right. I was only pointing out to you that the form of true worship of God was by sacrifice. The Old Law had both bloody and unbloody sacrifices.

Mr. J. It all becomes clear with a little explanation. I had supposed that the death of Christ on Calvary set humanity right with God, and gave to the Almighty the infinite worship which His justice demanded.

Father S. You reasoned correctly as far as the atoning effect of that sacrifice was concerned. But Christ, having instituted His religion first of all for His Father's glory, gave it a sacrifice, by which His Heavenly Father would be fittingly honored every day until the end of the world.

In the Mass, as on Calvary, Christ offers the sacrifice to adore God, to thank Him for His favors, to ask Him to bestow His blessings on all men, and to satisfy His justice for the sins committed against Him. The institution of the Mass made these grand aims possible. Through the Mass the merits of Calvary's sacrifice have been applied to individual souls throughout the ages.

Mr. J. Father, it is difficult not to become concerned when one thinks how many millions know nothing of this. As I see it the heavenly Father is honored by every Mass with a worship of no less value than the Sacrifice of the Cross, because the same person, His beloved Son, does the worshipping. It is of secondary importance, whether the offering is bloody or unbloody. Thus in the sacrifice of the Mass and the sacrifice of the Cross, the principal priest and the victim is the same, Jesus Christ. The main consideration in worship is "Who worships?" and it is Christ in both cases.

Father S. That's correct. The principal priest in every Mass is Jesus Christ, who offers to His Heavenly Father, through the ministry of His ordained priest, His body and blood which were sacrificed on the Cross.

Mr. J. Is there any difference between the sacrifice on the Cross and in the Mass?

Father S. The manner in which the sacrifice is offered is different. On the Cross Christ physically shed His blood and was physically slain, while in the Mass there is no physical shedding of blood nor physical death, because now Christ can die no more. On the Cross, Christ merited and satisfied for us, while in the Mass He *applies* to us the merits and satisfaction of His death on the Cross.

Before we close this evening, I would like to leave one other idea with you. The Mass is not a personal devotion, either of the priest or of the persons attending. It is a community act of worship, wherein God speaks to us through the *Liturgy of the Word* and shares His life with us through the *Liturgy of the Eucharist.* Christ died for all of us, and in the Mass, we as a Christian community offer the Son back to the Father.

As your understanding and appreciation of this central act of Catholic worship increases, Mr. Jackson, your reverence, attention, and devotion while present at Mass will no doubt increase. The best way to take part in the Mass is to unite yourself with Christ and the priest, His minister in offering the sacrifice, and to receive Christ in Holy Communion.

We can discuss this subject further at our next meeting.

Frequent Communion

Hearty endorsement is given to that closer form of participation in the Mass whereby the Faithful, after the priest's
communion, receive the Lord's body under the elements
consecrated at that very sacrifice. — *Liturgy, 55.*

Father S. We have seen that the Mass is the divinely established sacrifice by which Christ's followers were to worship
God in the New Law. We have observed that Christ's daily
self-immolation on the altar and His daily repeated prayer,
"Father forgive them," must explain the tolerance by God of a
wicked world.

Mr. J. Yes, that explanation clears up a matter which has
often perplexed me.

Father S. But the *secondary* purpose of the Mass is to
render Christ present under the form of *food,* in order that He
might be Emmanuel, which means "God with us," and be for
our souls the "bread of life."

There are four special effects produced by Holy Communion. It: (1) unites us intimately with Christ, and thereby
brings a great increase of Sanctifying Grace to the soul. This
effect is self-evident; because if all the sacraments impart
grace, that one surely does which unites the soul personally
with Christ.

(2) It makes us more eager to do good and strengthens

our will in that direction. If bodily food strengthens us for physical work, this spiritual food must strengthen us for spiritual work.

(3) It cleanses from venial sin and preserves from mortal sin. If God removes venial sin even upon our heartfelt expression of sorrow, His entry into our hearts, filled with sorrow and love, should surely cancel these smaller sins. When we fall into grievous sin it is because, left to ourselves, we are not strong enough to resist it. But with the divine help received from Holy Communion we should be stronger and better able to withstand temptation.

(4) The one who receives Holy Communion worthily is promised a glorious resurrection and everlasting happiness with God in Heaven.

Thus Holy Communion is the greatest aid to a holy life.

Mr. J. If all who die in the state of grace are to be raised to life at the end of the world and enter Heaven with body and soul, those most certainly will be thus favored whose bodies were made holy by visits of Jesus in Holy Communion. It would hardly even seem fair for them to miss Heaven, provided they live united to Christ throughout life.

Father S. I see that we shall never have to urge you to receive Holy Communion often.

Mr. J. Do you find it necessary to urge any Catholic to receive Holy Communion?

Father S. Yes, unfortunately, we do. Some seem to have no relish for the Holy Eucharist; they don't receive oftener than once in several months. There are even a few who will come to the Holy Table only once a year. However, since Vatican II the faithful on the whole are receiving Holy Communion more frequently. In fact, at most Masses the majority take full participation in the Sacrifice by receiving the Lord.

Mr. J. They must go at least once a year if they would be regarded as Catholics, must they not?

Father S. Yes, during Eastertime.

Mr. J. They certainly do not realize what they believe, or there would be more consistency between their belief and their practice. I should not even think that they would derive much benefit from Holy Communion, because surely Christ will do most for those who long for union with Him and accept His invitation to come to Him often.

Father S. You reason rightly. Christ wanted to be for man's soul what food is for his body — a "daily bread." The first Christians received Him daily, the Council of Trent urged people to receive every time they attend Mass, and the late St. Pius X asked that we admit children to Holy Communion at an early age, and then inculcate in them the practice of weekly or even daily Communion. Human beings can enjoy no other honor comparable to that which consists in personal union with God. Vatican II "endorsed" frequent Communion. (Liturgy 55).

Mr. J. As I look at it, man should need no invitation, because the benefits are all one-sided — they are in favor of the one who receives Holy Communion. Man should regard it as his greatest privilege to receive the Holy Eucharist.

Father S. Is there anything under this head about our teaching and practice, which you want to know more about?

Mr. J. Yes, Father, I must remind you of one more thing. You do not give the people Holy Communion under the form of wine, do you?

Father S. Yes, we do, when the bishop approves it. The meaning of *communion* is more evident when received under both forms. Vatican Council II's *Decree on the Liturgy* (55) leaves the decision of whether to allow distribution of Communion under both forms up to diocesan bishops, in accord with guidelines of the Holy See. The Missal used by the priest at Mass contains this statement in its introduction: "The faithful should be encouraged to desire Communion under both kinds...." All I want to repeat now is that it is not *necessary* to receive under both forms in order to receive the whole Christ. If the priest offers the Mass, he must receive under both forms, but if he does not offer the Mass, but goes to Holy Communion, he receives under one form only as laymen do, unless he is concelebrating.

Mr. J. What is concelebrating?

Father S. That is when several priests celebrate Mass together. Vatican II tells us that concelebration is a way in which the unity of the priesthood is fittingly made manifest. (Liturgy 57)

Mr. J. That's plain enough.

Father S. I do not recall informing you that ordinarily, besides being free from mortal sin, people intending to receive Holy Communion must fast from food and drink.

Mr. J. No, you didn't tell me that. Exactly what does it mean?

Father S. It is, of course, out of reverence for the Eucharistic food received in Holy Communion. Those who are to receive Holy Communion must fast for at least one hour from eating or drinking anything but water; water never breaks the Eucharistic fast. An exception is made for the sick and aged by limiting the fast to fifteen minutes, and for those caring for them who wish to receive with them but cannot fast for an hour without inconvenience. Those who are ill, even though not confined to bed, may take nonalcoholic beverages and liquid or solid medicine without any time limit.

Mr. J. Does that mean that you can drink ordinary water, but can take nothing else?

Father S. Yes, that is the present general rule, although until not so long ago, even water was not permitted. And I might add that special allowances are made for the sick who, even if not bedridden, may take nonalcoholic liquids and that which is really and properly medicine, either in liquid or solid form, before Mass and Holy Communion without any time limit.

Mr. J. Do Catholics ever have Mass except in the morning?

Father S. Yes, if they see good reason for so doing, especially to make the Mass available for those who could not otherwise attend. Late afternoon and evening Masses are becoming increasingly popular. I should mention that the bishop can give permission for the Sunday or holyday obligation to be filled by attending Mass on Saturday evening or the vigil of the holyday. Most dioceses now have Vigil Masses.

Mr. J. If a person attends Mass on Saturday evening and receives Holy Communion, may he or she also receive again on Sunday?

Father S. Yes. In fact, they could receive twice on Saturday by attending the Saturday Mass in the morning and then the Vigil Mass in the evening.

Priest at the Altar

For the Blessed Eucharist contains the Church's entire spiritual wealth, Christ Himself. — *Priestly Life, 5.*

Father S. You have told me that you are attending Mass every Sunday, and I can well understand that you become quite puzzled over many things. You see the priest clad in strange vestments. You hear bells. You see the people alternately kneel and stand and sit down. All this confuses the convert for some time, and makes him wonder whether he will ever be able to learn how to assist at the Mass intelligently, much less participate in it.

Mr. J. I have observed these things and have been awaiting your explanation.

Father S. The explanations are not difficult to understand once you realize that the priest deals directly with Almighty God and represents Christ. That is why he is clothed as he is. He wears vestments which are known as the *amice, alb, cincture, stole,* and *chasuble.* The vestments he wears are the *garments of sacrifice.* In the first centuries of Christianity these garments were the apparel of laymen in their daily lives. Since then fashions have changed, yet the Church retains these garments because they carry us back in memory to the early Church and the Last Supper. Each vestment has been given meaning and contains a lesson for the priest and for the people. You will understand the meaning from the prayer which the priest says, as he puts on each one.

The *amice* is a piece of white cloth which the priest touches to his head, then puts over his shoulders and around his neck. In early times it was protection for the head out-of-doors and was dropped to the shoulders indoors. While he adjusts it, the priest prays: "Place, O Lord, the helmet of salvation on my head to resist the attacks of the devil." The *alb* is a long robe of white linen which covers the entire body. In early times it was an ordinary outer garment. As he puts it on, the priest prays: "Make me white, O Lord, and purify my heart . . ." The *cincture* is a thick cord with which the alb is secured around the waist. As he ties it, the priest prays: "Gird me, O Lord, with the cincture of purity and extinguish in my heart the fire of concupiscence . . ." The *stole* is a long strip of colored cloth worn around the neck. Formerly it was a neckpiece which became a distinctive mark of duty and honor. As he dons it, the priest prays: "Restore unto me, O Lord, the stole of immortality which I lost through the sin of my first parents . . ." The last vestment is the *chasuble*, which is a large outer covering that served in ancient times as a sleeveless cape. Usually the chasuble has ornamentation. As the priest puts it over his head, the priest prays: "O Lord, who hast said 'My yoke is sweet and My burden light,' grant that I may so carry it as to merit your grace."

The *altar* itself represents Calvary. No matter how simple or how elegant the altar may be, the chief requisite is the *altar stone* placed in its center. In a small receptacle in this stone are sealed the relics of martyrs, because during the first three centuries of Christian times, when the people, because of persecution, attended Mass in the catacombs, the priests said Mass on the tombs of martyrs.

Immediately *back* of the altar of sacrifice in many churches one finds the permanent altar which was formerly used when the priest said Mass with his back to the faithful. This contains the tabernacle. If this altar is not present the tabernacle is on a shelf behind or to the side. The *tabernacle* is the Holy of Holies in which the consecrated bread, or the Holy Eucharist, is reserved for the worship of the faithful at any time.

Every altar has a crucifix near it, a reminder of the sacrifice of Calvary. The candles, which are made from beeswax, represent the virginal body of Christ, consumed for us. They also take us back to the days of the catacombs when it was necessary, even during the daytime, to have lights on the altar.

The *book* which the priest uses is called a *Sacramentary*. It contains the ordinary prayers, the Eucharistic canons, and prayers special to the day or feast. On a lectern in the sanctuary is another book called the *Lectionary*. In it are all the scriptural readings for the year.

Mr. J. This is all most informative. But I have noticed that vested boys assist the priest, that they ring the bell at certain times, and that the priest uses a golden cup, which at one part of the Mass he raises high.

Father S. The *servers* assist the priest. They bring him wine and water, help him to purify his fingers, and so on. One of them rings the bell to remind the congregation that the Consecration, or central act of the Mass, is approaching.

The golden cup, to which you refer, is called the *chalice*. It is usually made of silver and gold-plated, though any valued material may be used. Into this cup are poured wine and a few drops of water at the Offertory, which is later consecrated into the blood of Christ. Over the cup is a gold-covered plate, on which the unleavened bread is placed, which, too, is consecrated into the body of Christ.

Mr. J. I have also observed that the color of the garments worn by the priest is not always the same.

Father S. You are right. They are of six different colors.

Green, for the season of the year. It symbolizes hope.

Purple, for Advent and Lent; this color may also be used in Masses for the dead. It symbolizes penance.

Red, for Passion Sunday, Wednesday of Holy Week, Good Friday, Pentecost, feasts of the Passion of Our Lord, the Apostles and Evangelists, and martyrdom. It symbolizes the fire of the Holy Spirit and the blood of martyrdom.

Rose, in place of purple for the Third Sunday of Advent and the Fourth Sunday of Lent. It symbolizes joyful expectation.

White, for Christmastide, Eastertide, feasts of Our Lord (except Passion), those of the Virgin Mary, angels, saints who were not martyrs. All Saints and some other feast days, and also funerals and Masses of the Dead (Resurrection). White can be substituted for other colors in necessity. It symbolizes purity.

Gold, may be used for solemn feasts no matter the prescribed color.

Mr. J. I have known the importance which Catholics attach to the Mass itself, but I never dreamed that there was so much significance to the things associated with the Mass, such as the altar and its furnishings, the garments of the priest, etc.

Father S. Yes, and these things are of only minor importance as compared to the Mass itself. When you have that explained to you, you will not be surprised that the Catholic Church obligates her people to attend Mass every Sunday and on holydays. In fact, you will be surprised that most Catholics do not attend one or more Masses every day.

Cardinal Newman, the author of the hymn, "Lead Kindly Light," so frequently sung in Protestant and Catholic churches, after becoming a convert to the Catholic Church, and after becoming familiar with the great significance of the Mass, declared that he could attend Mass forever.

Participation in the Mass

We believe that the Mass, celebrated by the priest representing the person of Christ by virtue of the powers received
through the Sacrament of Orders, and offered by him in the
name of Christ and the members of His Mystical Body, is
the Sacrifice of Calvary rendered sacramentally present on
our Altars. — *Credo of the People of God.*

Father S. Every human being owes to Almighty God four
kinds of prayer, known as adoration, or worship; thanksgiving, or appreciation; reparation, or prayers of repentance; and
petition or supplication, or prayers for spiritual and temporal
help. An easy way to remember the forms of prayer is to recall
the word ARTS — standing for adoration, reparation, thanksgiving and supplication. That's also the order in which prayer
should be made. For too many people prayer is just the last,
asking for something.

You have already been told that no human being, *because
he is a human being,* is capable of giving to God the honor that
He fully deserves. But in the Mass, where Christ is the priest,
as He was at the Last Supper and on the Cross, He becomes
the victim, which those who attend Mass may offer to the
Heavenly Father in infinite adoration, reparation, thanksgiving and petition. At the same time, the people at Mass become
sharers in the fruits of Christ's Redemption. They may offer

this victim to fulfill all their own obligations to God, as well as for the benefit of others, both living and dead.

Mr. J. From what you say, I can now understand how the honor God receives through the Mass must compensate for the evil that is in the world.

Father S. Exactly. It is not likely that you and I would be alive today, because the world would probably long since have come to an end if it were not for the Mass. If this statement seems to surprise you, you must realize that mankind exists for the honor and glory of God. If God does not receive great honor and glory from the majority of His creatures — and He is certainly receiving everything else but that today — why should He not destroy the human race as He once did? The answer is that He receives from the Mass such glory and honor as offset the insult and dishonor He receives from hundreds of millions.

Mr. J. That seems very reasonable, Father. But now I should like to know whether there is more than one way of assisting at Mass.

Father S. Since the Mass is primarily community worship, and not individual worship, the form is fairly well set. In some parts we listen to the Word of God, in others we pray with the priest. The Mass is generally divided into six parts. First there is preparation which consists of greetings and an act of penance. Second is the Liturgy of the Word. This consists of three readings and the recitation of a psalm plus an alleluia verse. The first two readings, usually read by a lector, are taken from the Old Testament and one of the Epistles. The third reading, usually given by the priest, is from the Gospels. This is followed by a homily which seeks to give meaning and unity to the day's liturgy. This section of Mass closes with all reciting the Creed or Profession of Faith in which we remind ourselves of our basic beliefs.

The third part is the Preparation of the Gifts or Offertory. In ancient times the people would bring their gifts to the altar. Now this act is symbolized by the bringing of the wine, water and bread to be used at the Mass. The people make their gifts in money which goes to the support of the parish.

When the preparatory prayers are over, the fourth and central part of the Mass begins. It is called the Liturgy of the Eucharist. It begins with a preface, or special preparatory prayer. There are four Eucharistic canons from which the priest can choose. Usually the third is said on Sunday. The first and fourth are used on special feast days while the second is usually used on weekdays. In this section of the Mass the reenactment of Calvary takes place and the wine and water and bread become the Body of Christ. It is in this section, too, that the people recite the perfect prayer, the Our Father, taught us by Jesus Himself. At the end, the priest consumes the Sacred Species.

Next comes the Communion of the faithful. Finally Mass ends with closing prayers, a blessing and dismissal. Hymns are sung at various times principally at the Entrance, Offertory, Communion and Departure.

Mr. J. Wasn't Mass formerly said in Latin.

Father S. Yes, and it may still be. But in the Liturgical Reform after Vatican II permission was given to use the vernacular, thus making the Mass more understandable to the people. However, it is recommended that certain Latin parts be retained such as singing the Kyrie, Gloria, Credo and Pater Noster (Our Father). Unfortunately this wish of the Holy See is carried out in very few parishes.

Mr. J. Why do you say "unfortunately"?

Father S. The use of some Latin would preserve our ancient traditions and give a greater sense of unity to the Church. The few parts I mentioned can be easily understood by the people. However Latin was not the only language used in the Mass.

In Greece and Turkey the ancient Greek language is used in the Mass. In certain other countries, where other languages were developed, and where the ceremonies in Latin are not in use, the clergy have been permitted to retain the language in which the Mass was first offered in their respective countries.

Although the Liturgists would prefer us not to use Mass aids, let me suggest, Mr. Jackson, that you procure an English Missal, and use it when you attend Mass. Remember you will be slow at first, until you become familiar with the names and places of the parts of the Mass in the Missal. There is a certain propriety in the people joining themselves with the priest at the altar, saying the same prayers he does.

Mr. J. But, Father, you did not tell me what regulates the practice of kneeling, standing and sitting. I have been merely doing what the others do.

Father S. I am glad that you reminded me of this. There may be slight variations in different places due to local customs, but the practices are usually uniform in this country. We stand for the preparatory prayers, sit during the first two readings, stand for the Gospel, sit during the homily, stand for the Credo and sit during the Offertory. We stand again for the Preface and its response, then kneel through the consecration and following prayers. We stand for the Our Father and then kneel through Communion. We stand for the final prayers and blessing.

There are other questions, Mr. Jackson, which you will probably be prompted to ask, but you will usually find answers for them in Catholic pamphlets, and books, and in a Missal itself.

The main thing to keep in mind is that the Mass is not so much a prayer as a sacrificial *action*, in which Christ, through the priest, makes the same offering He made at the Last Supper, which has no less value than the offering He made on Calvary the next day, because a sacrificial offering has its value *from the object offered and from the dignity of the person offering it.*

At the Mass, as at the Last Supper and on Calvary, *Christ is the Victim* offered, and when the consecration of the Mass is effected by His representative, *He is the real priest Who makes His own offering.*

INSTRUCTION 38

Penance: Sacrament of Reconciliation

Those who approach the Sacrament of Penance obtain pardon from the mercy of God for offenses committed against Him. They are at the same time reconciled with the Church, which they have wounded by their sins, and which by charity, example, and prayer seeks their conversion. — *The Church, 11.*

Father S. Now, Mr. Jackson, we shall give some study to the sacrament which most non-Catholics find it most difficult to understand. They wonder why people should have to confess to a priest the sins they committed against God.

Mr. J. It would be difficult for me to accept such teaching if I had not already learned that confession is part of a *sacrament* and that the sacraments are administered by the duly ordained ministers of Christ's Church.

Father S. But ordinarily non-Catholics do not agree that Christ instituted a sacrament to take away sins committed after Baptism.

Mr. J. If He instituted a sacrament to take away original sin and sins committed before Baptism, why not one to take away sins committed *after* Baptism?

Father S. That's thinking straight, but they would answer you by saying that, while confession is necessary, it should be confession to God, not to man. However, that's the precise question. It has always been God's policy to deal with man through man. God gave him primitive revelation through the patriarchs, and they were commissioned to impart it to others. He gave the Ten Commandments to Moses, who was delegated to acquaint the people with them. The Son of God became *the Son of man,* in order to establish His Church among men; and the Bible emphasizes the fact that He forgave sins as the "Son of Man," as one sent by God (Matt. 9:5-6). When Saul was converted miraculously, Christ spoke to him: (Acts 9:6) "Get up and go into the city, where you will be told what to do." When the lepers implored Jesus to heal them, His condition was: "Go and show yourselves to the priest" (Luke 17:14).

Just as Christ commissioned His Apostles (and not others except their successors) to baptize, to preach the gospel, to consecrate the Eucharist, so He most explicitly delegated them to forgive sins in His name (John 20:23).

As you have already intimated, why should God institute a sacrament to forgive sins a first time, if there were not to be another sacrament to forgive the sins committed after one is baptized? Then, man needs external conditions to comply with. When the ceremony of Baptism is performed we know that our souls are cleansed. So for a feeling of security that the sins committed after Baptism are forgiven, we need certain external requirements to comply with. If I were to confess to Almighty God, and not hear in an audible way that I was forgiven, I would not be satisfied. I might *hope* that I am forgiven, but I should want a greater assurance in a matter of so great importance. When I am told that I must examine my conscience, be truly sorry, confess my guilt, resolve to amend, and then, by a delegate of God, have words of absolution pronounced over me, I feel that I can go away happy. I want as much assurance of forgiveness as Magdalen had from the words of Jesus Himself.

Mr. J. If sin be the only obstacle to salvation, I would want to feel assured that I was forgiven.

Father S. Then, too, it is somewhat natural to tell our conscience troubles to somebody, even if we have already confessed to God. Many a non-Catholic unburdens himself to a priest, because he wants to tell someone and has heard that the priest is obliged not to reveal what is confided to him as a confession. Only recently a gentleman sat down with me on the plane, and after a half-hour's conversation said: "You are used to hearing confessions, and I am going to tell you some things which have been troubling me; I know that I shall feel better." I presume you know that the priest never reveals anything he hears in confession.

Mr. J. I have been told so, and I am sure he would not violate so sacred a trust.

Father S. So sacredly is confession regarded that if my father had been recently murdered, and you confessed to me that you were the murderer, I would not be allowed to report you; more than that, I would not be permitted to allude to it, nor act differently toward you, if you called at my house immediately after the confession. Information which I receive in the confessional I am not allowed to use or to act on in any way.

Mr. J. This assurance should take fear away, and establish confidence. We expect doctors and lawyers to observe confidentiality, how much more the priest to whom is revealed a man's innermost secrets.

Father S. Then we are not obliged to ask a single question in the confessional, and do not, unless we feel that the penitent has not properly examined his conscience. Our non-Catholic friends should get their information about the confessional from the people who go to confession, and not from the ones who find it profitable to misrepresent it. I presume you know that the priest himself goes to confession?

Mr. J. I suppose he does, if he sins.

Father S. It's not just a question of sin. Priests, bishops, and the Pope go to confession since they must save their souls and need God's grace like any other member of the Church. The Sacrament of Penance, like the other sacraments, confers grace even when the penitent has but little to confess. The holiest people go to confession frequently. Now would priests themselves go to confession, and would they go miles in bad weather to hear the confessions of the sick, go even to the bedside of a man dying of smallpox or cholera, if they did not believe in the divine institution and the forgiving power of this sacrament?

Mr. J. You answer your own questions. Is the Rite of Penance always the same?

Father S. There are accidental variations. Some people prefer to see the priest face to face to discuss problems, others prefer the anonymity of the confessional box. But no matter how the rite is administered certain parts must be retained — the confession of sins, the acceptance of the act of penance, the invitation to contrition, the form of absolution and the dismissal. However, in case of immanent death all this is shorten and the priest may merely say, "I absolve you from your sins in the name of the Father and the Son and the Holy Spirit."

Before you go home today, I shall take you over to the church and show you the confessional. Any of your non-Catholic friends are also welcome to examine it. They will find that it offers no occasion for evil, that the priest does not even know who is the penitent. I did not intend to dwell so long on the reasonableness of the sacrament and on these many side issues, but probably it is good that I did. In our next instruction, we shall talk about the divine institution of the sacrament of Penance.

However, what I would like you to remember especially from our discussion this evening is this: By deliberate sin, a person separates himself or herself from God. Yet out of love for us, God has given us a sure way to reconcile ourselves to Him again. This way is the Sacrament of Penance, which the Church also calls the Sacrament of Reconciliation.

Scripture Proof for Penance

(The Church) is therefore holy, though she has sinners in her bosom, because she has no other life but that of grace; it is by living by her life that her members are sanctified; it is by removing themselves from her life that they fall into sins and disorders that prevent the radiation of her sanctity. — *Credo of the People of God.*

Father S. Since you are favorably disposed towards the belief that Christ committed to His Church the power to forgive sins, the Scripture authority on this point will have great weight.

Mr. J. I'll be glad to have it pointed out to me.

Father S. In Chapter 20, verses 21, 22, 23, St. John tells of our Savior's appearance to the Apostles on the day of His Resurrection, when He greeted them with the words He had never used before: "Peace be with you!" After repeating the greeting, "Peace be with you," the Savior transferred to the Apostles the great mission which He descended from Heaven to perform: "As the Father has sent Me, so I send you."

Mr. J. And Christ was sent by the Father primarily to reconcile sinful man with God?

Father S. Surely. The angel who announced His coming to Joseph said: "And you are to name Him Jesus. Because He shall save His people from their sins" (Matt. 1:21). By His words and parables He made that plain. "For I have come to call not the self-righteous, but sinners." (Matt. 9:13); "The Son of Man has come to search out and save what is lost" (Luke 19:10). In the parables of the "Prodigal Son," of the "Good Samaritan," and of the "Good Shepherd," He taught that His mission was to call to repentance and to forgive the individual sinner. Christ absolved only individuals, such as Mary Magdalen, Zacchaeus, the penitent thief, the Samaritan woman at the well.

Mr. J. If that was Christ's chief mission, and He express-ly stated that He was transferring it to the Apostles, that should settle the matter.

Father S. It certainly should. But the plainer declaration of Christ, following immediately the words quoted above, re-moves all doubt. St. John continues: "Then he breathed on them and said: Receive the Holy Spirit" (John 20:22). To my mind this was so significant that non-Catholics should see through the institution of the Sacrament of Penance with their eyes shut. Holy Scripture says that God *breathed* into Adam's newly created body a living soul — a spirit. By breathing on the Apostles, Christ communicated to them the Holy Spirit; in fact, He expressly says so, "Receive the Holy Spirit" while in the act of breathing on them. This was evidently to empower them to fulfill their God-given mission. Then following these words and this act came the clearest transfer of power: "If you forgive men's sins, they are forgiven them; if you hold them bound, they are held bound." One who will not be convinced by these plain words of Jesus surely does not want to be con-vinced.

Mr. J. I should like to have an argument for those who might say that while Christ did confer such a commission on the Apostles, He promised nothing to bishops and priests of a later age.

Father S. What would be the difference whether succes-sors of Apostles were called "bishops and priests" or whether they were called by some other name? Christ surely intended that the work of absolving repentant sinners should be continued until the end of the world. Following the death of the Apostles, others must succeed to this office, otherwise one must hold that the Church of Christ was to endure only through one generation of people, and that sin came to an end with the death of the Apostles.

Mr. J. It seems clear that the remedy for sin must last as long as the disease, sin, exists in the world, and that will be until the world's end. I can see that the power to forgive sins in the name of God should remain and continue to be exercised by those properly ordained, but where does confession of sin come in?

Father S. Note well that the power was of forgiving and *retaining* or refusing forgiveness. They were to forgive or withhold forgiveness as they judged the person worthy or unworthy. This meant that they had to know what they were forgiving, the disposition of the sinner, his resolutions for the future, his willingness to repair the harm done to the neighbor by his sins. Who could make this known except the sinner himself? Sin and sorrow for sin spring from the heart.

Why, confession was known even in Old Testament times. It was *the Sacrament of Penance* which Christ instituted. But the practice of confession of sin was even then a condition for forgiveness. We read in the book of Numbers 5:5-7: "If a man (or woman) commits a fault against his fellow man and wrongs him . . . he shall confess the wrong he has done, restore his ill-gotten goods in full, and in addition give one-fifth of their value to the one he has wronged."

Mr. J. I never thought of it that way.

Father S. That is the way in which the Church has always believed and acted, for Christ made it an important matter. The confession of mortal sin is a requirement for eternal salvation. Does that answer your question?

Mr. J. Yes, it does.

Father S. Have you ever heard that Catholics pay for the forgiveness of sin?

Mr. J. Yes, Father, but I was never foolish enough to believe it.

Father S. Then I presume you have also heard that Catholics may run to confession, be absolved, and start out to commit new sins — much as a child can fill his slate with figures, erase them, then fill it up again?

Mr. J. I have heard that. I have even heard that sins are forgiven in advance, and that licenses to commit sin may be granted by the Pope or priest.

Father S. Yes, this is the notion of "indulgences" that so many falsely entertain. We shall discuss it in one of our next instructions as well as the resolution needed to amend one's life.

Now let me explain the effects of this wonderful sacrament. When you receive it, you receive Sanctifying Grace and the forgiveness of your sins; the everlasting punishment due to them is remitted if you had committed mortal sins, and even part, at least, of the temporal punishment due to your sins is remitted. God's grace received through this sacrament helps you to avoid future sin. Moreover, you are given the opportunity to receive spiritual advice and instruction from the priest.

Contrition and Confession

In the spirit of Christ the Shepherd, priests should train them (the Faithful) to submit their sins with a contrite heart to the Church in the Sacrament of Penance. Thus mindful of the Lord's words: "Repent, for the kingdom of God is at hand" (Matt. 4:17), the people will be drawn ever closer to Him each day. — *Priests, 5.*

Father S. We have learned that Almighty God forgives actual sin through a sacrament, just as He forgives Original Sin through a sacrament. We have seen that even babies should receive the sacrament of Baptism in order that the Holy Spirit may enter their souls and remit Original Sin by giving them Sanctifying Grace. There is no need for one to confess or even to be sorry for Original Sin, because it was not personally committed by the one who seeks its removal through Baptism.

But it is different with "actual" sin, or those sins which we commit ourselves. They are not taken away unless the one who commits them acknowledges them, is sorry for them, and resolves to reform.

Mr. J. According to what you say the mere confessing of sins does not take them away.

Father S. You are right. You might go to confession to a priest, to a bishop, to the Pope, and acknowledge in detail the various ways in which you have offended God, and still remain unforgiven.

Mr. J. What would be especially wanting in that confession?

Father S. Supernatural sorrow and a firm resolution of amendment. Evidently God is not going to forgive sins for which we have no sorrow, or when we have no intention of changing our lives. Our sorrow must be *supernatural,* which means that with the help of God's grace it must flow from a heart that is sorry for having offended God or for having deserved His punishment in the next world. We must be prompted by motives that spring from Christian faith.

The very theological term used for sorrow expresses this fact. It is called "contrition," which implies "a tearing of the heart." Contrition is either perfect or imperfect. It is *perfect* when it is prompted by the love of God, which means that we are sorry for our sins because they offend God who is so deserving of our love and we grieve for having been so disloyal and ungrateful as to defy His law.

It is *imperfect* when we are sorry chiefly because by our sin we deserve to lose Heaven and to be punished in Hell. There is, as you can see, considerable self-interest in this kind of sorrow. Yet it is *supernatural,* because we believe Heaven is what it is because God is there; and Hell is chiefly what it is because God is *not* there.

We know that our sorrow is genuine when it is internal, coming from the heart, not merely from the lips; when we are sorry for all the mortal sins that we may have had the misfortune to commit; when we are willing to endure anything rather than offend God in the future.

Imperfect contrition is sufficient for a worthy confession, but you should try to have true perfect contrition. In fact, anyone who commits a mortal sin should make an act of perfect contrition at once and go to confession as soon as possible. Such a person should not receive the Holy Eucharist until after confession.

Mr. J. What about venial sins?

Father S. We should try to be sorry for our venial sins

when we go to confession because they are displeasing to God and may lead us to mortal sin. It is not necessary to confess venial sins, but it is better to do so. If we have only venial sins to confess we should have the firm purpose of avoiding at least one of them in the future. However, in every confession we should have the firm and sincere purpose of avoiding mortal sin in the future, and as far as possible the near occasions of sin.

Mr. J. Non-Catholics certainly have a wrong notion about confession. I never heard people say that Catholics believe the *Sacrament of Penance* forgives sins, but rather that confession does. I have always heard them say that confessing sins to a priest insures their forgiveness, whether they intend to reform or not.

Father S. Yes, unfortunately, they entertain unfounded prejudices against this most consoling sacrament precisely because they do not understand it. If I were told a priest could forgive sins of his own power, or that the mere confession of sins to the priest would procure their forgiveness, I would have the same prejudice.

It is the *sacrament* that takes away sins committed after Baptism, just as there is a sacrament which takes away all the sins you have committed prior to your Baptism. Baptism is not repeated every time one sins, but the Sacrament of Penance was instituted to be applied frequently. Confession is only a part of the Sacrament of Penance. We are told that *five things* are required of us for the worthy reception of the Sacrament of Penance, namely, the examination of one's conscience, the arousing of supernatural sorrow, the firm purpose of amendment, the confessing of the sins, and the fulfillment of the penance imposed by the priest.

Mr. J. For fear I do not understand you fully, would you explain what is meant by the *examination of conscience?*

Father S. It means that the one who would receive the Sacrament of Penance must reflect, stir up the memory, and ask God's help to determine in what ways He has been offended since one last received the sacrament. And, in the case of mortal sin, the *number of times* the sin was committed.

We can make a good examination of conscience by going over in our minds, or with the help of a prayer book, the Commandments of God and of the Church, our various duties, the vices (such as pride, envy, sloth, intemperance in eating and drinking, and greed), and by asking ourselves if we have sinned in their regard.

Mr. J. Isn't it difficult to determine the number of times with exactness?

Father S. Yes, it can be, but not for those who go to confession frequently, and who seldom commit a mortal sin. But when it is practically impossible to determine exactly, it is necessary only to determine the number of times as nearly as possible. If one has contracted the habit of committing a certain sin and has been away from the Sacrament of Penance for three months, say, one is obliged to tell the priest "about" how often the sin was committed each week, on average.

Mr. J. After this examination of conscience, when the person has a sort of bird's-eye view of his or her conduct since last receiving the sacrament, is presumably the time to awaken sorrow for having been so wicked.

Father S. Yes, sorrow for one's sins should certainly be awakened before one enters the confessional — that's why the Church wants us to make an act of contrition before receiving the Sacrament of Penance. Of course, saying an act of contrition merely *expresses* that sorrow; saying only the words, purely from memory, without any sorrow of heart, would not mean much.

In the confessional, before a person receives absolution from the priest, he or she confesses sins, humbly and frankly and entirely — their kind, the number of times, and any circumstances that might alter the character of a particular sin.

Mr. J. And if a person should forget to tell a mortal sin?

Father S. If a person accidentally forgets to confess a mortal sin, he or she can receive Holy Communion but should mention the sin in the next confession. Deliberately to conceal a mortal sin in confession is an abuse of the sacrament (which itself is a sin of sacrilege), and no sins are forgiven. In such a case, one is obliged to confess that one has made a false confession, mention any sacraments received since that confession, and confess any mortal sins committed since one's last "good" confession. Only then can a priest grant the person absolution.

Mr. J. Can you explain a bit more about absolution?

Father S. After a penitent finishes the confession of sins, the priest offers advice and counsel and then pronounces forgiveness of the sins. The words of this *absolution* are: "I absolve you from your sins, in the name of the Father and of the Son and of the Holy Spirit."

Mr. J. You said that one must also perform some penance after the confession.

Father S. Yes, it is customary for the priest to give the penitent a penance to perform. It is usually very easy, but because it is a *sacramental* penance, it has considerable value before God by way of atonement for our sins, and by way of satisfaction for the temporal punishment due to them. God requires temporal punishment for sin to satisfy His justice, to teach us the great evil of sin and to warn us not to sin again.

Mr. J. When is this penance performed?

Father S. If it consists of saying certain prayers, then it should be taken care of immediately after confession, before one leaves the church. Sometimes the person may be asked to perform some good action. In that case, the penance should be fulfilled as prescribed.

Mr. J. Would you now kindly tell me, Father, just how the penitent should make his confession?

Father S. After one has made an examination of conscience and awakened interior sorrow for one's sins, one is ready to enter the confessional. Do you remember how a confessional is arranged?

Mr. J. Yes, I noted that the confessional is so constructed that while one person is occupied with his confession at one side of the priest, another is in waiting on the other side.

Father S. Do you know why there is always one in waiting?

Mr. J. I presume it is to prevent the delay which would otherwise be required for one penitent to follow another.

Father S. That is correct. Frequently there is a line of people preparing to go to confession at the same time and the reduction of any delay is certainly helpful.

Mr. J. How does a penitent start his confession?

Father S. Make the Sign of the Cross and ask for the priest's blessing, saying, "Bless me, Father. I have sinned." Then tell how long it has been since your last confession. After the priest welcomes you, you confess your sins in the manner we have just discussed. When you have finished, the priest will offer you spiritual advice and assign you a penance. This would be the time when you would ask the priest any questions you have, perhaps about a personal problem the priest might be able to help you solve. The priest will then pronounce the words of absolution.

Indulgences

"I will entrust to you the keys of the kingdom of heaven. Whatever you declare bound on earth shall be bound in heaven; whatever you declare loosed on earth shall be loosed in heaven." — *Matt. 16:19.*

Father S. Tonight our instruction will be on the much misunderstood subject of "indulgences." It might be best for me to explain first that the conception which the generality of non-Catholics have of indulgences is most erroneous.

Mr. J. What do they believe to be the Church's teaching?

Father S. Many of them suppose that an indulgence is a pardon of sin for money, or even a license to commit sin.

Mr. J. I told you the other night that I had heard this, but do you really think that many hold such notions?

Father S. I am sure of it; recently an aged minister, one who preached for years, but who is now drawing a pension as a retired minister, told me that the universally accepted definition of "indulgence" by the non-Catholic world is "a license to sin for a remuneration."

Mr. J. Where did they get such ideas?

Father S. Well, it is maintained that the so-called Reformation of the sixteenth century was occasioned by the sale of and traffic in indulgences; this, they say, is evidence that they are, or were, sold. Then the plain meaning of the word "indul-

gence" is, they say, "a yielding to excess," a "favor granted,"
"a license." Therefore it is a license to sin for a contribution of
money.

Mr. J. How do you answer their charge?

Father S. The ecclesiastical meaning of the Latin word
"indulgentia" is *"pardon,"* but *not* a pardon of *sin,* much less
a license to sin. In fact, it has no reference to sin at all, which is
pardoned by the worthy reception of the Sacrament of Penance. It is not a pardon of sin, but of the *temporal punishment*
due to sin already forgiven.

Mr. J. What is meant by "temporal punishment" still
due after the sins are forgiven?

Father S. Let us suppose a case: You have committed a
grievous sin which renders you liable to eternal punishment.
But you sincerely repent of and confess the sin and receive
absolution.

Mr. J. Yes, Father.

Father S. By your good confession the guilt of the mortal
sin was removed, and also the eternal punishment which you
deserved. But if your sorrow was not as earnest and intense as
God would have from you, you might be punished for a brief
period in Purgatory. This would be the *temporal* punishment
deserved for your sins. The temporal punishment can be removed by the performance of penances, good works, and
prayer; and also by an "indulgence" the Church applies to
your soul through the merits of Christ for the expiation of your
fault. Even *forgiven* sins demand some expiation — if not here
on earth, then before one enters heaven.

A Scripture example will make the case clearer. David,
many of whose psalms are outburst of repentance for two
grievous sins he committed, received assurance from God,
through the prophet Nathan, that his crimes were forgiven,
but that nevertheless his son would be taken from him. This
was to be his temporal punishment after he repented and his
sin was forgiven.

Mr. J. If the temporal punishment is not endured here, or

is not removed by penance or good works, it will be inflicted in Purgatory. Am I right?

Father S. Yes; unless remitted through the application of Christ's merits to the soul by the Church, by the grant of an indulgence.

Mr. J. The indulgence is not granted at the time of confession?

Father S. No; the Church attaches indulgences to certain prayers, or good works, which become effective if performed by a person who is in the state of grace (free from sin) and otherwise properly disposed. An indulgence is either plenary of partial: that is, either calculated to remove *all* or *only part* of the temporal punishment. Partial indulgences are usually attached to prayers, while for a plenary indulgence it is nearly always required that the person receive Holy Communion and pay a visit to the church, where he must say more prayers for the success of God's interests on earth, especially as they are in the mind of the Pope.

Mr. J. Compliance with such conditions always secures the plenary of indulgence?

Father S. Not always. If the person be somewhat attached to the sin for which temporal punishment would be due, if his sorrow be not sufficiently intense, he would not gain the indulgence *in all its fullness*.

Mr. J. Since an indulgence can be gained only after the person's sins are wholly forgiven, I suppose, if a plenary indulgence be actually gained before one's death, that one avoids Purgatory, and has assurance of immediate entrance into heaven, does he not?

Father S. Yes.

Mr. J. Can a person gain an indulgence for someone else?

Father S. We cannot gain indulgences for other *living* persons, but we can gain them for the souls in Purgatory, since the Church makes most indulgences applicable to them.

Mr. J. And money is never paid for an indulgence?

Father S. No; as I have said, works of penance, prayers,

Holy Communion, visits to a church, and so on, may be among the conditions named for the gaining of an indulgence; and since the Bible recommends alms as a work pleasing to God, the offering of an alms might be asked, but not in return for the indulgence.

Remember that a person who has not confessed and repented of his sin could not gain an indulgence for any amount of prayers, alms and good works. Let us refute the case of "indulgence-traffic," of which the so-called Reformer accused the Church. Pope Leo X, at the beginning of the sixteenth century, when all Europe was Catholic, decided to erect in Rome a cathedral church such as should exist in the capital city of the Christian world. He asked for small contributions from Catholics throughout Europe, and promulgated a plenary indulgence to all who should *pray* for the success of the cause, *go to confession and receive Holy Communion worthily,* and *contribute an alms towards the erection of the great cathedral.* Now any instructed Catholic knows that the indulgence *could not be given* in return for an alms, no matter how great, without previous confession and Communion.

I have told you that even today, some good work, such as visiting a church, is required for the gaining of a plenary indulgence, even after confession and Communion. The good work specified in that instance was an alms, but the papal letter expressly declared that the poor could gain the same indulgence by performing good works of another nature.

Mr. J. To me this instance is much the same as the frequent announcements from Protestant pulpits that Almighty God will grant special favors and blessings to those who contribute for home or foreign missionary work.

Father S. It was quite the same. But to explain the grounds for the non-Catholic contention that indulgences were *sold:* At that time there was no telegraph service, there were no daily newspapers to acquaint the people of Europe with the desire and the project of the Pope. It had to be done by sending preachers to the several countries. John Tetzel, head of the

Dominican order of priests, was commissioned to preach the indulgence in Germany. It might be that *uninstructed Catholics thought* that the indulgence was given in return for their alms. We shall even grant, for sake of argument, that Tetzel himself abused his charge, but that would not implicate the Church. It would never have justifed Luther of the Augustinian order of priests, to repudiate his vows, and attack the Church.

Mr. J. No, John Tetzel was not the Catholic Church.

Anointing of the Sick

By the sacred anointing of the sick and the prayer of her priests, the whole Church commends those who are ill to the suffering and glorified Lord, asking that He may lighten their suffering and save them (cf. James 5:14-16). — *The Church, 11.*

Father S. The Catholic Church has divine help to benefit man from the cradle to the grave. It administers a sacrament to the infant soon after birth, and after caring for her children all through life, it has a sacrament for them when they are seriously ill. However, even the aged can avail themselves of this sacrament, even though they may not be sick. It is known as Anointing of the Sick.

In this sacrament the priest anoints the sick person with oil, which is blessed once a year for this sacrament by the bishop. The oil is applied in the form of a cross to the forehead and hands while the anointing is accompanied by a prayer that God may help the patient through the Holy Spirit and save him and raise him up.

Mr. J. Does the Bible make reference to the practice of anointing the sick?

Father S. Yes. In the Epistle of St. James (5:14-15) we read: "Is there anyone sick among you? He should ask for the presbyters of the Church. They in turn are to pray over him, anointing him with oil in the name of the Lord. This prayer uttered in faith will reclaim the one who is ill, and the Lord will restore him to health. If he has committed any sins, forgiveness will be his."

The Protestant version calls "elders" what we call "presbyters" or "priests." But why should lay persons be called in to pray for and to anoint the dying with oil?

The Greek word used is "presbyteros" and that it signifies "priest" is clear from the fact that in the ceremonial of the first Christians the word for "priesthood" is "presbyteratus." This comment may be a little heavy but it may help you if you ever need the information.

Mr. J. From that I judge that only a priest can administer the Anointing of the Sick.

Father S. That's right.

Mr. J. I wonder why oil was chosen for this sacrament.

Father S. Because Anointing of the Sick was to act on the soul as oil does on the body: it strengthens and heals. The Good Samaritan poured oil on the wounds of the man who had fallen among robbers.

Mr. J. That text from St. James seems to imply that the sacrament works a physical cure for the person.

Father S. It sometimes does that, as every priest and many physicians have witnessed. But its primary purpose is to heal and strengthen the soul and prepare it for eternity. It does this by increasing Sanctifying Grace, giving strength against temptation, remitting venial sin and cleansing from the remains of sin. Thus it is a preparation for death, if God wills that the person should die, and it hastens a restoration of health if God be pleased to let the person recover.

Mr. J. Therefore, when the priest is called to administer Anointing of the Sick, the Catholic need not conclude that he is surely to die?

Father S. Not at all, though some Catholics do wait until too late. Viaticum is for the dying. Anointing is for the living, not for the moment of death.

Mr. J. When should Anointing of the Sick be given?

Father S. The sacrament is meant for all who are dangerously or seriously ill, or the aged.

Mr. J. Then not only those who are about to die should receive this sacrament.

Father S. That is correct. The Church urges us to pray for those who are ill. Christ's ministry to the sick is continued in the Church. The sick are anointed so that they might be restored to health, be enabled to bear their suffering in union with the passion of Christ, and be prepared for death which eventually comes to all of us.

Mr. J. What happens when a person dies suddenly and unexpectedly?

Father S. In that case, the priest should always be called, because he can give absolution and Anointing of the Sick conditionally (on condition that the soul may not have left the body) for some time after death has apparently taken place.

Mr. J. How old must the person be to receive this sacrament?

Father S. Any person who is capable of sinning should receive it, since the sacrament completes the work of confession. Often the sick, because of pain, or half-unconsciousness, are unable to make a complete confession; and Anointing of the Sick remits the sins which the sick person was unable to confess providing he was at least imperfectly sorry for them.

Mr. J. May Anointing of the Sick be given only once to the same person?

Father S. If a person recovers but falls ill again, the anointing is repeated; even in the same illness, it is repeated if the illness worsens.

Mr. J. How should a sick person prepare for this sacrament?

Father S. If possible, one should receive the Sacrament of Penance, renew one's faith, hope and love in and for God, and resign oneself to God's will.

Mr. J. Has the Church any other help for the dying?

Father S. Yes. The Church empowers the priest to impart a plenary indulgence by what she calls a "last blessing." But this is not effective if the person should recover. After receiving this blessing the dying person kisses the crucifix and pronounces verbally, if possible, or at least in his heart, the name "Jesus."

Mr. J. I presume that certain things must be prepared for Anointing of the Sick in the room of the sick person?

Father S. Yes. There should be a stand or table near the foot of the bed, covered with a clean cloth, and on the table a lighted candle, crucifix, holy water, and a little salt or piece of bread or cotton.

Mr. J. What is the bread or salt for?

Father S. The priest uses it to cleanse his thumb from the holy oil, after which the salt or bread is burned.

Mr. J. Is the anointing followed by Holy Communion?

Father S. Yes, though not always immediately. We might confer Anointing of the Sick in the afternoon or evening and bring Holy Communion the next morning.

Mr. J. What preparation is made at the home when Holy Communion is brought to the sick?

Father S. The table is prepared in the same manner as for Anointing of the Sick, with this exception: no salt or bread is needed. But there should be a glass of water and a spoon, and a napkin to place under the chin of the sick person.

Mr. J. What are the water and spoon needed for?

Father S. The priest purifies his thumb and index finger, which touched the Sacred Host, in a spoon filled with water. This is then received by the sick person.

Holy Orders

Those of the faithful who are consecrated by Holy Orders are appointed to feed the Church in Christ's name with the Word and the grace of God. — *The Church, 11.*

Father S. Tonight we shall give some study to that sacrament which is needed to empower a person to administer most of the others. It is known as *Holy Orders.*

No man could forgive sins except by delegated power; no man could change bread and wine into the Body and Blood of Christ without being empowered by Christ Himself. Hence it was necessary for Christ to institute a sacrament, whereby the supernatural authority and power needed to carry on His redemptive work would be conferred. This is done by bishops, priests and other ministers of the Church.

Mr. J. I see; no one could become a self-appointed priest, and presume to forgive sins.

Father S. Certainly not. Christ said to His Apostles: "It was not you who chose me, it was I who chose you" (John 15:16); and St. Paul says: "Every high priest is taken from among men and made their representative before God. . . . One does not take this honor on his own initiative, but only when called by God as Aaron was" (Heb. 5:1,4).

Mr. J. When did Christ institute the sacrament of Holy Orders?

Father S. At the Last Supper, when after exercising the priesthood "according to the order of Melchisedech," He empowered the Apostles to do the same: "Do this in remembrance of Me." Then on the day of His Resurrection, He empowered His Apostle-priests to forgive sin in His name: "If you forgive men's sins, they are forgiven them; if you hold them bound, they are held bound." Finally, immediately before His return to Heaven, He commissioned them to teach and baptize in His name.

Mr. J. Is there any record of the Apostles conferring Holy Orders on others?

Father S. Yes, as a matter of fact, four successive generations of priests are mentioned in the New Testament. In Acts 13:3, we read of the (1) *Apostles* laying hands upon (2) *Paul* and Barnabas, bishops; and 2 Tim. 1:6, tells of Paul having elevated Timothy to the same dignity. Then Paul writing to (3) *Titus,* says: "My purpose of leaving you in Crete was that you might accomplish what had been left undone, especially the appointment of (4) presbyters in every town" (Titus 1:5). Read also Acts 14:22.

Mr. J. How is this sacrament conferred?

Father S. In a very impressive ceremony a bishop, and only a bishop, who himself is a legitimate successor of the Apostles, lays his hands on the candidate for ordination, calls down upon him the Holy Spirit, anoints his hands, and presents him with the sacred vessels and Sacramentary used at the Mass, and commissions him to offer Mass for the living and the dead, to forgive sin, to bless and consecrate.

Mr. J. How old must one be to receive this Sacrament?

Father S. Twenty-four.

Mr. J. How long is the course of training in preparation of Holy Orders?

Father S. Usually 12 years.

Mr. J. The student has to begin his studies pretty young then?

Father S. Of course, one may be ordained at any age after

24. Some boys begin their studies for the priesthood soon after they finish the elementary school. However, in recent years older boys are sought, after high school or college.

Mr. J. Are there any other requirements?

Father S. Yes, the man should be called to Holy Orders by his bishop. He should have the intention of devoting his life to the sacred ministry. Of course, he should be in the state of grace when he receives this sacrament because it gives him an increase of Sanctifying Grace and also sacramental graces through which he has God's constant help in the ministry.

Mr. J. You said before that Holy Orders confers a character that lasts forever.

Father S. Yes, once a priest, always a priest. The character is a special sharing in the priesthood of Christ and gives the priest the special priestly powers which I mentioned at the beginning of our instruction.

Mr. J. What are some of the obligations of the priesthood? Of course, I know that the priest is bound to remain unmarried. But in recent years we hear of priests leaving the priesthood.

Father S. Yes, we touched on the obligation of celibacy before. As for priests leaving, the Holy See allows a priest to return to the lay state for sufficient reason. This may or may not involve a remission of the vow of celibacy. Some enter the priesthood who are immature or not even certain of their vocation. The Church seeks total dedication that such men cannot give. Rather than hold them as disgruntled and unhappy priests, the Church relieves them of all responsibilities and privileges of the clerical state and allows them to return to the life of a layman.

Mr. J. Would you mind telling me what some other duties of the priest are?

Father S. There are many other duties; for instance, he must be ready to go on a sick-call at any hour and to any patient, no matter if the dying person be quarantined against everybody else. Then in large parishes, he must hear confessions every Saturday and on other days of the month. This is really a *burden* to the priesthood, no matter how non-Catholics may view it. It goes without saying that he must deny himself many worldly amusements.

Mr. J. I presume, too, that because of his self-consecration to God's work, he feels that he has considerable responsibility?

Father S. Precisely; he feels in a measure responsible for every soul committed to his care, and is pained when any one of them leaves the path of virtue. Of course, he enjoys abundant consolation, nevertheless.

Mr. J. I see now why Catholics feel they should revere and honor their priest as a representative of Christ.

Father S. Yes, they should. They should also interest themselves in his work because due to the need for more priests, only with the aid of his people can the priest hope to bring to all under his charge the knowledge of Christ and His Church. A good priest is a servant of the people.

Christian Marriage

Christian spouses, in virtue of the Sacrament of Matrimony, signify and partake of the mystery of that unity and fruitful love which exists between Christ and His Church (cf. Eph. 5:32). The spouses thereby help each other to attain to holiness in their married life and by the rearing and education of their children. And so, in their state and way of life, they have their own special gift (cf. 1 Cor. 7:7) among the People of God. — *The Church, 11.*

Father S. Every unmarried person should wish to be familiar with the attitude of the churches towards marriage, and should particularly be desirous of knowing how the oldest Christian Church — the Catholic Church which did all the marrying for so many centuries — views the marriage union.

Mr. J. That is true, because most people will eventually enter married life. How does the Church regard marriage?

Father S. According to the Church, it is the sacrament by which a baptized man and a baptized woman bind themselves for life in a lawful marriage and receive the grace to discharge their duties. The Church contends that God Himself is the author of the marriage bond, and that both parties to the contract are bound by it until the death of either one of them. Because divorce is common in our country, it is taken as much for granted as marriage, despite God's emphatic declaration on both marriage and divorce.

Mr. J. Does the Bible speak of God as the author of marriage?

Father S. Yes; in the book of Genesis, 2:22-24, we read of God uniting Adam and Eve to be "two in one body." And in Matt. 19:6, and Mark 10:9, Christ is reported as saying that it is God who "has joined" the two who are validly married.

Mr. J. Was marriage a sacrament before the coming of Christ?

Father S. No, it was a merely natural contract; only *baptized* people receive any sacrament, and baptism was instituted by Christ.

Mr. J. Well, is marriage always a sacrament for baptized people?

Father S. Yes. Our Lord plainly and emphatically stated that the husband cannot, during the life of his wife, have another wife, nor the wife, during the life of her husband, have another husband. "Therefore, let no man separate what God has joined" (Matt. 19:6). "Whoever divorces his wife and marries another commits adultery against her; and the woman who divorces her husband and marries another commits adultery" (Mark 10:11-2). Luke (16:18) uses almost the identical words. Likewise the Apostle Paul said: "A wife is bound to her husband as long as he lives" (1 Cor. 7:39).

Mr. J. So there may be no separation for any cause?

Father S. *Separation,* for good reasons is allowable, but the right to remarry is not allowed. St. Matthew (5:32) mentions "lewd conduct" as a reason for separation; and many persons understand him to mean that absolute divorce might be granted for that cause, but the other plain declarations, which we have just quoted, prove that *separation only* can be referred to by St. Matthew. From the time of the Apostles until the sixteenth century, the right to remarry after separation was never tolerated among Christian people. Even when Henry VIII, King of England, threatened to sever a whole nation from the Church unless he were given the permission to put away his lawful wife and marry another, the Church denied his request. In the face of God's evident will, the Church could not do otherwise.

Mr. J. Then the divorce laws of different states, and the divorce courts of thousands of countries may not dissolve a valid marriage?

Father S. Not at all. A couple validly married in the eyes of God remain validly married despite any civil laws which pretend to annul the marriage. The Church alone has the right to make laws regulating the marriages of baptized persons because the Church alone has authority over the sacraments and over sacred matters affecting baptized persons.

Mr. J. Has the state any rights in this matter?

Father S. As far as the marriage of baptized persons is concerned, the state has authority to make laws concerning the merely civil aspects of marriage: the civil registration, license, etc.

Mr. J. Comparatively speaking, are divorces as numerous in other countries?

Father S. No, some countries allow no divorce by law. Even our neighboring nation, Canada, is much more strict. We now have as many divorces as all the rest of the Christian nations combined, and more than any pagan country.

Mr. J. Is it true that the Catholic Church does not recognize as valid any marriage which the priest does not perform?

Father S. It is not true. The Church legislates *only for her own* members. For them marriage is a sacrament, and hence should be contracted before the priest, who is the proper person to witness a sacramental marriage.

Mr. J. Why do you say the priest "witnesses" the marriage?

Father S. Because he is not the minister of the sacrament, but only the Church's official witness. The bride and groom minister this sacrament to each other.

Mr. J. What would you say are the chief duties of husband and wife in the married state?

Father S. Their chief duties are determined by the very

purpose of marriage. They must be faithful to each other and should provide in every way for the children God may give them.

Mr. J. What is required of Catholics who wish to get married?

Father S. They are required to call on the parish priest at least three weeks before the date set for the marriage, in order to have the banns (announcement) published in church on three consecutive Sundays. They will also receive certain instructions on Christian marriage. Then they are to be married by the parish priest in the presence of two witnesses.

Mr. J. What if the man and the lady belong to two separate parishes?

Father S. Then the banns are supposed to be published in both churches, but in practice it is usually only in the church where the wedding will take place. The marriage ceremony should take place in the church which the bride attends. In fact the banns should be published in every place where the person has lived for six months. However, this practice is not followed strictly, instead, when the priest has any doubts, he makes discreet inquiries.

Mr. J. What is that for?

Father S. In order to elicit information concerning their freedom to marry. One of the parties may have been married and divorced and the priest requested to perform the marriage would have no evidence except the party's own word. Even in court one may not be his own sole witness.

Mr. J. Marriages are always held in the morning, are they not?

Father S. No, they can be held at any time. The Church wishes her children to be married in connection with a "Nuptial Mass," and, of course, Mass can be said in the afternoons and evening, as well.

Mr. J. The idea of being present at a Mass when being married is grand.

Father S. Not only is the couple present at Mass, but the

Mass is offered for them, and while Jesus is personally present on the altar, He is implored to bless the union and make it enduring and happy. Moreover, the bride and groom receive Jesus as their first food as husband and wife.

Mr. J. That kind of wedding surely resembles the marriage of Cana, which was blessed by Jesus.

Father S. It surpasses the marriage of Cana, for Christ had not yet elevated marriage to a sacrament, nor did He nourish that couple with the Eucharist. The Catholic couple is married when they are in the state of grace, and the sacrament increases Sanctifying Grace and imparts special helps for husband and wife to love each other faithfully, to bear with each other's faults, and to bring up their children properly.

Mr. J. It could not be improved on, Father. I surely would not wish to be married in any other way. May I ask you another question here?

Father S. Surely.

Mr. J. You explained why priests do not marry, but if I am correct, nuns do not marry either?

Father S. You are right. They even take a vow to live in chastity throughout life — for the simple reason that they consecrate their persons to Christ, and make a life's profession of serving Him in schools, hospitals, houses for the aged, the poor, the orphan, etc.

Mr. J. Would I be right in assuming that people outside the religious orders would do better to remain unmarried if they consecrated their lives to the service of God?

Father S. Yes. St. Paul (1 Cor. 7:38) speaks of the state of virginity *embraced for love of God* as a higher state than marriage. In verse 34 he had said: "The virgin — indeed, any unmarried woman — is concerned with things of the Lord, in pursuit of holiness in body and spirit. The married woman, on the other hand, has the cares of this world to absorb her and is concerned with pleasing her husband."

Purpose of Sacramentals

Holy Mother Church has, moreover, instituted sacramentals. They are sacred signs which bear a resemblance to the sacraments; they signify effects, particularly of a spiritual kind, which are obtained through the intercession of the Church. . . . Thus for well disposed members of the Faithful, the liturgy of the sacraments and sacramentals sanctifies almost every event in their lives. — *Liturgy, 60.*

Father S. Well, Mr. Jackson, we are nearing the end of our instructions. I am glad that you were so interested in the treasures which the Church possesses in the seven sacraments. Tonight our lesson will be on the "sacramentals," which, as the word implies, must bear a *certain likeness* to the sacraments because these sacraments are holy things or actions of which the Church makes use to obtain for us from God, by her prayers, spiritual and temporal favors. The sacraments were instituted by Christ Himself, while the Church is the author of the sacramentals.

Mr. J. Is there any difference?

Father S. Yes; the sacraments give or increase Sanctifying Grace, while sacramentals do not.

Mr. J. What are the sacramentals for then?

Father S. Chiefly, the pious use of them disposes the person to receive grace.

A clearer way of expressing the difference might be as follows: The sacraments were instituted by Christ as means whereby He conveys Sanctifying Grace to the soul. Hence they cause grace independently of what we deserve because of our good dispositions. Even when good dispositions are not possible, nor supposed, as when an infant is baptized, the sacrament gives grace. The sacramentals do not cause grace. For example when we bless ourselves with holy water, we receive actual grace partly through the prayer of the Church used in blessing the water and partly through the good sentiments with which we use the holy water. Thus in using the sacramentals, the prayer of the Church is assured, and it depends upon our good dispositions that we receive grace.

Mr. J. You said that their *chief* benefit to us is grace. Are there other benefits that can be obtained by their use?

Father S. There are others, such as: The forgiveness of venial sins; the remission of the temporal punishment due to sin; protection from evil spirits; health, and other material blessings.

Mr. J. What are some of the sacramentals?

Father S. Well, certain approved prayers lead the list, such as the Lord's Prayer and the Sign of the Cross. Next come things blessed by the Church, such as holy water, candles, palms, ashes, crucifixes, images of Our Lord, the Blessed Virgin and of the saints, medals, rosaries and scapulars, and others.

Mr. J. I never knew there were so many.

Father S. Yes, and their use often seems strange to converts, but not after they become familiar with them. Of course, you can use sacramentals as you choose.

Mr. J. Tell me how the use of these things excites pious sentiments, which move God to bestow grace.

Father S. When making the Sign of the Cross, we are moved to gratitude for the great blessings of the Incarnation and Redemption, and glorify the Trinity; in using holy water, we are reminded of the need of being cleansed more from sin;

the sight of a lighted blessed candle revives the faith of a dying person, and sends his thoughts heavenward. In the blessing of things to be used as sacramentals the Church first exorcises the objects; that is, she prays that they may be withdrawn completely from any power which the evil spirit, according to the Bible, has over creatures; then she prays that, on the contrary, the blessed objects may have power against the devil and his temptations. Hence, the pious use of sacramentals is salutary against temptations.

Mr. J. Is there any Biblical warrant for such sacramentals as holy water, etc.?

Father S. There is an abundance of it. In the Old Law, which Christ came not to destroy but to fulfill, the use of many blessed objects was of obligation, such as holy water, salt, oil, and others. Read Numb. 5:17; Levit. 14:51; Job 42:6; Dan. 9; Exod. 30:31-35; Levit. 2:13. St. Paul says: "Everything God created . . . is made holy by God's word and by prayer" (1 Tim. 4:4-5).

Mr. J. When is holy water used?

Father S. It is used in connection with the blessing of a church, school, home, and with the blessing of many objects. On occasion, before the Mass on Sunday the priest, walking down the center aisle of the church, sprinkles the people with it as a reminder that all worldly thoughts should be suppressed. As people come into the church at any time they bless themselves with holy water contained in vessels near the entrance. People also keep holy water in their homes with which to bless themselves and their homes.

Prayer

The spiritual life is not confined to participation in the liturgy. The Christian is indeed called to pray with others; but he must also enter into his own room to pray to the Father in secret (Matt. 6:6); in fact, according to the teaching of the Apostle Paul (1 Thess. 5:17), he should pray without ceasing. — *Liturgy, 12.*

Father S. We have seen that the sacraments are the great sources or means of grace. They were instituted by Jesus Christ to convey the merits of His passion and death to each individual. But there is another means of grace of which all people, Catholic and Protestant, Jew and Gentile, are obliged to make frequent use. It is *prayer.* No duty is more imperative than that of prayer, and there is nothing of which man stands in greater need.

Mr. J. The way in which you insisted that I pray often made me think, and I have several questions that I would like to ask.

Father S. Fine! Let's have them.

Mr. J. Well, why is it that prayer and religion always go together? What's the connection?

Father S. It is because prayer is the most common and most natural act of religion.

Mr. J. What do you mean by "natural"?

Father S. I mean that prayer is what religious people do instinctively as a dictate of common sense. When human help fails or is wanting, don't we instinctively say "God help you" or "God help me"? Sometimes we do not think what we are saying, but it seems to be the natural thing to say. But maybe I should have said *human*. It would be inhuman to travel across the country in an automobile with another person and not to speak with him. Isn't it just as inhuman to travel through life depending upon God for life itself, for everything, and never to speak to Him, recognizing that fact?

Mr. J. But just what does God get out of my prayer?

Father S. It isn't so much what God gets out of it—it is what *you* get out of it. You are better off for having prayed, even though your prayer isn't answered precisely the way you want it. It's rather hard to explain, but it is something like this: When you stop to think of God, when you go in mind to Him and mentally kneel before Him, you can never be as far from Him as you were before. You are closer, nearer to Him; and when you believe that you were meant to meet Him in another life, getting closer to Him in this life is bound to help you. There is comfort, consolation, a changed outlook on life, a feeling of having done your duty, a little stiffening of the will to put up with life.

Mr. J. I have heard it said that if God knows our needs, there is not much point in telling Him about them.

Father S. Don't think that we pray to inform God of something He doesn't know. He doesn't require us to pray in order to find out what we need. He knows all that, and He could give us all without our inviting Him to do so. But He has good reason for requiring our prayers. As long as we pray, we can never forget who we are, Who He is, and what He does for us. We too easily forget our dependence upon Him and feel that we have a *right* to everything. It is easy to think that what He gives and what He could withhold is *due* to us. When He requires our prayer, He prevents our being forgetful of Him and enables us to recognize Him as our Creator and Lord.

Can't you see that to pray to God in the right way is really acknowledging Who He is and who we are, and is a constant reminder that we should be grateful to Him as well? He is really a kindly Father who looks to our interests in requiring us to pray and in so doing protects us from ourselves, from our neglect and ingratitude.

Mr. J. What about those people who do not know how to pray?

Father S. It is difficult to conceive of such a person, if he has the use of reason and believes in the existence of a Supreme Being. One need not be educated in order to pray. One needs but to raise his mind and heart to God. You might not understand the meaning of a form of words uttered by an illiterate person, but God surely does. He reads the person's thoughts and intentions.

Mr. J. I hadn't looked at the matter in that light, but it sounds very reasonable.

Father S. St. Augustine says: "Begin to pray well, and you will cease to sin; cease to pray, and you will begin to sin." Many prayerbooks are called "The Key to Heaven," because prayer is the key by which we can open the treasures of God's graces and favors. It is the established means of communication with God. Just as I can send a message from New York to San Francisco and reach any person in that populous city, so I can send a message to my Heavenly Father, and receive a favorable answer. Prayer resembles the wire message, and just as government employees must keep in constant touch with Washington, so should we be in constant communication with God. The words, spoken or sung, on TV, are heard by people thousands of miles away. So we can never be too far away from God to be heard. God is always near. When we are in the state of grace, He is especially close to us.

Mr. J. You make the idea of prayer appear beautiful.

Father S. It is beautiful, and if people only realized the power and the pleasure of prayer, they would use it more regularly.

Mr. J. Do you mean to say that all prayers are answered?

Father S. Yes; all prayers said in the *proper spirit* are answered. We might not receive the precise favor we ask for nor reap the benefits of our prayer at once, but no prayer is altogether lost; it will bring us some return, sometime.

Mr. J. What is the proper spirit which God expects?

Father S. He expects us to pray with attention to what we are doing, with the conviction of our dependence upon Him, with a desire for the grace necessary to save our souls, with trust in His goodness, and with perseverance.

Remember that our prayers are not always answered in the precise manner that we expect. God understands our needs better than we do, and hence will not grant what might *appear* to *us* to be good, but what *He knows would be really harmful* to our spiritual welfare.

Mr. J. Prayers need not be long?

Father S. No; God cares rather for quality than for quantity.

Mr. J. Nor do they need to be the approved prayers, such as the Lord's Prayer and the Hail Mary?

Father S. No; these prayers have a great value because they practically came from Heaven and bear the Church's highest endorsement, but we are likely to say with distraction prayers which we know by heart; hence it is good to pray also in our own words, such as spontaneously spring from the heart.

Mr. J. Prayers said from memory, I imagine, cannot be worth much if the mind is not on them?

Father S. Well, if the distractions are not willful, the prayer has value. In fact, when we must struggle with distractions in order to pray well, our prayer has a very great value, because of the greater effort it costs us to pray.

While I think of it, let me warn you not to get into the habit of making in a distracted manner the Sign of the Cross with which we usually begin and end our prayers. This act should express the spirit of faith which should permeate our prayer, because when we say, "In the name of the Father, and of the Son, and of the Holy Spirit" we express our belief in the three Divine Persons, and when we make the form of the cross on ourselves, we profess our belief that the Son of God became man and redeemed us by His death on the Cross.

Mr. J. In case we pray long for a special favor without receiving it, does that mean that we should cease asking for that particular thing?

Father S. No; even the saints prayed for years for certain favors before the requests were granted. It took St. Monica thirty years of prayer before her son, Augustine, was converted, and he became an illustrious saint. In that event our prayers accumulate, pile mountain high, and, as it were, take Heaven by storm; then the answer will be far beyond our expectation, because of having been so long withheld.

Mr. J. Father, I have heard you speak of meditation. What is that?

Father S. You see, there are two kinds of prayer: mental and vocal. Vocal prayer is the kind we have been discussing. It comes from the mind and heart and is spoken by the lips. In mental prayer, or meditation, we unite our hearts with God while thinking of Him and what He has done for us and revealed to us. There are formalized systems of meditation, such as the Sulpician Method or the Ignatian Method. You can find out more about them if you are interested. The interesting thing is that young people today think they have discovered something in transcendental meditation when it has been around as long as the Church.

Mr. J. What is the highest form of prayer?

Father S. Adoration of God: Its object is to please God first and to benefit us second. By worship we feel our littleness and God's majesty; we express our love and loyalty and we acknowledge His supreme dominion over us and our entire dependence on Him. This is the first purpose of prayer.

Mr. J. What is next in order?

Father S. Thanksgiving: By this we give God all the credit for the big and little blessings with which our daily lives are filled; by it, too, we subordinate self to God.

Mr. J. Therefore, *petition,* or *supplication,* in which there is principally self-interest, is a lower form of prayer?

Father S. Exactly. There is one other form of prayer which is loftier than petition: it is that of *reparation,* whereby we express our regret at having offended God, and determine to serve Him better. Then petition might be concerned about both spiritual and temporal favors. That which importunes God for spiritual help is to be rated higher than that which seeks only worldly assistance.

Mr. J. Just what part has my prayer in obtaining a favor from God?

Father S. Your prayer of petition has a necessary part. God does not change His mind when you pray, thus deciding to give you something which He wasn't going to give you. In His eternity, He has decided that there are certain things He will give you *on the condition* that you pray for them. This is what makes your prayers necessary. When you pray, you are fulfilling a condition which He has laid down, and which you are free to comply with or disregard. "Ask"—there is the condition; "and you shall receive"—there is the promise.

Mr. J. I imagine that more prayer for *temporal* favors go forth to God than all other kinds.

Father S. That is true, and it explains why God does not seem to hearken to them. Many people are beggars only; they pray only when they are in need of material assistance. They are not concerned about God's honor and glory, nor about their own soul; when things go smoothly with them in worldly matters, they forget all about God, and what they owe to Him.

Mr. J. Yet I suppose they are the most impatient ones, if they are not heard at once?

Father S. Your surmise is correct, and I shall show you how the Lord's Prayer subordinates man's needs to God's great designs, and how spiritual help must be considered before material assistance.

Beauties of Prayer

With their parents leading the way by example and family prayer, children and indeed everyone gathered around the family hearth will find a readier path to human maturity, salvation and holiness. —*The Church Today, 48.*

Father S. In our instruction on "prayer," I stated that I would show that the prayer taught to us by Our Lord Himself is a perfect model for our prayers to copy. It is a prayer of perfect and unselfish love.

Mr. J. Why do you say that?

Father S. In saying it we offer ourselves entirely to God and ask from Him the best things, not only for ourselves but also for our neighbor. Brief as it is, it contains worship of God, petitions for the furtherance of the great interests of the Almighty, and for our own spiritual and temporal needs. Its opening words inspire confidence: "*Our* Father, Who art in Heaven." It suggests that we pray in union with Christ and all fellow-members of the Mystical Body.

Mr. J. That sentiment is certainly beautiful; it represents the child, who is an exile on earth, lifting his mind and heart to an all-powerful, all-loving Father, Who is in Heaven, yet intensely interested in the welfare of His helpless child on earth.

Father S. Then it represents the child deeply concerned about the honor and glory of that Heavenly Father: "hallowed be Thy Name, Thy kingdom come," etc.

Mr. J. I do not know what the word "hallowed" means.

Father S. It is an old English word, meaning "honored"; the petition put in other words would be: "May Thy holy name be *honored* (revered) by Thy creatures."

Mr. J. In these days of profanity and blasphemy, such a petition is certainly in order.

Father S. Those four words, therefore, are a prayer both of petition and reparation.

Mr. J. I am not sure that I grasp the full significance of the other three-word petition: "Thy kingdom come."

Father S. God's kingdom on earth is His Church—His kingdom of grace which He wishes to *come* to all people of all nations, in order that, through its help, people may *come* into eternal possession of His kingdom in Heaven. The way to God's kingdom in Heaven is through this kingdom on earth.

Mr. J. How significant! These three words contain a prayer which is concerned about the highest interests both of God and man.

Father S. "Thy will be done on earth as it is in Heaven." What love is contained in these words! They ask that we on earth may love God and serve Him as willingly as His angels and saints in Heaven do.

Mr. J. When people are prompted to pray in their own words, they probably seldom think of petitioning for the furtherance of the great interests of God.

Father S. That's true. Our own petty interests, no matter how important they appear to us, are not worthy of consideration as compared to the great interests which God Almighty has in this world. In our prayers God should come first.

Mr. J. I get what you mean by saying that the Lord's Prayer is a model prayer.

Father S. Now come petitions in our own behalf in the second part of the prayer: "Give *us* this day our daily bread, and forgive *us* our trespasses, as we forgive those who trespass against *us,* and lead *us* not into temptation, but deliver *us* from evil."

Mr. J. Since all the other petitions are so condensed, I wonder why the words "this day" are used, since the sentiment would be expressed by the words "Give us our daily bread."

Father S. No, the same sentiment would not be expressed; the words "this day" were designedly used. Christ would emphasize the requirement of *daily* prayer. We pray for the needs of today: should we want God's blessings tomorrow, they are worth asking for again.

Mr. J. I take back my remark.

Father S. It shouldn't be necessary to remind you that the word "bread" here is not to be taken in its narrowest meaning; it stands for "all our needs," spiritual and bodily needs. Of course, in Christ's mind the spiritual needs were foremost.

Mr. J. In the next petition, I presume the word "trespass" means sin.

Father S. It means our "debt" with God. We ask God to forgive us on the ground that we forgive the offenses which others commit against us. We, therefore, include love of neighbor in our prayer, which is the surest way to win love and favors from God.

Mr. J. Why do we say "and lead us not into temptation, but deliver us from evil"?

Father S. We pray that God will always give us the grace to overcome temptations to sin and that He will always protect us from harm, especially harm to our spiritual welfare.

Mr. J. I never realized how much was in that prayer. I'm going to try to think of what I am saying hereafter.

Father S. Do this, and your prayers "will pierce the clouds," and your temporal interests will not suffer. Too many people are praying for health, more remunerative work, even silly things, while never putting in a word for the conversion of sinners and for the spread of the Church. Many, otherwise good parents, are greatly grieved when some temporal misfortune overtakes their boy, but are not disturbed when he misses Mass or remains away from the sacraments for months. We want favors from our Heavenly Father, but forget that He has a standing request for us to do some one thing that will please Him. Be good to God, and He will be good to you; "I love those, who love Me."

THE HAIL MARY

Father S. Just as the Lord's Prayer comes from Heaven, inasmuch as it was composed by Christ Himself, so did a portion of the "Hail Mary."

Mr. J. I fail to grasp that.

Father S. The words, "Hail, full of grace, the Lord is with thee, blessed art thou among women" are the words with which the archangel Gabriel greeted Mary; and the Bible expressly states that the angel addressed Mary as a messenger of God: "The angel Gabriel was sent from God" (Luke 1:26). Then Holy Scripture also declares that Elizabeth spoke under the inspiration of the Holy Spirit, when she greeted Mary with the words: "Blessed art thou among women and blessed is the fruit of thy womb."

Mr. J. Hence, when we say the "Hail Mary," we are certainly employing words which are pleasing to God?

Father S. That is the Church's reason for embodying them in a prayer of which she wishes her children to make daily use.

Mr. J. I have observed that Catholics almost invariably say the "Hail Mary" immediately after the Lord's Prayer; one would almost suppose that they belonged together.

Father S. Their relation is intimate. We greet our Heavenly Father and implore Him to help us; then we greet our Heavenly Mother and entreat her to offer her powerful prayers in our behalf.

Mr. J. What a beautiful idea, and it must please Christ, Who, when dying on the cross, besought us to regard Mary as our mother.

Father S. There is no question about it.

Mr. J. The invocation in the "Hail Mary": "Holy

Mary, Mother of God, pray for us sinners now and at the hour of our death," is a Scripture passage, too?

Father S. No, these words were added by the Church, which would remind people to address themselves every day to their Heavenly Mother for present needs, and especially for the greatest favor God could grant them, the blessing of a happy death. Left to themselves, people would not pray as regularly as they should for this undeserved grace.

Mr. J. What do you mean by a "happy" death, Father?

Father S. Death in the state of grace. There may be sorrowful circumstances surrounding a person's departure from this world, but if he or she is a child of God through the possession of His grace at that moment, it is truly a happy event and a sign of His everlasting love.

PART IV

Approved Devotions
and
Religious Associations

"For where two or three are gathered in my name, there am I in their midst." Matt. 18:20.

"How different the man who devotes himself to the study of the law of the Most High!" Sirach 39:1.

"Proclaim the greatness of his name, loudly sing his praises." Sirach 39:15.

"Therefore will I proclaim you, O Lord, among the Nations." Ps. 18:50.

"It is God's will that you grow in holiness." 1 Thess. 4:3.

"All ages to come shall call me blessed." Luke 1:48.

"There is your mother." John 19:27.

And if anyone asks him, "What are these wounds on your chest?" he shall answer, "With these I was wounded in the house of my dear ones." Zech. 13:6.

"I will set my dwelling among you." Levit. 26:11.

The Rosary

Placed by the grace of God, as the Mother of God, next to her divine Son, and exalted above all angels and men, Mary played her part in the mysteries of Christ. Rightly she is honored . . . While honoring the Mother of Christ, these devotions make her Son rightly known, loved and glorified, all His commands obeyed. — *The Church, 66.*

Father S. You have probably heard about the rosary.

Mr. J. Yes; and I have already purchased one. Are you ready to tell me how to use it?

Father S. Let me first explain that the rosary is a special form of prayer. It is like a bouquet of roses that we offer to God in honor of His Mother. The beads are merely a device for keeping count of the prayers, and are called rosary beads because they are used in this special form of devotion. The complete rosary devotion consists of fifteen groups of Hail Marys, ten to each group, which is commonly called a decade. Each group of prayers is associated with a special mystery in the life of Our Lord and His Blessed Mother. Hence with beads as you have them the complete rosary would be said by going over them three times.

Mr. J. Yes, I have only five groups of ten beads, each separated by a larger bead. And it has an appendage containing a crucifix, a large bead, three small beads, and another large bead.

Father S. Prayers are said on every bead and on the crucifix, but those recited on the crucifix and on the five beads which you have referred to as an appendage are only *introductory* to the rosary itself, and are not essential to the rosary.

Mr. J. What prayers are said as we finger the crucifix, and all the beads?

Father S. On the crucifix we make a profession of faith by reciting the Apostles' Creed. On the larger beads we recite the Lord's Prayer, and on all the smaller beads, the Hail Mary.

Mr. J. Do you mean that when the complete rosary is said, the "Hail Mary" is said 150 times?

Father S. Exactly; they correspond with the 150 psalms of David, which are a part of the Bible.

Mr. J. Would you mind explaining the relationship?

Father S. Well, from the earliest days of Christianity, the psalter, or book of psalms of David formed the main prayer of the monks in monasteries and of other pious people who could read. Those who could not read would recite some other prayers, approved by the Church, usually the Lord's Prayer, in the place of the psalms. They kept count of the number by little pebbles or beads. This explains the 150 beads. Later the "beads-prayer" became a devotion in honor of the Blessed Virgin, when the Hail Mary was substituted for the Our Father. St. Dominic, who lived at the beginning of the thirteenth century, propagated the rosary as we now have it, principally with a view to check a heresy of that age. Then the Church authorities took the prayer in hand, improved its form, made it both a mental and a vocal prayer, indulgenced it, and urged its general introduction throughout the Catholic world.

Mr. J. How did the Church improve its form?

Father S. She divided the complete Rosary into three parts, 50 beads each, divided the 50 into five decades or groups of ten, headed by a larger bead, on which the Lord's Prayer would be said. Then the prayer of the rosary would be begun by a profession of faith — the recital of the Apostles' Creed, and three times the Hail Mary for an increase of faith, hope and charity. The Our Father is said on the larger beads. This would constitute the "oral" or vocal part of the rosary.

Mr. J. But you say that it is both a *mental* and a *vocal* form of prayer?

Father S. Yes, while reciting the prayers of the various decades orally, we meditate on the important mysteries of our faith. We rehearse the whole life of Christ in our thoughts, and draw therefrom salutary lessons.

Mr. J. Would you please explain that a little more fully?

Father S. Well, the important events in our Savior's and His Blessed Mother's life are reduced to 15, and these are classified among three groups of five each, which we call the five *joyful,* the five *sorrowful,* and the five *glorious* mysteries. When we recite the complete rosary, our meditation covers all these mysteries; but since it is customary to carry a string of beads comprising only five decades, we choose for our meditation any one of the three groups of mysteries. Those who say the rosary every day meditate on the five *joyful* mysteries on Monday and Thursday; on the five *sorrowful* mysteries on Tuesday and Friday; and the five *glorious* mysteries on Wednesday and Saturday.

Mr. J. You left out Sunday.

Father S. On Sunday it is customary to meditate on that group of mysteries which corresponds with the ecclesiastical season at hand; for instance, during Advent, the five *joyful;* during Lent, the five *sorrowful,* and during the rest of the year, the five *glorious* mysteries.

Mr. J. What a perfect arrangement! And how your explanation refutes the charge that in the rosary Catholics merely "count beads"!

Father S. If people who make that charge only reflected a bit, they would know that the old Church is too wise to have *silly* devotions.

Mr. J. What events in Christ's and Mary's life are recommended for our meditation?

Father S. The five *joyful* events are: The Annunciation,

the Visitation, the Birth of Jesus, the offering of Jesus in the Temple, the finding of Christ in the Temple when He was twelve years old.

The five *sorrowful* mysteries are: The Agony in the Garden, the Scourging, the Crowning with Thorns, the Carrying of the Cross, and the Crucifixion.

The five *glorious* mysteries are: The Resurrection, the Ascension, the Descent of the Holy Spirit, the Assumption of Mary into Heaven, her Coronation in Heaven.

Mr. J. I have always regarded the rosary as a form of prayer for the uneducated, but I see that one must be instructed in his religon before he can say it properly.

Father S. Indeed, the educated *could* profit by it most, because they should be able to meditate best; the rosary has been the favorite prayer of priests, Popes, scholars and kings.

Mr. J. The oral prayers, however, must be only mechanical, if the mind is to occupy itself with serious thinking on those events.

Father S. Not exactly; the oral prayers are those with whose contents we are most familiar; it is not the same as if we were reading some prayer which we never saw before, while having our attention elsewhere.

Mr. J. I see. But can children and the uninstructed derive any benefit from the rosary?

Father S. Most assuredly. The Church dispenses the merits of Christ, and adjusts her terms to the capabilities of her people. And you may be assured that God in His infinite justice and mercy, and His Blessed Mother in her loving kindness, hear the prayers of and reward children and the uninstructed in the fullest measure. It is they, you know, who are often the most sincere and earnest in their devotions.

Mr. J. I believe you said the rosary is an indulgenced prayer?

Father S. Highly so. The string of beads is blessed and an indulgence may be gained for every Our Father and Hail Mary, if five consecutive decades are said.

Mr. J. Must the beads be touched as the prayers are said?

Father S. Yes, in the private recital of the rosary; if, however, one leads in prayer and many others respond, it is necessary only that the one who leads have a rosary.

Mr. J. Which is the best way to meditate?

Father S. Let your imagination represent to the mind a picture of the mystery under consideration, and think of its relation to you. Then, when distractions come, the mind can always go back to the picture.

Mr. J. Are Catholics expected to say the rosary every day?

Father S. There is no obligation for them to do so, but good Catholics recite it daily. In many homes it constitutes a family evening prayer, especially during October, the month dedicated to the "Mother of the rosary." When the rosary is said in a church where the Blessed Sacrament (the Holy Eucharist) is reserved, one may gain a plenary indulgence.

In many parishes the *Confraternity of the Holy Rosary* is established, with which any member may become affiliated. More commonly the women of the parish belong to it, and it is called the *Rosary Society*. But men and children may also have membership in it.

Way of the Cross

Popular devotions of the Christian people, provided they are in accord with the laws and norms of the Church are warmly commended, especially those devotions called for by the Apostolic See. — *Liturgy, 13.*

Father S. You have frequently noticed the set of fourteen framed pictures mounted by crosses of wood which ornament the walls of our church?

Mr. J. Yes, Father. Somebody told me that they are called "Stations," which word did not mean much to me.

Father S. Well, they represent fourteen scenes of our Savior's sufferings, including His death and burial, and are more properly called "The Way of the Cross." Separately the pictures or figures are called "Stations," because the person practicing the devotion *stops* and meditates briefly before each.

Mr. J. He meditates on the Passion of Christ?

Father S. Yes, and usually expresses his sorrow for his sins and his love for Jesus before each.

Mr. J. I was present at this devotion several times during Lent; the priest, accompanied by altar boys, led in prayer, and I was deeply touched by the meditations that he read; only it looked somewhat like worshipping the pictures, because the knee was bent in worship before each.

Father S. But did you not observe that when the genuflection was made, the priest said: "We adore Thee, *O Christ*"? The act of worship was directed to Christ, Who is God, and not to the picture.

Mr. J. I must have paid too much attention to the act and too little to the words.

Father S. The Way of the Cross may be made at any time privately as well as publicly, and it is a most richly indulgenced form of devotion. The early Christians made great sacrifices to visit the Holy Land and follow the way their Redeemer walked under the weight of the cross to Calvary. But, many centuries ago, the Turks or Moslems got possession of the holy places, and it became dangerous for pious people to go there. Then the Church authorized the erection of representations of scenes of Christ's sufferings in her churches and substituted this beautiful devotion for such pilgrimages to the Holy Land.

Mr. J. The Church never permits her members to suffer spiritually as a result of the persecutions of their faith, does she.

Father S. No, she has the treasury of the merits of Christ to apply to souls in different ways.

Mr. J. What prayers must accompany the meditations before the Stations?

Father S. No prayers *must* accompany them although it is customary, in public devotions, to recite the Our Father, Hail Mary, and Glory be to the Father, etc., after each meditation.

Mr. J. Hence, although only a few could actually visit the Holy Land to make the Way of the Cross, all Catholics, except the sick, may gain the same benefit now in their parish church.

Father S. There is a substitution offered even to the sick. They may gain the indulgence of the Way of the Cross by reciting twenty times the Our Father, etc., while holding the crucifix, properly blessed, in their hands.

Mr. J. Wonderful privilege, indeed; but why a repetition of these prayers twenty times?

Father S. Fourteen times to correspond with the fourteen stations, five times in honor of Jesus' five wounds, and once for the intention of the Holy Father.

Mr. J. Just what are the indulgences, which may be gained?

Father S. A *plenary* indulgence is offered for the entire devotion of fourteen Stations; and a *partial* indulgence is granted for each Station if the devotion should be interrupted.

Eucharist Outside Mass

In the house of prayer the most holy Eucharist is to be offered and reserved. There the Faithful gather and find help
and comfort in venerating the presence of the Son of God,
our Savior, offered for us on the sacrificial altar. — *Priestly
Life, 5.*

Father S. I wish to speak with you about the reservation
of the Eucharist apart from Mass.

Mr. J. I have seen the tabernacle where it is kept and
have noticed the red light burning before it. In fact, I often
pray there.

Father S. Good! That is most praiseworthy. That is
where the Blessed Sacrament is reserved — Emmanuel, God-
with-us. Day and night Christ physically makes His home
with us. The Blessed Sacrament is a source of life and grace for
us.

Mr. J. This can set up a very personal relationship with
Christ.

Father S. Exactly. The reason for the tabernacle is that
the Eucharist was originally reserved for the dying, and that is
still its primary purpose. But because the Lord is there, people
naturally express their faith before the sacrament.

Mr. J. I understand that the Blessed Sacrament is exposed for the veneration of the faithful at certain times.

Father S. Yes. The Blessed Sacrament is sometimes placed in a gold monstrance and exposed for the worship of the people. This might last for a day or for a shorter period. However, when the Sacrament is exposed the Church requires that suitable numbers of the faithful should be present.

Mr. J. I have heard people speak of Benediction.

Father S. Benediction as Benediction is not allowed under the liturgical renewal. However, the Church encourages short periods of exposition of the Eucharist which include readings from the word of God, songs, prayers and silent meditation. At the end, the priest blesses the people with the eucharist. This is the benediction.

Mr. J. You call the beautiful receptacle, containing the consecrated Host, the monstrance?

Father S. Yes, or ostensorium—a Latin word, signifying the precious receptacle in which Jesus is exposed to the public.

Mr. J. What is the meaning of the smoking vessel which the boy swings?

Father S. It is called the censer, and contains burning charcoal on which incense is placed. Incense is used at many services as the symbol of prayer. Even in the Old Law, it was so used at the direction of Almighty God Himself. David prayed, "Let my prayer come like incense before you" (Psalm 141:2).

Mr. J. Several weeks ago I attended a devotion when the Blessed Sacrament was exposed for a full hour, and many prayers were recited and a short sermon was delivered before the Benediction service began.

Father S. That was what we call a "holy Hour" — an hour of Scripture readings, prayer, meditation, and singing of hymns in the presence of the exposed Blessed Sacrament. Some parishes have the custom of a monthly all-night vigil before the Sacrament.

Knights of Columbus

Father S. Have you heard of the Knights of Columbus?

Mr. J. Yes. It's some sort of men's club, isn't it?

Father S. In a way, but it's much more than that.

Mr. J. In what way?

Father S. Primarily, it is a fraternal benefit society for Catholic men.

Mr. J. What does that mean?

Father S. When it was started in 1882, its purpose was to make inexpensive insurance available to Catholic working men. Since then, its purposes have become much broader.

Mr. J. What are its purposes now?

Father S. While insurance for its members is still a very important part of the Knights of Columbus program, its primary purpose now is to be of service to the Church, the family and the community.

Mr. J. Could you give me some examples?

Father S. Over the past 25 years or more, they have sponsored a Catholic advertising program in national secular publications. Through this, more than 600,000 persons have enrolled in instruction courses in the Catholic faith. The Knights have also given generous support to a wide variety of Catholic and community projects. They sponsor boys' homes, projects to benefit youth, the aged and the underprivileged, plus educational programs and many other charitable and community projects.

Mr. J. How widespread is the organization?

Father S. It has about 1.2 million members in more than 6,000 local councils, located in every state, Canada, the Philippines, Cuba, Mexico, Puerto Rico, Panama, Guatemala, Guam and the Virgin Islands.

Mr. J. It sounds like a Catholic version of the Elks or Moose.

Father S. In some ways, that's true. But to become a Knight of Columbus, a man must be a practical Catholic, and the organization's entire orientation is to Catholic principles. Thousands of Catholic clergymen belong to it. Each local council is directed to have its own priest-chaplain, and the different "degrees" of the organization are designed to teach charity, unity, fraternity and patriotism.

Mr. J. It sounds like a good organization for a Catholic man to join.

Father S. It is.

Retreats, Missions, Novenas

Father S. Do you know what a retreat is, Mr. Jackson?

Mr. J. No, Father, I do not.

Father S. Just as Christ went to the desert to pray and meditate for forty days before He began His public ministry; just as He asked His Apostles to come with Him "to a desert place" (Mark 6:31) to rest a while, to join Him in serious contemplation of the things of the soul and of eternity; just as the Pope, busy as he is, retires to some quiet place for a whole week every year to commune with his God for his own benefit and for the benefit of his entire world-flock; just as the bishop takes his priests away from their parishes periodically to some institution to spend several days in meditation and prayer and silence, just as the Sisters, who labor in parochial schools and institutions of charity, go to their motherhouse to spend from four to eight days in group prayer, meditation and spiritual exercises, so do many lay people leave their work a few days each year to occupy their minds and their hearts exclusively with matters pertaining to their sanctification. Such spiritual exercises are called "retreats."

It is customary, as you know, for businessmen to take an inventory every year, to have their books audited to ascertain how this year's business compared to last year's, whereupon they consider measures of improving their business. So should every person have his accounts with God audited from time to time, to ascertain whether he has been going forward or backward in his business of salvation.

In many cities there are *Houses of Retreat,* to which men and women are invited for weekend recollection, prayer-conscience-audit, and to receive spiritual stimulation which will enable them to pursue their personal sanctification.

In recent years two movements have given impetus to retreats. One is called the Cursillo (or Little Course) which began in Spain and which involves a three-day weekend aimed at Christian renewal and individual apostolic activity through an intensive religious experience. The other is called Marriage Encounter and is made by husbands and wives on a weekend. It too is an intensive religious experience aimed as forming a better Christian Marriage.

Mr. J. If the clergy and the good Sisters, and even the Pope, observe annual retreats, it would seem that the man or woman of the world, who mingles daily with the pagan-minded, needs such retreats far more.

Father S. Since it is impossible for all the people to leave their homes and go to *places* of retreat, it is customary for pastors to invite periodically a specially-trained missionary to conduct a series of morning and evening services continuously for a week or more in the parish church. These are called "missions." During a mission all parishioners are expected to so arrange their work that they may attend the principal sermons and devotions, to receive the sacraments of Penance and Holy Eucharist with great earnestness, and to resolve in the future to use those means necessary to overcome their predominant faults.

Mr. J. I see that the Church provides for the strengthening of the faith and piety of persons in every walk of life. At one of the churches in our city there is being held a rather lengthy devotion in honor of St. Jude. Is that a mission?

Father S. No, that is a novena.

Mr. J. What's a novena?

Father S. You will recall that just before our Divine Savior returned to Heaven He asked His Apostles and disciples to assemble at a certain place and to engage in prayer to the Holy Spirit for *nine* days. He had promised that He would send the Holy Spirit to them, which He did on the tenth day. Following the example of the Apostles, Catholics observe *nine* days of prayer and devotions, and call the same a "novena." The word "novena" is taken from the Latin word "novem," which means "nine." Sometimes by extension the novena is held once a week for nine weeks.

.. ..

Well, Mr. Smith, this concludes our instruction. By reading Catholic books and other publications, you can further your knowledge of the Church and its beliefs. We must now begin arrangements for your baptism.

Mr. J. Thanks very much, Father. I have profited greatly from our meetings.

Some Scripture Texts Often Overlooked

Therefore, just as through one man sin entered the world and with sin death, death thus coming to all men inasmuch as all sinned. (Rom. 5:12)

I solemnly assure you, no one can enter into God's kingdom without being begotten of water and Spirit. (John 3:5)

The pair upon arriving imposed hands on them and they received the Holy Spirit. (Acts 8:17)

Do this as a remembrance of Me. (Luke 22:19)

This is My body . . . this is My blood. (Matt. 26:26-28)

And everywhere they bring sacrifice to my name, and a pure offering. (Mal. 1:11)

Then he breathed on them and said:
"Receive the Holy Spirit. If you forgive men's sins, they are forgiven them; if you hold them bound, they are held bound." (John 20:22-23)

Is there anyone sick among you? He should ask for the prebyters of the church. They in turn are to pray over him, anointing him with oil in the Name of the Lord. (James 5:14)

If he ignores them, refer it to the church. If he ignores even the church, then treat him as you would a Gentile or a tax collector. (Matt 18:17)

All ages to come shall call me blessed. (Luke 1:48)

There shall be one flock then, one shepherd. (John 10:16)

Jesus replied, "Blest are you, Simon son of Jonah! No mere man has revealed this to you, but my heavenly Father. I for my part declare to you, you are 'Rock,' and on this rock I will build my church, and the jaws of death shall not prevail against it. I will entrust to you the keys of the kingdom of heaven. Whatever you declare bound on earth shall be bound in heaven; whatever you declare loosed on earth shall be loosed in heaven." (Matt. 16:17-19)

My purpose in leaving you in Crete was that you might accomplish what had been left undone, especially the appointment of presbyters in every town. (Titus 1:5)

Thus they are no longer two but one flesh. Therefore, let no man separate what God has joined. (Matt. 19:6)

This is a great foreshadowing; I mean that it refers to Christ and the church. (Eph. 5:32)

This incense shall be treated as most sacred by you. (Exod. 30:36)

In an earthen vessel he shall meanwhile put some holy water. (Numb. 5:17)

He fasted forty days and forty nights, and afterward was hungry. (Matt. 4:2)

None of those who cry out, "Lord, Lord," will enter the kingdom of God but only the one who does the will of my Father in heaven. (Matt 7:21)

I warn you, you will not be released until you have paid the last penny. (Matt. 5:26)

Out of my sight, you condemned, into the everlasting fire prepared for the devil and his angels! (Matt. 25:41)

Appendix
Date of Origin of the Principal Churches in the United States

The True Church Must Date Back To The Time Of Christ
Statement of the Comparative Age of the Catholic Church and of the
Non-Catholic Denominations

Name	Place of Origin	Founder	Year
CATHOLIC CHURCH	JERUSALEM	JESUS CHRIST	33
Adventists	Dresden, N.J.	William Miller	1831
Assemblies of God	Hot Springs, Ark.	Evangelizing Missions banded together	1914
Baptists	England	John Smyth Thomas Helwys	1611
Brethren, Plymouth	England	John Nelson Darby	1830
Christian Scientists	Boston, Mass.	Mrs. Mary Baker Eddy	1879
Church of God	Pittsburgh, Pa.	John Weinbrenner	1830
Church of God and Saints of Christ	Lawrence, Kans.	M. S. Crowdy	1896
Church of the Nazarene	Pilot Point, Texas	Methodist dissenters	1908
Congregational and Christian Churches	London, England	Robert Brown	1560-1633
Disciples of Christ	Lexington, Ky.	Alexander Campbell Barton W. Stone	1832
Evangelical Church	Leicestershire, England	Jacob Albright	1803
Friends	Pennsylvania	George Fox	1648
Latter Day Saints (Mormons)	Palmyra, N.Y.	Joseph Smith	1829
Lutherans	Germany	Martin Luther	1517
Mennonites	Holland	Menno Simons	1525
Methodists	Oxford, England	John and Charles Wesley, George Whitefield	1729
Moravians	Kunwald, Bohemia	Peter Chelczicky	1467
Pentecostal Holiness Church	Anderson, S.C.	Originated from Methodists	1898
Presbyterian Church	Scotland	John Knox	1560
Protestant Episcopal Church	American Colonies	Samuel Seabury	18th Century
Salvation Army	London, England	William Booth	1865
Unitarians	Boston	Liberal Christians	1785
United Brethren	Susquehanna Valley	Philip Otterbein	1766

Common Prayers

The Sign of the Cross

In the name of the Father, and of the Son, and of the Holy Spirit. Amen.

The Lord's Prayer

Our Father, Who art in heaven, hallowed be Thy name; Thy kingdom come; Thy will be done on earth as it is in heaven. Give us this day our daily bread; and forgive us our trespasses as we forgive those who trespass against us; and lead us not into temptation, but deliver us from evil. Amen.

Hail Mary

Hail Mary, full of grace; the Lord is with thee; blessed art thou among women, and blessed is the fruit of thy womb, Jesus. Holy Mary, Mother of God, pray for us sinners, now and at the hour of our death. Amen.

The Apostles' Creed

I believe in God, the Father Almighty, Creator of heaven and earth; and in Jesus Christ, His only Son, our Lord; Who was conceived by the Holy Spirit, born of the Virgin Mary, suffered under Pontius Pilate, was crucified; died and was buried. He descended into hell; the third day He arose again from the dead; He ascended into heaven, sitteth at the right hand of God, the Father Almighty; from thence He shall come to judge the living and the dead. I believe in the Holy Spirit, the Holy Catholic Church, the communion of saints, the forgiveness of sins, the resurrection of the body, and life everlasting. Amen.

The Confiteor

I confess to Almighty God, to blessed Mary, ever Virgin, to blessed Michael the Archangel, to blessed John the Baptist, to the holy Apostles Peter and Paul, and to all the Saints, that I have sinned exceedingly in thought, word and deed, through my fault, through my fault, through my most grievous fault. Therefore, I beseech blessed Mary, ever Virgin, blessed Michael the Archangel, blessed John the Baptist, the holy Apostles Peter and Paul, and all the Saints, to pray to the Lord our God for me.

May the Almighty God have mercy on me, forgive me my sins, and bring me to everlasting life. Amen.

May the Almighty and merciful Lord grant me pardon, absolution and remission of all my sins. Amen.

An Act of Faith

O my God, I firmly believe in Thee and in all the sacred truths which the Catholic Church believes and teaches because Thou hast revealed them Who canst neither deceive nor be deceived.

An Act of Hope

O my God, I firmly hope in Thee and trust Thou wilt grant me pardon of my sins, grace to observe Thy commandments faithfully in this life, and the glory of paradise in the next, through the merits of my Lord and Savior, Jesus Christ.

An Act of Charity

O my God, I love Thee with my whole heart and soul above all things because Thou art all-good and deserving of my love and for Thy sake I love my neighbor as myself. Mercifully grant that having loved Thee here on earth, I may love and enjoy Thee forever in heaven. Amen.

An Act of Contrition

O my God! I am heartily sorry for having offended Thee and I detest all my sins, because of Thy just punishments but most of all because they offend Thee, my God, Who art all-good and deserving of all my love. I firmly resolve, with the help of Thy grace, to sin no more and avoid the near occasions of sin. Amen.

To the Blessed Virgin

Remember, O most gracious Virgin Mary, that never was it known that any one who fled to Thy protection, implored Thy help, or sought Thy intercession, was left unaided. Inspired with this confidence, I fly unto thee, O Virgin of virgins, my mother; to thee I come, before thee I stand, sinful and sorrowful. O Mother of the Word incarnate, despise not my petitions; but in thy mercy hear and answer me. Amen.

Hail, Holy Queen

Hail, holy queen, mother of mercy, our life, our sweetness, and our hope; to thee do we cry, poor banished children of Eve, to thee do we send up our sighs, mourning and weeping in this valley of tears. Turn then, most gracious advocate, thine eyes of mercy towards us, and after this, our exile, show unto us the blessed fruit of thy womb, Jesus. O clement, O loving, O sweet Virgin Mary!

The Blessing Before Meals

Bless us, O Lord! and these Thy gifts which we are about to receive from Thy bounty, through Christ our Lord. Amen.

Grace After Meals

We give Thee thanks for all Thy benefits, O Almighty God, Who livest and reignest forever; and may the souls of the faithful departed, through the mercy of God, rest in peace. Amen.

INDEX

Pleased?